SEARCH for a FATHER

SEARCH
for a
FATHER

Sartre, Paternity, and the Question of Ethics

ROBERT HARVEY

Ann Arbor
THE UNIVERSITY OF MICHIGAN PRESS

Published in the United States of America by
The University of Michigan Press
Manufactured in the United States of America
1994 1993 1992 1991 4 3 2 1

Distributed in the United Kingdom and Europe by
Manchester University Press, Oxford Road,
Manchester M13 9PL, UK

Library of Congress Cataloging-in-Publication Data

Harvey, Robert, 1951–
Search for a father : Sartre, paternity, and the question of ethics / Robert Harvey.
p. cm.
Includes bibliographical references (p.) and index.
ISBN 0-472-10225-7 (cloth : alk. paper)
1. Sartre, Jean Paul, 1905– —Characters—Fathers. 2. Sartre, Jean Paul, 1905– —Ethics. 3. Fathers and sons in literature. 4. Paternity in literature. 5. Ethics in literature. I. Title.
PQ2637.A82Z726 1991
848′.91409—dc20 91-27474
CIP

British Library Cataloguing in Publication Data
Harvey, Robert
Search for a father : Sartre, paternity and the question of ethics.
1. France. Philosophy. Sartre, Jean-Paul 1905–1980
I. Title.
194

ISBN 0-472-10225-7

to Jim and Cherry

Acknowledgments

The protagonists of *Search for a Father* do not so much fail as they fall victim to an absence: turning for guidance they encounter a void. Without the common presence of many individuals—at once readers and friends—the study that follows would not have acquired shape and substance.

For their own inspiring work and unflagging counsel in the earliest stages, my gratitude to Denis Hollier, Ann Smock, Martin Jay, and Leo Bersani has no bounds. Discussions and debate with Benny Lévy, François George, and Michel Contat have proven as indispensable as their generosity. More recently, some of the arguments found here have benefitted from the critical eyes of Dick Howard, Hugh Silverman, David Allison, and François Raffoul. And my personal thanks would not be complete without the names of Hélène Volat and Jean-François Lyotard.

Much of my preliminary research was carried out under fellowships from the University of California at Berkeley. With this support I was able, over an extended period of time, to avail myself of the staff and research facilities of the Ecole Normale Supérieure and the U.E.R. de Sciences de Textes et de Documents at Paris VII. The State University of New York at Stony Brook granted me a 1989 Summer Stipend allowing me to expand and revise the original manuscript.

Acknowledgments

With the encouragement of E. Ann Kaplan, director of the Humanities Institute at Stony Brook, I presented an earlier version of chapter 1 in the context of the Institute's Faculty Seminar Series in 1989. The second half of chapter 10 revises a paper I delivered at the Seventh Annual Colloquium in Twentieth Century Studies in 1990. Chapter 5 appeared in slightly different form in *SubStance* 64 (1991).

Contents

Part One

Introduction

There is uncanny simplicity and consistency in the efforts of humans to establish a peaceful and equitable functioning of civil society. Whether by prescriptive or descriptive approximations, we quest for an elusive body of law acceptable to all persons. Once revealed to us, this canon would serve as a regulatory system (prescriptive) or as a clarification of natural virtues (descriptive) with which humanity would then be able to tutor itself. In either case, our search takes the form of an inscription, as if by writing the evolution of ethics we were lending more weight to the endeavor and more permanence to the results.

Literature and philosophy are the two principal discourses of this ethical inscription. While confluences between literature and philosophy on questions of ethics abound, it has most often been the vocation of philosophy to anticipate rules of behavior, whereas we appeal to literature to represent models of equitable relations within lived experience. Neither discourse is superior in characterizing the ethical quest. And the present study makes no claim at preferring one over the other, for indeed both seem indispensable to our efforts at creating a civil society.

The attempts of one writer to envision an ethics through the ambiguous lens of the relation to the father are dissected here. However, to view Sartre's focus on paternity merely as the residue of an upbringing in colonialist, industrial-capitalist Europe where patriarchy ruled unchecked would be historically shortsighted, for identifying the family as the measure of all ethical relations is a connection as old as the stories of Cain and Abel, and of Jacob and Isaac. Sartre's search for a father projects him well beyond the bounds of mid-twentieth-century European thought—of which he is nevertheless paradigmatic—to insert him within the ethical genealogy of which we are all offspring.

The wisdom that Shakespeare recommended fathers acquire in knowing their child is gained through the willingness to nurture a bond that mothers are undoubtedly aware of from the moment of conception. Sartre, though an advocate of enlightenment or self-effacement on the part of fathers, demands much more from humanity if it is ever to become ethical, universally advocating the prophecy of Wordsworth that "the child is father of the man."

CHAPTER 1

The Unbearable Weightiness of Being

> Pères, ne l'oubliez pas, vos
> enfants sont votre unique avenir.
> Il dépend de vous que vous les
> massacriez ou qu'ils vous sauvent
> du néant: car vous ne vous sauverez
> pas tout seuls, je vous le dis.
>
> —Sartre[1]

Ever since Descartes, the Western philosophical tradition has been characterized by the resistance to accepting an assumed incommensurability of subject and object. At the heart of France's foulest moment, in the midst of the Nazi occupation, armed with the investigatory and descriptive methods of Husserlian phenomenology,[2] Jean-Paul Sartre set out on an ontological crusade, announced in the opening pages of *Being and Nothingness*,[3] to unify the two components of being. However apt to succeed he must have thought it to be, Sartre's mission ended in one of modern philosophy's most well-known failures. Referring to the unrequited desire of humans to achieve a plenitude of being that objects appear to us to possess, Sartre ends the treatise by declaring that "man is a useless passion" (1943, 678). In the same vein four years later, the Paris stage actor playing Garcin in Sartre's *No Exit*[4] would sardonically declaim the line that "hell is other people" (1960c, 182), confirming that the rift between "me" and the rest of the world is just as impossible to narrow as that "nothingness" that separates subject and object.

The popularity of Sartre's writings and the admiration that they had once inspired had begun to wane as early as 1963 and 1964, well before his death in 1980. As a series of thinkers from Lévi-Strauss and Barthes to Foucault, Althusser, and Lacan rejected Sartre's humanism implicitly or explicitly, successively finding themselves at center stage in France's intellectual theater, Sartre came to symbolize the repudiated forefather whose thinking was invoked only with contempt. Yet a certain fascination has endured for this figure whose more than prolific polygraphy is rife with aporia in its philosophical manifestation, with crabbed repetition in its literary products, and is everywhere revelatory of consistent political foibles. Just as Sartre claimed that Marxism was the "unsurpassable philosophy of our time,"[5] the unique worldview of this quintessentially engaged man of letters, who remains one of the most widely read and quoted authors a decade after his death, is an unavoidable step in our reflection on the world today.

There are at least two negative judgments about Sartre's thought that, having been expressed frequently in the heyday of existentialism, continue to creep into our minds today with the insistence of commonplaces: (1) if he is not profoundly immoral, Sartre is, at the very least, a profoundly demoralizing thinker, and (2) as a general advocate of a freedom so unlimited that the human subject must owe allegiance to no one and forge its own destiny out of nothing, Sartre is not only skeptical about the beings who engender us, he quite specifically and unequivocally condemns fathers. Though still exercizing considerable influence, the first of these clichés has come under some revision by the critical work of the past thirty years, revealing how consistently Sartre's work is predicated upon questions of moral judgment within the framework of radical freedom. Thus, although he never elaborated an ethical system, Sartre's work is profoundly moral. The assumption, however, that Sartre abhors all family-grounded interpersonal relationships as epitomized by paternity is a much more tenacious one.

As is frustratingly true of much of Sartre's thought, the opposites of these two persistent criticisms are not only coherent and supported by evidence, but they are fused in Sartre's thought in a way that actually promotes his ethical reflection. In positing such a paradoxical fusion, I am proposing to go against the grain not only of several critiques of Sartre as moralist but also to go against the grain of Sartre himself. In order to move in this direction, it is necessary, first, to question the assumption that Sartre abhors fatherhood by showing how his writings consistently link the constitution of the ethical subject with the problems endemic to the most difficult interpersonal relation of all: that between fathers and sons. Rather than dismiss, once and for all, the possibility of a tolerable paternity, Sartre became truly obsessed by it—perhaps on a private level, but certainly as a thematic in his literary work. What I intend to show in this study is that Sartre ties this preoccupation with paternity to his search for a paradigm for all ethical interaction between human subjects. Never either condemning paternity nor endorsing it, Sartre remains ambivalent in the extreme about its negative effects on human freedom. Yet this very ambivalence fuels his abiding interest in the relationship's ethical potential.

Finding Meaning between Discourses

As something of the Victor Hugo or the Voltaire of the twentieth century, Sartre engaged in almost every type of writing conceivable.[6] Having specialized in his early career on consciousness and the imagination, Sartre wrote two major philosophical treatises in which he attempted to wed the Marxist political theory of the second with the existentialist ontology and epistemology of the first.[7] In the concluding remarks of both of these philosophical projects, he dangled before his readers the promise of an ethics that would lend practical support to the metaphysical system. To the frustration of many of the unconditional Sartreans, however, he never formalized this promised ethics into a treatise of its own, although all of his work is profoundly ethical in its considerations.

Although Sartre's ethical thought is not absent from his written legacy, I contend that the core of this ethical thought is not to be found in the posthumously published *Notebooks for an Ethics*, but rather in a rhetorical interworld situated between Sartre's philosophical discourse and his literary discourse. This rhetorical interworld can be fixed and decoded. The voice Sartre assumed both in his theoretical writings and in the literary illustrations of his philosophy that are the loci of his philosophical *language*—that voice, though perhaps not what one could actually call poetic, is often lyrical and fraught with metaphor and tropes of which the most frequent is by far the chiasmus.

The constant play in Sartre's rhetorical usage should incite anyone to hesitate before taking his reputation for spleen, philosophical aporia, and unfinished projects at face value and to look elsewhere *within* his works rather than *beyond* them (i.e., in posthumous volumes) for his deepest expression. I have adopted the method of weaving back and forth between his philosophy, on the one hand, and his fictional and political writings on the other, making of the present book a sustained commentary on the patterns that this hermeneutic method renders. Recent continental philosophy has demonstrated the heuristic value of shattering traditional barriers separating discourses,[8] and indeed I am convinced that just such an intertextual weaving was a method that Sartre himself put to profit through his own polygraphic practices: by his habit of writing simultaneously in several registers, he sought paths beyond his own apparent dead ends in the ethical realm.[9] From my experience in reading Sartre's corpus, I have concluded that the reader must shuttle between the various genres or discourses that the "pen-wielding hyena"[10] practiced in order to avoid the shortsighted impression of Sartrean contradiction and to grasp most clearly his meaning.

Sartrean "Passion": Useless or Necessary?

It is rarely observed that, in *Being and Nothingness*, Sartre's ontological story of irretrievably split being stands parallel to an ethical version of the same dilemma for whose two parts, one could argue, he found a much more felicitous reconciliation through their parallels in his literary discourse. This literary voice also has a major part in the famous treatise. How else could it happen that, in spite of the pessimism infusing *Being and Nothingness*, the consensus of Sartre's readers come to hold a generally positive view of the work? Was Sartre's popularity merely the by-product of a particularly disabused and morbid postwar generation? On the other hand, how does a pathos-filled concluding statement like "man is a useless passion" resolve, in any positive manner, the ontological project of regluing Cartesian being as Sartre announced it in the treatise's first pages? What blinds most of Sartre's readers, then, to an all-too-obvious despair infusing the words "useless passion"? And may we assume that "passion" has something to do with the proposed rewelding of being? If so, what? And why is the project doomed to fail, that is, why is man destined to become a vain longing for the unattainable? What, finally, are we to make of the highly suggestive multiplicity of meanings in a word like *passion* employed prominently in the philosophical context?

The first stirrings of viable answers to these questions appear when nontechnical expressions like *useless passion* are allowed their polysemantic potential through a hermeneutics of discursive dialogue that I suggest as one of the most fruitful methods of reading the work of any writer, but especially that of a polygraph like Sartre. In so doing we discover that, between Sartre's relentless ruminations on paternity and his striving to locate an ethical unification of split being, there exists the same link as that of problem to solution. The sheer massiveness and wordiness of Sartre's oeuvre, sometimes daunting, sometimes annoying to the critic, cloaks a raw material that Sartre forged into an ever-renewable tool of thought. His seemingly eclectic work invites us to become engrossed in a flow of words and imagery common to virtually all of his "voices"—words and imagery that dissolve the traditional barriers between his discourses.

Some preliminary clues about man's "useless passion" should come as no great surprise to readers who have already had the stamina to wade through the nearly seven hundred pages of Sartrean logorrhea constituting *Being and Nothingness*. *Passion* connotes the irrepressible desire of humans for that totality of being which modern man has come to believe he lacks. Heidegger, whom Sartre had only read rather superficially until spurred (and spurned) by the former's "Letter on Humanism,"[11] theorized about a lost state of wholeness that he calls *Being* with a capital *B* (*Sein*) for which today's atrophied *being-there* with a lowercase *B* (*Dasein*) stands as a mere nostalgic longing. It is to that lost state that Sartre refers when he speaks about man's attempt to commune with the other side of being.[12] "The real goal of man's search," writes Sartre, "is being as the synthetic fusion of the in-itself with the for-itself" (1943, 691). What Sartre designates as man's "passion" is an emotionally charged quest for that wholeness, completeness, or totality which, through endless deferrals and ultimate inconclusiveness, Sartre only teases us into thinking may be realizable.

If we consider the context of the passage in which Sartre's bleak conclusion occurs, passion takes on axiological connotations that throw its declared *uselessness* into question. Putting the crabbed repetititiveness of Sartre's philosophical prose to hermeneutical use, we find him stating that "man loses himself as man in order for God to be born" (678): God only exists, in other words, to the extent that man renders himself capable of self-nihilation. Varying his terms only slightly, he writes that "man makes himself man in order to be God" (690): the nihilating act, the sine qua non of for-itselfness, infuses human consciousness with an illusion of omnipotence. In yet another version, "man loses himself in order for *causa sui* to exist" (690): the Spinozan spin-off of Sartre's notion of God is, once again, the only positive residue of man's work of self-nihilation. What is striking in these three declarations in the form of oracular maxims is how obviously Sartre, through the notion of passion, signals religious inclinations in the for-itself—inclinations that he is noted for vehemently rejecting elsewhere.[13] Through an extension of this choice of metaphor, carrying out the decision to assume responsibility takes on the demeanor of an obligatory act of mortification. Sartre thus bids us to recall and ponder the passion of Christ in living out our existence.

Christ's passion was an acceptance ritual of universal responsibility leading from the bearing of a cross to death by crucifixion. The passion of the subject of modern philosophy would thus represent a martyrdom of the ultimate responsible agent—the final agony of godless man before the telos of an unattainable total being. Not only in the context of his ontology but throughout his work, Sartre displays an unflagging fascination with a link between the human act of negation (or nihilation) and the heroic risking of life that he feels is intrinsic to our nature. This theme of a perilous scrape with death is of central importance in Sartre's ethical ruminations.

Ethics before Ontology before Politics

Despite the explicit pledge of his title to provide a "phenomenological ontology," the author of *Being and Nothingness* slips willingly, almost prematurely, into the mode of the moralist. The last hundred pages of the treatise are essentially devoted to what one *must do* rather than what one *is,* that is, what one does presumably after coming into being. With the categories of freedom and responsibility replacing the dodging and weaving dialectic of for-itself and in-itself, Sartre tries to elucidate his quandary over the completion of man's being in ethical terms. But what is imperative to note is how, in this last part of *Being and Nothingness,* the language and imagery of the passion of man assumes the axiological and even theological dimensions that I have suggested and preserves, by the same stroke, the unresolved tension in man's longing for totality.

The very being of man *is* a constant risking of life to become God. Yet the crux of Sartre's ontology—the principle of existentialism—is that human existence is a *becoming* before it is a *being:* "existence precedes essence." The human in flux, the human of becoming, remains in the realm of the obligatory ethical problem of the relationship with other humans until such time as the difficulties of this relationship are solved. In other words, the ontological stumbling block of the 1943 treatise is subtended by the absence of true ethical foundations even though the ethical edifice gets partially built. In the ethical language that subsumes the ontological vocabulary in the last part of *Being and Nothingness,* the absolutely unfettered freedom for which Sartre was attacked by critics is, by its very nature, linked to a primordial, inescapable responsibility. Such a responsibility establishes a constraining force enchaining me to freedom prior even to the question of for what or for whom I am responsible interpellates me. Sartre tirelessly repeats his oxymoronic maxim that "we are condemned to freedom" as if, from the very moment this priceless gift is granted us, a law imposed also from outside our consciousness (i.e., outside our authority) were commanding our action, guaranteeing that it takes the other into consideration first.

"Condemned to be free," man is immediately (i.e., from his moment of inception) confronted with the precarious and life-threatening situation of "carry[ing] the weight of the entire world on his shoulders: he is responsible for the world and for himself insofar as [this is his] manner of being" (1943, 612). This moral duty to others is, Sartre contends emphatically and repeatedly, "overwhelming" and even "unbearable" (*insoutenable*) but must be borne as if it were a destiny. Moral responsibility for the entire world is a burden of immense weight that each of us must bear.

An ethics that somehow renders compatible radical freedom and universal responsibility must be instituted before the ontological aporia of duality can be confronted. In turn, the relative ease with which Sartre wrote of current affairs would seem to indicate his propensity for viewing the ethical prerequisite as a political problem, leaving the metaphysical resolution of dualities in suspense. Sartre strove continually, through a series of positions ranging from aloofness to radical leftist militancy, to resolve the political avatar of his ethical premises through commitment. Man would be condemned to being a "useless passion" only as long as the grounding of an ethics devoid of predetermined normativity had not yet been worked out in political terms.

Yet *ontological* completeness, which in Sartrean terms would consist of the "synthesis of the for-itself and the in-itself," requires *ethical* maturity—an equilibrium between one subject and the rest symbolized by the fitting together and welding of freedom with responsibility. Virtue in politics, in the form of commitment—a realm of action set into motion by what Sartre calls the *act*—depends on ethics. To guarantee morally responsible political action, the realization of the subject's full ethical potential must be achieved prior to the moment of the act. It is in this ethical a priori that the greatest paradox of Sartre's project lies. In fact, the concerns expressed in most of Sartre's fiction allow us to argue that the ontological and political registers of the human being are more or less synchronic in their coming to maturity while they are *subsequent* to the resolution of ethical questions. The subject's being-in-the-world, being in the polis, his or her political positioning must stand upon an ethical grounding located in the *oikos*—and for Sartre, this *oikos* is, indeed, the home. Beginning with this hypothesis, one may perhaps begin to explain the arguably irresponsible political decisions Sartre constantly found himself making. For without an ethics based on a reliable model for intersubjectivity, the Sartrean political act ("existential Marxism" or otherwise) risks being as reckless as Sartre's more vehement detractors claimed it was.

. . . and Paternity before Ethics

The idea of a nonprescriptive ethics might at first seem absurd. If one eliminates the possibility of rules for guaranteeing virtuous behavior, then man must simply be presumed to be good by nature and, unless it be considered descriptive only, there is no need of constructing an ethics at all. For Sartre, virtue as well as evil are bequeathed to individuals through family (or culture) and for even a nonprescriptive ethics to work, that individual must have a model. As a leitmotiv in virtually all of his theater and fiction, and as the principal force behind his literary biographies, Sartre consistently displays various aspects of a lifelong rumination on paternity. The problems, as Sartre views them, that set fathers and sons against each other find expression in precisely the same allegorical terms of relative weightiness or lightness of being as are found in the descriptions in *Being and Nothingness* of how freedom and responsibility theoretically unite. An uncanny similarity between the allegory of Atlas bearing the ethical weight of the world on his shoulders and an image Sartre used to illustrate his contention that the father-son relationship is fundamentally warped incited my hypothesis that reflection on paternity helped him to nurture his belief in the possibility of an ethics. If the title of my study alludes to *Search for a Method* (Sartre's theoretical foundation for the *Critique of Dialectical Reason*), it is because, for Sartre, to conceive of a father with whom a son could establish a viable and equitable relationship is to find the linchpin of the Ethics he never wrote.

By a cursory examination of evidence about Sartre's childhood, as he provides it in his autobiographical *The Words*,[14] and evidence about his private adult life rendered so highly public through his interviews and Simone de Beauvoir's intimate writings,[15] as well as the famous couple's correspondence,[16] we readily grasp how violently opposed to paternity Sartre wished to have himself appear. Avoiding the role with apparent care, it is further known that Sartre never became a biological father. He is thus consistent when he creates a fictional character like Mathieu who, in *The Age of Reason,* is in the position of becoming a father and whose freedom is thus in imminent danger of being restricted.[17] Sartre has that character seek, by any means possible, to get the child's mother to have an abortion. Yet, paradoxically, as I will show in a later chapter, even though Sartre "was" Mathieu in the late 1930s as he "had been" Roquentin earlier in the same decade, it is Marcelle who serves, in a certain sense, as Sartre's mouthpiece in the novel.[18] In a sententious opening passage of *The Words,* Sartre pronounces a sweeping yet very ambiguous condemnation of fatherhood. Several of Sartre's literary treatments of father-son configurations, on the other hand, show him favorable to what would be a utopian paternity for him. Whether rejecting paternity on behalf of fictional sons or refusing paternity when speaking from the position of fictional fathers, Sartre returns incessantly to the relationship, as to the core of his ethical thought, as if it were the foundation of ideal intersubjectivity. But also as if it were, at the same time, an impossible burden for either father or son to bear.

Surrogate Fatherhood

In his real life (which, in this case, does have a bearing on much of the literary and philosophical creation), Sartre encouraged and cultivated an attachment that a series of rootless young men felt toward him. These part professional, part affective relationships tended to inspire ambivalently fatherly sentiments in Sartre. In turn, these free souls like Jean Genet, André Gorz, Francis Jeanson, and Benny Lévy acted out truly filial behavior with their "surrogate father," either in the form of piety or rebellion. One of these very protégés, Olivier Todd, wrote a book entitled *Un fils rebelle.*[19] Much earlier, Francis Jeanson, observing the Sartrean father-son paradigm even in his own case, coined the phrase "social bastards" to describe them all.[20] Sartre developed a truly morbid fascination with Jean Genet[21] and Goetz, a bastard by Jeanson's definition in Sartre's play *The Devil and the Good Lord,*[22] was modeled directly after the scandalous playwright. So is Edmund Kean, the English actor reincarnated in Sartre's adaptation of Alexander Dumas's *Kean.*[23] Between Genet and Jeanson, Sartre had met André Gorz, the Viennese political philosopher whose early career he sponsored by prefacing the autobiographical *The Traitor*[24] and who later composed *Foundations for an Ethics.*[25] Finally, late in Sartre's life, the young Benny Lévy,[26] an exiled Egyptian Jew leading the Maoist Proletarian Left, so much intrigued Sartre that he virtually adopted him, employing him as his last secretary and kindling Beauvoir's jealousy (Beauvoir 1981). In short, Sartre may have, like his creation Mathieu, refused to have a child, but he certainly sought a kind of spiritual paternity in his relations with younger men.

In the lives of these "social bastards" considered eminently free men, Sartre's rejection or condemnation of conventional paternity, his emphasis on their bastardy, constituted an ethical challenge. Sartre wagered that, of all individuals, these fatherless "sons" were best equipped to invent a new ethical mode of behavior for themselves—a moral life after which the rest of the world could model itself in turn. Unrestricted by any normative model handed down by a father, bastards are best at eluding established powers in building a new moral code. Sartre's message in *The Words* was that for a son to have a father is to be needlessly emburdened and thus inhibited in existence as if by enormous weight. Other literary works by Sartre show, however, that the more "weightless" a subject's being is, the more chance he has of being free as well as moral. This challenge, sent out through much of Sartre's work to all "bastards" within earshot, has both axiological and psychological repercussions.[27]

An ethics of the integrally free soul, the ethics of a sort of fatherless son, the basis of a *Sartrean ethics,* is to be found within one's self. The Sartrean man is a "self-made man" in the strongest sense of the phrase: he creates his model through the nihilating act, then creates himself based on the "clean" image. Thus Jeanson became the first to attempt to write the "unwritten" Sartrean ethics in 1965 with a book whose title is quite ironic for someone supposedly "fatherless": *The Ethical Problem and Sartre's Thought.*[28] In the late 1970s, Benny Lévy, who was later to compose an ethical dialogue with Sartre,[29] was trying to generate enough energy in a dying Sartre to deliver himself of the ethics he still had not written at the eleventh hour of his life. André Gorz, at the beginning of his *Foundations for an Ethics,* asks rhetorically (and in autobiographical words reminiscent of *The Traitor*), "starting from nothing, that is from oneself, can one restore and reconstruct everything?" (Gorz 1977, 11). As early as the second paragraph, Gorz describes the enunciator of that question (himself) as a "social bastard" according to Jeanson: "a stateless exile, without family, past or future, with no reason to be 'here' any more than anywhere else or to act in one way any more than any other" (11). Restoring and reconstructing everything indeed constitutes the challenge of Sartrean ethics, as Gorz goes on to explain: "When the randomness of birth and history cause you to belong to no people or group, when no culture, ideology, class or value strike you as being your own, can you come to prefer a certain class, value, action or behavior over all others and if so, based upon what criteria?" (11). In other terms, if the free subject that Gorz's statelessness (and hence his fatherlessness) allow him to be could answer these questions with any certainty, then the ethics devoid of predetermined normativity that Sartre could only dream about might be possible.

Lending Weight to Being

The feeling of weightlessness in one's being is a recurrent theme in Sartre's writings, systematically undermining the individualistic foundation for ethics that readers are often hasty to extrapolate from *Being and Nothingness.* The discomfort of weightless being gives way to a pluralistic foundation for Sartre's ethics. In *The Unbearable Lightness of Being,* Milan Kundera emphasizes how pervasive metaphors of heaviness are for expressing our compulsion for responsible lives. Not only are burdens an ever-present reminder of our sense of moral destiny, but "the heavier the burden, the closer our lives come to earth, the more real and truthful they become."[30] Whether Sartre truly rejoiced, as he insists in *The Words,* at not having been emburdened by a father or whether, on the contrary, his father's premature death left an incommensurable lack (*manque*) in Sartre's life, the situation was dramatic enough for his writing to be haunted with metaphors not of heaviness, but rather of lightness. Indeed, we must ask, as Kundera does, "Is heaviness truly deplorable and lightness splendid?" (1984, 5). In any case, it is to sons *with* fathers that Sartre reserves metaphors of heaviness. It is *they* who are overwhelmingly emburdened by fathers.

Daring right after the Liberation to claim that "we were never freer than under the German occupation,"[31] Sartre envisioned the possibility, and one might say the necessity, of radical freedom even in the most repressive social or political conditions. Yet if we search through his theater, we find that several of Sartre's freewheeling protagonists, who describe themselves as weightless, suffer intensely from freedom's consequential *lightness of being*. Orestes complains of feeling so lightweight that he is *literally* out of touch with reality: as he treks toward Argos, he is unable to feel the sharpness of the stones that should press against his feet.[32] Hugo, the "social bastard" in *Dirty Hands*,[33] whines about his weightlessness too. As in the case of Orestes, Hugo's problem finds remedy in a murder that is nothing less than a symbolic parricide. In Sartre's most un-Sartrean work, *Bariona*,[34] the decision to embrace paternity brings upon the hero a feeling of weightiness of which he previously suffered the lack. With predictable regularity, then, Sartre's literary production frames a relationship between the absence of moral responsibility, on the one hand, and an absent father or the lack of paternal sentiment in a potential father on the other. Those deficiencies, in turn, cause the existential uneasiness that Sartre's characters experience as an anxiety-filled weightlessness. Just as predictably, the Sartrean agent unravels the problem by an act that brings him perilously near death, but that lends the weight required to properly establish the subject's being and make him feel complete. Thus, the fertile image of man's "passion" indeed entails suffering and approaches death without, nevertheless, delivering on the bliss of a theological afterlife.

In apparent contradiction with the antipaternity pronouncements of *The Words*, being exempt from responsibility is never an enviable state, since it causes the subject to endure a highly uncomfortable lightness of being. Sartre's glorifications of freedom tend to overshadow what is perhaps the most important aphorism of *Being and Nothingness*, namely that being a "radical freedom" implies man's *condemnation* to responsibility for all other subjects. This forced accountability to others precisely reduplicates the ethical stance that Dostoyevsky conceived in order to compensate for the moral shortcomings he observed in humans. In *The Brothers Karamazov*, Markel declares on his death-bed that "every one of us is responsible *before* everyone else, responsible *for* everyone else, in every way . . . and I most of all."[35] Emmanuel Levinas, Sartre's contemporary who had learned of phenomenology well before him,[36] posited this Dostoyevskian concept of responsibility as the foundation of ethical intersubjectivity precisely because of its asymmetrical quality. For Dostoyevsky, Levinas, and Sartre, being ethical means that the individual must take the entire world of others into consideration with each act and without any expectation of reciprocity.

In *Being and Nothingness,* this overwhelming responsibility is the price the subject must pay for attaining complete being. But universal responsibility proves also that man's passion, at least on the level of being as interaction, is *not* useless. The most astounding contradiction in Sartre's resolution of ethical duality appears to be that the unavoidable burden upon the ethical Atlas is, by virtue of congruent allegories, identical to the paternal albatross that he rejects out of hand in *The Words* and which any number of other works seem to uphold. Is there any difference at all, one is then in a position to ask, between the universal responsibility that ballasts an otherwise excessively light existence in freedom and a father who weighs his son down and stifles his freedom? Obviously, yes: otherwise Sartre could not embrace one image as expressive of the very foundation of his ethics while rejecting the other as the greatest iniquity one individual can inflict upon another. Yet it cannot be denied that the allegories and linguistic imagery Sartre deploys to convey both situations confirm that the constitution of total being and the problem of paternity are intertwined in his overall thinking on ethics. The imbalance, asymmetricality, or, to put it in down-to-earth terms, the unfairness that Sartre praises in the theoretical and condemns in the empirical constitutes the unresolved tension lending my study its impetus, just as that imbalance was, I believe, the principal force in Sartre's ethical thought.

Crisscross

Asserting one's place in the world without upsetting a balance between claim and concession is the goal of a Sartrean ethics. A fusing of choice and destiny, ethical intersubjectivity must reaffirm each subject's integral freedom. The worlds described in *Being and Nothing-*

ness and in *No Exit* are images of the world as it exists today and, as such, are not the worlds of a Sartrean ethics. Glimpses of that utopian world, however, came to Sartre through the image of the unbearable weightiness of being brought upon a subject by having to face the parent-child bond. This bond is one that combines a condemnation to responsibility with a free choice of that responsibility. As the legacy of the late Freud informs us, a study of links between ethical and familial relationships inevitably entails many of the premises of psychoanalysis. However, beyond the Oedipal triangle that forms the basis of Freudian theory, the Sartrean search for a father shifts willingly to a configuration equally familiar to the Western mind consisting of savior, virgin mother, and faithful subject. Contrary to what one expects from an atheist thinker, Sartre's pronouncements on ethics and on paternity almost always, at some level of language, carry religious overtones.

While the degree of responsibility devolving to Sartre's subject far surpasses that of everyday Christian morality, Sartre finds certain Christian models useful and the qualities he deems necessary for assuming universal responsibility are reminiscent of those imputed to Christ. For example, in the elements of the legend of Saint Christopher, one can circumscribe a redoubled image of shouldered responsibility that illustrates the paradoxical reciprocity for which Sartre seems to search, at least as far as we can gather from *Being and Nothingness.* As the repository for everyone's sins, the boy Christ was thought to incorporate immeasurable weight. In the case of Sartre's ethical Atlas (the allegorical image that will aid us throughout this study), responsibility is not a state of originary being (as with Christ) but is rather an *assumed* responsibility in the manner of Christopher, Christ's carrier (*christos phoros*). Capable of ferrying any passenger, no matter how cumbersome, across the river he commanded, Christopher was nearly overcome by the weight of the Son of man when he hoisted him upon his shoulders to facilitate his passage. Only Christopher's conversion to Christianity, occurring in midcourse, saved the giant from drowning beneath the burden of the world's sins. Sartre envisions a utopian father-son relation in terms similar to the Christopher/Christ configuration—a relation in which the burden of the world (symbolized by the father) miraculously *supports* the bearer of that burden. This ideal father-son relationship, which would serve each individual as model for any other intersubjective link established in life, must be a *doubly asymmetrical bond*. The responsibility assumed by either member of the pair for the other must be *equally overwhelming*.[37]

At the deceptively simple level of syntactic organization and linguistic play, Sartre's unusually pervasive use of chiasmus functions as a textual reminder of this double asymmetricality founding the ethical bond. Sartre came closest to envisioning an ethical paternity when he figured the relationship as one of reciprocity between two bipolar beings fused in chiastic fashion—crisscrossed, as it were, like two magnets whose poles must be reversed in order to allow them to be joined. A rhetorical figure organized in the shape of a cross (x), the term *chiasmus* explains, expands, extends the Christian hues of Sartre's ethical thought. For it to overcome uselessness, the passion of one individual, which is his or her responsibility for others, must be reciprocal like the chiasmus—reciprocal just as in the mutuality and reversibility of father's and son's roles that would ultimately have permitted Sartre to lift his ban of paternity. The weightiness of one's being in responsibility must only *approach* the unbearable: others, whom Sartre personally perhaps never really considered otherwise than as hell, are meant in utopia to shoulder the rest of the burden.

Notes

Throughout the text, quotations from Sartre's works will be identified by year and page. Complete citations are listed in the Bibliography.

1. "Fathers: don't forget that your sons are your sole future. Whether you massacre them or they save you from nothingness depends on you. You won't save yourselves alone: this I say to you" (Jean-Paul Sartre, "Le droit à l'insoumission," in the pamphlet *Dossier des "121"* [Paris, n.d.], 32 [my translation]).

2. Sartre was introduced to phenomenology in 1933. However, accounts differ about how he first learned of the strain of thought that originated in Germany: either it was through Raymond Aron (according to the famous anecdote of Simone de Beauvoir, *La Force de l'âge* [Paris: Gallimard, 1960], 156–57) or through reading Emmanuel Levinas (*La Théorie de l'intuition dans la phénoménologie de Husserl* [Paris: Alcan, 1930]), which Beauvoir says he bought just after the Aron revelation. In any case, he was soon off to Berlin

(1933–34) on a scholarship. There he immersed himself in Husserl's teachings.

3. Jean-Paul Sartre, *L'Etre et le Néant* (Paris: Gallimard, 1943). Translations are my own and have been checked against *Being and Nothingness*, trans. Hazel E. Barnes (New York: Philosophical Library, 1956). *L'Etre et le Néant* was written in less than two years, although Sartre had started writing notes for it in late 1939. On the genesis of this work, see Michel Contat and Michel Rybalka, *Les Ecrits de Sartre* (Paris: Gallimard, 1970), 85–87; Annie Cohen-Solal, *Sartre: 1905–1980* (Paris: Gallimard, 1985), 252–55.

4. Jean-Paul Sartre, *Huis clos* (1944) in *Théâtre, I* (Paris: Gallimard, 1960).

5. Jean-Paul Sartre, *Questions de méthode* (Paris: Gallimard, 1967), 44.

6. Contrary to common belief, Sartre also dabbled in poetry: Beauvoir has transmitted to us two lines of an elegy written by Sartre (Beauvoir 1960, 53); on this particular poem, see also Josette Pacaly, *Sartre au miroir* (Paris: Klincksieck, 1980), 147. I relate these lines to Sartre's evolution as perceiver of the cinematic work of art in "Sartre/Cinema: Spectator/Art Which Is Not One," *Cinema Journal* 30, no.2 (1991): 43–59. See also the Jean-Paul Sartre, *Ecrits de jeunesse* (Paris: Gallimard, 1990).

7. Jean-Paul Sartre, *Critique de la raison dialectique* (Paris: Gallimard, 1960); see also Mark Poster, *Existential Marxism in Postwar France: From Sartre to Althusser* (Princeton, N.J.: Princeton University Press, 1975), 72–105, 264–305.

8. Individual works need not be enumerated; it should suffice here to invoke the names of Gilles Deleuze (with Félix Guattari), Jean-François Lyotard, Michel Foucault, and Jacques Derrida.

9. This method, though left unnamed in this capacity by the author, is analogous to the progressive-regressive method of historical or biographical analysis that Sartre first described in *Questions of Method* and notably put to use in the *Critique* and *The Family Idiot*. The progressive-regressive method itself was borrowed from Marxist sociologist Henri Lefebvre (see Sartre 1967, 73n), and modified to fit Sartre's purposes (119ff.).

10. Fadeev, quoted at the Moscow Congress, August 1948, by Contat in Jean-Paul Sartre, *Oeuvres romanesques* (Paris: Gallimard, 1981), lxvii.

11. Sartre first read *Being and Time* in 1934. Heidegger's "Letter on Humanism," published in French in 1947, stirred up more general interest in Heidegger there and served as a corrective for many skewed interpretations (see note 12). The literature on this subject, especially in the wake of renewed debate in France over Heidegger's allegiance to Nazism, is voluminous.

12. According to Heidegger, Sartre, as well as many other French philosophers, wrongly overemphasized the importance of *Dasein* in his thought, having been misled about its meaning by the poor translation as *réalité humaine*. See Martin Jay, *Marxism and Totality* (Berkeley: University of California Press, 1984), 335.

13. Despite his reputation for atheism, evidence of Sartre's serious reflec-

tion about religion through conversations with "a young vicar and a Jesuit novice" he met in a German prisoner of war camp in 1940 may be found in Jean-Paul Sartre, *Lettres au Castor* (Paris: Gallimard, 1983), 299–300, and Beauvoir 1960 (540, 584–85, passim).

14. Jean-Paul Sartre, *Les Mots* (Paris: Gallimard, 1964).

15. In the present study, information will be gleaned from the second and last of the several volumes constituting Beauvoir's memoirs: Beauvoir 1960 and Simone de Beauvoir, *La Cérémonie des adieux* (Paris: Gallimard, 1981).

16. For Sartre's letters to Beauvoir, see *Lettres au Castor;* Simone de Beauvoir, *Lettres à Sartre* (Paris: Gallimard, 1990).

17. Jean-Paul Sartre, *L'âge de raison* (1945) in *Oeuvres romanesques* (Paris: Gallimard, 1981), 391–729.

18. I wish to thank Richard Moreland who pointed this out to me and illustrated it with his analysis of Rosa Coldfield in William Faulkner's *Absalom! Absalom!;* see Richard Moreland, *Faulkner and Modernism: Rereading and Rewriting* (Madison, Wis.: University of Wisconsin Press, 1990).

19. Olivier Todd, *Un fils rebelle* (Paris: Grasset, 1981). The author had been close to the "Sartre family" since 1948, when he married Paul Nizan's daughter.

20. See chapter 8.

21. This fascination was demonstrated by Sartre's "monstrous" introduction to Jean Genet's complete works; see Jean-Paul Sartre, *Saint Genet, comédien et martyr* (Paris: Gallimard, 1952).

22. Jean-Paul Sartre, *Le Diable et le Bon Dieu* (Paris: Gallimard, 1951).

23. Jean-Paul Sartre, *Kean* (Paris: Gallimard, 1954).

24. André Gorz, *Le Traître* (Paris: Seuil, 1958).

25. André Gorz, *Fondements pour une morale* (Paris: Galilée, 1977); quotations are translated by me.

26. Benny Lévy was known during his Left extremist years, that is, during the period in which he worked with Sartre nearly every day, under the pseudonym Pierre Victor.

27. An idea that will be developed in Part 5 is that Sartre's ideas on bastardy directly defy psychoanalytic theory, which would claim, in accordance with Freud's *The Ego and the Id,* that ethics is the social dimension of superego formation, that is, the subject's gradual introjection of the law of the father.

28. Francis Jeanson, *Le problème moral et la pensée de Sartre* (Paris: Seuil, 1965).

29. Benny Lévy, *Le Nom de l'homme: dialogue avec Sartre* (Paris: Verdier, 1984).

30. Milan Kundera, *The Unbearable Lightness of Being* (New York: Harper and Row, 1984), 5.

31. Jean-Paul Sartre, "La République du silence," in *Situations, III* (Paris: Gallimard, 1949), 11.

32. Jean-Paul Sartre, *Les Mouches* (1943) in *Théâtre, I* (Paris: Gallimard, 1960), 7–121.

33. Jean-Paul Sartre, *Les Mains sales* (Paris: Gallimard, 1948).

34. Jean-Paul Sartre, *Bariona, ou le Fils du tonnerre* (1940) in Michel Contat and Michel Rybalka, *Les Ecrits de Sartre* (Paris: Gallimard, 1970), 565–633.

35. Fyodor Dostoyevsky, *The Brothers Karamazov* (Harmondsworth: Penguin, 1958), 1:339.

36. See note 1.

37. Another contemporary work of fiction built upon the theme of burden carrying is Michel Tournier, *Le Roi des aulnes* (Paris: Gallimard, 1970).

Part Two

Paternity Rejected

The first step in Sartre's search for a father requires a leap from the aporia of *Being and Nothingness* to the more felicitous experimental field of Sartre's literary discourse. This part explores Sartre's largely unsuccessful attempt to unite being or to posit man's completeness in order to show that project's link to Sartre's most commonly known attitude toward the family. The key to this welding of being would have been the ethics alluded to at the end of the 1943 treatise and which Sartre never wrote. However, the allegorical imagery Sartre used to describe that proposed ethics corresponds precisely to the allegorical imagery he used everywhere else in his work to describe relationships of paternity.

Paternity is not reducible to the biological or legal condition of he who occupies the position of father: it is a fundamental duality signifying the paternal relation as viewed from the standpoint of the child as well as from the viewpoint of the parent. To think paternity without considering both the father's relation to his son as well as the son's relation to his father would be to theorize in an incomplete manner. Accordingly, Sartre, who wrote unflaggingly about paternity throughout his career, always took both the paternal and the filial positions into consideration. Just as the relation involves two distinct individuals whom Sartre often prefers to call a "genitor" (*géniteur*) and an "offspring" (*rejeton*), so the term carries meanings specific to their respective positions. Paternity signifies a way of looking upon the other, a way of perceiving, a *regard*—in the sense of thought, attention, concern, respect, deference—from each of the two vantage points.

Although, as we shall see, he castigates what he calls the "*bond* of paternity" in *The Words,* Sartre emphasizes the potential force in this dual and ideally reciprocal relation between beings. At the most immediately accessible (often polemical) level of his writings, Sartre abhors paternity, calling it the single most harmful relationship that most of us, as offspring of some living genitor or another, must endure. As is often the case with Sartre, this polemical position is vividly imaged. In *The Words,* he proposes a representation of his rejection of paternity, claiming that it is the destiny of sons to eternally carry their fathers on their backs. Any conceivable liberation of those sons would come about only when they *rejected* (literally *threw off*) their paternal burdens. In *The Age of Reason,* he demonstrates, conversely, that, whenever possible, fathers reject biological paternity in an effort to preserve personal freedom. If ever that rejection proves impossible, they then attempt to reject legal paternity. Yet despite these dismal prognoses for the "bond of paternity," Sartre returns to various aspects of the relationship in work after work, not so much in an effort to reprove those who advocate it but as if it were the only space where, in some utopian moment, "producer" and "produced" might coexist on an equal footing.

Sartre expresses the paradox of paternity in metaphors of weight. Sons are represented as unwanted burdens on their fathers; fathers are unwilling nurturers and crush their sons under a weight of guilt and obligation. But without their family counterpart, both fatherless sons and childless men experience their being as something so light as to become insignificant or weightless. Because paternity, as it appears in Sartre's literary imagination, always creates problems of relative weights, the bond of paternity becomes the concrete correlate of the allegory of the ethical subject as Atlas that was left in suspense at the close of *Being and Nothingness.* Had Sartre indicted paternity once and for all, simply never mentioning it again, the present study would have no conditions for existence. However, the texts in which he tears apart the relationship seem to open up experimental fields in works that echo them—experimental fields upon which the father-son relation is reconsidered for revision or improvement. Putting those reconsiderations to philosophical use, Sartre gradually realizes that the key to establishing ethical intersubjectivity in the realm of concrete relations is the very "bond," with its potential force of reciprocity, that he vehemently rejected in his autobiography.

CHAPTER 2

Sons Rejecting Fathers: Paternity Condemned

Haste, my dear father, 'tis no time to wait,
And load my shoulders with a willing freight.
Whate'er befalls, your life shall be my care;
One death or one deliverance we shall share.
—Virgil[1]

Sartre may have adopted a grown woman late in his life, making her his legal daughter and thus becoming a true surrogate father, but when he writes about paternity it is usually as a son whose father is absent.[2] Then, how and for what purpose does Sartre persistently condemn paternity?

Having already written the bulk of his philosophical texts, fiction, drama, and literary biographies—all equipped with their distinctively Sartrean, existentially bumbling male protagonist—Sartre published his autobiographical *The Words* in the early 1960s. In this uncharacteristically succinct work, Sartre recounts the lived conditions (*le vécu*) in which he himself (as prime source of empirical information contributing to his philosophical and fictional subject) had made his way from cradle and pacifier to café table and pen. One is immediately struck by the fabulously legendary details contained in the dramatization Sartre unfolds of his own conception, birth, infancy, and childhood, and how these events supposedly threw him and his father into mute mortal combat.

Sartre expects us to believe that Poulou's[3] first sign of existence operated like a tacit cue for his father to start hitting the road: "Jean-Baptiste [Sartre's father] made a child on the run (me) and tried to take refuge in death" (1964a, 16).[4] But because "dying isn't easy," the autobiographer sardonically adds, the death of this ever-so-ephemeral paterfamilias did not occur immediately.[5] As a consequence of Jean-Baptiste's protracted illness, Anne-Marie, the newly wed mother, spent herself not only in caring for her neonate but also in nursing a husband in failing health whom she had barely had time to know.[6]

The cruelty with which he relates his father's "hesitant" death under an eager filial gaze results less from Sartre's admiration for his mother's sacrifice or from relief at *her* having survived the ordeal (even though her survival meant that she could now care for him unswervingly) or even from resentment at Jean-Baptiste's escape *away* from him into death, than from a narcissistic awe at the mortal danger he putatively faced.[7]

> The sleepless nights and worries exhausted Anne-Marie. Her milk dried up and I was handed over to a wet-nurse. . . . I applied myself to dying too—of entiritis and perhaps of resentment. (1964a, 16)

Entiritis caused by the ingestion of another mother's milk had obviously little to do with this incipient devitalization. Sartre's insistence that Poulou applied himself to dying is transparent proof that the author is peddling another fantasy wherein, at six months, he was already a jealously murderous Oedipus. Had his attempts to usurp his father's position aborted, the new-born underdog contender for Anne-Marie's love would have had to fade out of the picture: the Sartre household was just not big enough for father and little son.[8]

However, miraculously, Poulou emerged victorious from the dilatory moves toward death and Jean-Baptiste, after long illness, appeared forever silenced. The future author of *Being and Nothingness* was now free to say, do, and eventually, as we all know so well, write whatever he wanted. Sartre's moment of inception was not Poulou's birth but rather Jean-Baptiste's death.[9] The schoolboy fascination with mortal danger that pervades Sartre's work derives from a narcissistic awe for a sudden availability made possible by his father's premature death, his own ability to make himself into the writer of *The Words* and thereby become the very "self-engendered being" that is at the core of his thought.

Père: Néant

In his autobiography, Sartre stages an absurdly premature Oedipal conflict culminating in the son's outrageous triumph that I have just described.[10] Yet this tale of attempted suicide by means of willful resentment and Sartre's dwelling on his mother's maidenliness (and, thus, on the proximity of their ages, hinting at incestuous possibilities) seem not quite so simply to be one more in a series of fictions concocted to satirize psychoanalysis. It is true that from the earliest moments in his career, Sartre often heavy-handedly rejected any multilayered model of the psyche, especially as elaborated in Freud's theory of the unconscious.[11] His position on many other aspects of psychoanalytic theory, however, proved more supple and open to inflection. By the time he was writing *The Family Idiot*,[12] for example, he seemed quite at home using a psychic topography of the subject not unlike that posited by the later Freud of *The Ego and the Id*.[13] It is impossible to determine to what extent Sartre's repeated staging of the Oedipal schema in grossly exaggerated fictional settings can be attributed to his squabble with psychoanalysis over the existence of an unconscious. But these repetitions, like the workings of the repetition compulsion—a deliberate reinsertion into painful situations[14]—might just as easily point to his own difficulties in surmounting childhood crises.[15] It is fairly clear, in any case, that Sartre's early loss of his real father governs his abiding fascination with the Oedipal configurations experienced by *other* sons.[16]

Beyond any propensity of psychoanalytic critics to place Sartre's paternal bond or lack of it at the center of their approach, Sartre himself would claim that the strife between fathers and sons is the single most important series of events of man's existence. To this son, now transformed into an adult writing the saga of his infancy, the father's death was the break of a lifetime: "Jean-Baptiste's death was my life's big venture" (1964a, 18). But Jean-Baptiste's passing is not primarily valued for having allowed Poulou an undeterred maternal affection, which he already possessed in abundance. Sartre implies that there is something in this type of loss that signals nothing less than the dawn of existence. The narrator wastes no time in revealing the contours of that beginning: "Jean-Baptiste's death, while putting my mother back in chains, gave me freedom" (18). Sartre contends that Poulou's precocious fatherlessness—being "orphaned of the father,"[17] as he puts it—delivered him into a state of unmitigated freedom that other sons never experience.

His father's death was auspicious because it afforded Poulou the quality of existence that would become the hallmark of Jean-Paul's philosophy: radical individual freedom. A victim of the patriarchal order, the woman in this tale passes from one male to another. Widowed, his mother must return to shackles under the parental roof her father built, while Poulou, "orphaned of his father," is unconditionally free to begin life. The weight upon Anne-Marie, symbolized by her chains, emphasizes by contrast the lightness that now characterizes her exceptional son in his newfound freedom. As Poulou becomes fatherless, so he becomes weightless: "Instead of letting me think I was the son of a dead man, I was told I was a miracle child. That's undoubtedly where my *incredible lightness* comes from." (1964a, 20; italics added).[18] This ontological lightness, felt at the beginning of life, would become the crux of Sartre's reflection on ethics throughout his career.

For virtually all other sons, the competitive self-destruction, beyond whose preliminaries Poulou and his father never advanced, results in a stalemate where both survive to impair each other's freedom. But while the father's life is difficult in this forced cohabitation, Sartre adjudges the son's position to be absolutely intolerable. The father-son relation is depicted as an endless struggle in which the father maintains the upper hand because a culturally assured generational ascendancy constitutes his being as a crushing burden that the son is condemned to support. Rejoicing at his own good fortune in possessing a uniquely granted freedom around which he would build an entire philosophical edifice, Sartre, in the name of all sons, unleashes his famous condemnation of paternity:

> There is no good father, that's the rule. Don't lay blame on men but on the bond of paternity which is rotten. To *make* children: nothing better; to *have* them: what iniquity! Had my [own] father lived, he would have lain on me full length and crushed me. As luck would have it, he died young. Amidst Aeneas and his cohorts, bearing their Anchises on their backs, I move from shore to shore, alone and hating those invisible genitors who bestraddle their sons all their life long. I left behind me a young man who didn't have enough time to be[come] my father and who today might be my son. Was it a good or a bad thing? I don't know, but I readily subscribe to the verdict of an eminent psychologist[19]—I have no superego. (19)

Does This Condemnation Speak to Another Text?

In *The Aeneid,* Virgil only has his hero carry his crippled father, Anchises, for the time it takes him to escape a burning Troy—a burden that Aeneas takes on with loving willingness.[20] Perhaps the most striking feature in Sartre's distorted application of the famous Virgilian scene is that, along with his vehement indictment of paternity, it is possible to detect an implicit desire to vicariously experience the very suffering of "Aeneas and his cohorts" that he has escaped and rues.

Because Sartre is fatherless, he carries no burden and thus considers himself dispensed from even having to bother contemplating the rejection implicitly advocated here. He can only *imagine* the frustration sons who have fathers must feel when they learn that full rejection of paternity (barring patricide) is a project doomed to failure. But since he can *only* imagine this predicament, he ends up writing about it constantly. The real struggle with a father, missing from Sartre's childhood, does not find expression in the unlikely fiction of an oedipally precocious infant, but in the final sentence of the passage where, with Sartrean hubris, he denies having a superego.[21] In this denial, we witness a Sartre who sincerely, I think, takes the later Freudian topos to its literal limits: possessing a superego means permanently having a father perched on one's back. The very vehemence of Sartre's denial points us in the direction of the writer's trajectory with respect to paternity: from total rejection on all fronts, he will eventually attempt every conceivable method of advocating another, unheard-of paternity.

While he considers himself fortunate not to labor under the weight of an Anchises, joyously free to proceed in any direction through life, Sartre strains to gain awareness of the struggle his peers must confront. This is a positioning repeated throughout Sartre's career whenever he defends the oppressed or the pariahs of society. Only through the act of writing can he take it upon himself to go through the rebellious motions of an unfilial Aeneas, casting off the paternal burden in fiction. But were he to constrain himself to imagining, through writing and revising the father-son relation, condemnations of paternity such as this (where he vilifies "invisible genitors who bestraddle their sons"), Sartre would be admitting that there is little anyone, including himself, can do about this "rule" of the rotten bond. This would parallel his despair at there never being quite the appropriate atmosphere for an ethics.

And if there is nothing to be done, then what purpose is served by the ambiguities in this famous condemnation? With regard to my hypothesis of a thematic of relative weights pervading his work, Sartre confronts us with a fundamental contradiction: the exceptional family circumstances that liberated Poulou from the paternal millstone are in direct opposition to the representation of an ethical Atlas emburdened with responsibility in *Being and Nothingness*. In that fleeting prelude to a Sartrean ethics at the end of the 1943 ontology, an *application*—not a removal—of burden was required for the constitution of the ethical subject. Here, in the 1964 autobiography, to be free is first to be fatherless. And that fatherlessness brings on the weightless characteristic of radical freedom, which is a freedom from responsibility. The condemnation in *The Words* directly challenges and problematizes the allegory of ethical being proposed in *Being and Nothingness*. Sartre thus opens his field of literary experimentation with conflicting appreciations of congruent images.

It's Not Dads, It's What They Do

Sartre is, of course, the offspring of some genetic father, if only the product of a thoroughly random coupling. He is unlike those Aeneas-like sons for whom he does battle, however, because he is not and never has been a son where *son* signifies an individual who is crushed by another. "My father made a child on the run." In stressing Poulou's victorious single combat, Sartre allows to slip through the screen of self-censorship a pathetic expression of his loneliness at having been excluded from everything that makes an offspring a true son of his father. Elsewhere in *The Words,* he speaks of the feeling of being left out of other boys' games, watching them from a distance either in the Jardin du Luxembourg or from high up at his apartment window.[22] His pride at standing alone and observing hides, however, an implicit longing to fuse, if only momentarily, with the others in their games and perhaps even commiserate in their struggles with the "invisible genitors."

The freewheeling action Sartre described in the passage as "moving from shore to shore" *empty-handed* is a recurrent image of the radically free subject. But unless a burden is borne—a condition that, in *Being and Nothingness,* he said was inescapable—life's "crossings" remain meaningless and without ethical grounding. According to the "rule" of the father-son relationship, were Sartre to have had a father who survived long enough *to be* a father to him, he would have been crushed, and the freedom to which he was released would have slipped away from him. According to Sartre's condemnation of paternity, no freedom is allowed with a father about. Yet in *Being and Nothingness,* the very consequence of being free was assuming the Atlas posture and carrying around the weight of the world. There seems to be no middle ground between being crushed by paternal weight and the absolute freedom that burgeons and flourishes when a father dies at childbirth. In Freudian terms, either an offspring is equipped with a built-in superego or he is not a son. And if he does not possess this putative determining attribute of a son, he must be Sartre searching for the ideal father.

Although he claims that the father-son relation is always deleterious, Sartre hedges on where to place the blame. This censure that shifts between father and son cannot, however, be inferred from the first sentence of the condemnation: "There are no good fathers, that's the rule." What could seem more clear than that Sartre is aiming reprobation at all men who become fathers: one thing is for certain, a good father doesn't exist. In the next breath, though, Sartre lifts the onus from individuals and places it on the very *link* binding fathers and sons: "Don't blame men, but the bond of paternity which is rotten." An umbilical cord unites the two family members, connecting the generations. Because tradition precludes the potentially unhealthy tie from ever being severed, it becomes infected. What exactly takes place, then, in the creation of a "bond of paternity"? What is the link between subjects based upon and what makes it oppressive for one or both of them? And who or what is to blame for its inevitable failure, its incurable disease, its putrefaction?

Sartre differentiates sharply—here and elsewhere in his work—between two "productions" of children. By using distinct verbs in parallel constructions, Sartre apparently stresses the contrast between, on the one hand, a biological "making of children" (*faire des enfants*) and a more socioeconomic, one might say, "having" or "possessing of children" (*avoir des enfants*). To the former activity, Sartre lends his whole-hearted approval ("nothing better"), whereas for the latter he reserves the qualifier "iniquitous." With this distinction underscored, we should promptly observe that Sartre's own father fits into the approved category of those who simply make or sire a child, then quickly vanish. All other fathers (the Anchises who survive to crush their sons) are possessors of their sons, appropriating and enslaving them as capitalists do with proletarians and as colonists do with the colonized.

Yet because Sartre indicts an abstract "bond of paternity" rather than individual humans, fathers must be considered as much the victims of this economy as the offspring they end up oppressing. It is because, in nearly all of its manifestations, the bond of paternity is an appropriation and possession of children rather than a creation that the iniquitous bond rots. And, since it is the only intersubjectivity possible between the vast majority of fathers and sons (and nevertheless the model for all other interpersonal relations), no *ethical* intersubjectivity can, at present, be envisioned by Sartre. Paternity cannot yet be the ethical praxis (*faire*), the healthy bond that gives rise to all other healthy bonds, because fathers who survive the birth of their sons survive only to oppress them. For the present, the only acceptable fathers are those who, like Poulou's, make children, in the primitive sense of siring pups, only to abandon the bastards. Sartre considered his father of this type: he simply acted as an agent of a pregnancy, then conveniently disappeared into death. All other forms of fatherhood constitute iniquitous breaking of the originary will to freedom that takes place allegorically on the son's back.

Making versus Having

> To you your father should be as a god;
> To whom you are but as a form in wax,
> By him imprinted, and within his power
> To leave the figure, or disfigure it.
> —Shakespeare, *A Midsummer Night's Dream*

As closed to appeal as this condemnation of paternity would appear, Sartre leaves the destiny of the relationship open to improvement by not blaming any individual but rather a norm (that of "having children") to which fathers cannot help but conform within patriarchal society. Sartre leaves man's nature, in other words, free from blame, and its propensity for change intact. His persistent returns to the idea of process or praxis (*faire*) in order to replace stasis (*avoir*) are expressions of hope that Sartre's critics have often considered absent from his thought.[23] Sartre banks his hopes in praxis almost as often as he discusses some aspect or another of paternity.

The passage condemning paternity in *The Words* is not the first time *avoir* and *faire* have taken on philosophical import in order to be set in opposition to each other. Fleshing out his presentation of "existential psychoanalysis" with a discussion of desire in *Being and Nothingness,* Sartre opposes the two verbs in explaining their epistemological applications.[24] Predictably, since he had already done so in describing Husserlian intentionality,[25] he denounces *avoir* as an extension of a philosophical tradition that considers human knowledge to be an assimilative or "digestive process" (1943, 639). *Having* is a project of appropriative desire that, since it is grounded in "bad faith," is doomed to failure. Conversely, Sartre views *doing* as the principle feature of a rather sublime notion combining with freedom to form a game playing that he likens to Kierkegaardian irony. Diametrically opposed to *having, doing* is entirely dissociated from the rights of appropriation of being (641), which will eventually lead to Sartre's sociological critique of "birth right." *Doing* serves as a sort of gratuitous mirror in which absolute freedom admires itself:

> The act is not its own goal. Its goal is not its explicit end, representing its goal and its deep meaning either. But the act's function is to manifest freedom and to make it absolute—freedom, which is the very being of the individual—to make it present [*présentifier*] *to itself.* (641)

So, although the ideal and free subject is not actually in possession of its being, it nonetheless procures pleasure from the contemplation of its image. Seventeen years later, the avatars of *faire* in the *Critique of Dialectical Reason* would be revolutionary praxis and the desire for permanent "group in fusion," while *avoir* would be the heading under which bourgeois appropriation, ownership of property, and accumulation of capital are assembled for summary execution by the Sartrean pen.

The Words, then, is no exception to the consistently prominent place that Sartre reserves for diametrically opposed worldviews represented by the verbs *faire* and *avoir.* As in the philosophical texts, the former is acceptable, even moral, while the latter is oppressive and scandalous. *Avoir* is the rule ("there is no good father, that's the rule"), and *faire* the exquisite exception. *Faire* may, as in the *Critique,* only be the tenuous activity whose end is an ephemeral utopian *Mitsein* that Sartre calls the "group in fusion," or it may gropingly imply a Sartrean ethics that never materialized—in either case it is always lent a positive value.

Paternal Weight

Read in a casual manner, the famous paragraph from *The Words* comes across as a straightforward statement against paternity. Counterposed to Sartre's agressive response to fathers' repression of their sons is his own gleeful story of how he escaped the ineluctable rule of rotten paternity. In light of his Anchises-Aeneas paradigm for father-son relations, the description of Sartre's situation with his own father is far from clear. For Jean-Baptiste's death to have been a true liberation for Poulou *from* the burden of fatherly influence, the weight of that burden would already had to have been felt—Jean-Baptiste would already have had to be performing his prescribed role as Anchises, the prototypical father. If Sartre is so hasty to assure us that Jean-Baptiste "didn't have the time to be [his] father," then his father never had time to stifle his freedom—there was never any fatherly burden for Sartre. This should prompt us to ask whether what Sartre calls "[his] life's big venture" was, in fact, a liberation *from* nothing and therefore *for* nothing? Does this possible lack of a repressive situation from which to escape (which would evolve into Sartre's "single combat" on behalf of other oppressed sons) conceal a regret or nostalgia for the father? Would this nostalgia for ballast not be the impetus behind such descriptions of his own ethereal lightness as: " . . . I feel nothing but a rhythm, an irresistible impulse, I am taking off, I've taken off, I'm moving up, the engine's purring. I feel the speed of my soul" (1964a, 208)?

Sartre describes a bizarre distortion taking place in the relative ages of two people when one of them dies. This strange scenario problematizes his condemnation of paternity. In order to evoke, in most poignant fashion, the vast difference between his forty-nine years at the time of writing *The Words* and his barely postpartum age when his father died,[26] Sartre concocts this reversal: "I left behind me a young dead man . . . who today might be my son" (19). It is as if Jean-Baptiste's death initiated some miraculous arresting of his aging process rather than an abrupt end to, or absence of, life. Sartre has done nothing less than create a fiction wherein his "departed" father is suspended in time to be included among the "invisible genitors." It enables him to utter the fantastic anachronism that, today, he could be his own father's father. The mere mention of an imagined paternity of one's own father signifies both a regret at missing paternity and a willful confusion of the two senses of the phrase: regret at missing a father and regret at never having been immersed in the bond of paternity by being a father. This nostalgia for kinship (which will be examined through other texts and in greater detail in Part 2) is also evident in such disquieting formulations at the close of the book as: "I am [today] a man . . . who no longer knows what to do with his life" (212). A few years later, incidentally, at age sixty, he adopted Arlette El Kaïm.

Finally, this passage leaves unspecified what precisely results from the emburdening effect of fatherhood on offspring. The degree of freedom that a free subject enjoys is translated here into capacity for movement: "he would have lain on me full length" (19). Equipped with a father, Sartre would have been immobilized. The norm—sons *with* fathers—should logically be characterized by the same immobilization. But in his description of Aeneas' cohorts, Sartre attenuates the paternal burden to the point where these supposedly "unfortunate" sons can actually transport their burdens around. Sartre seems bent on exaggerating paternal oppression for polemical effect, but the burden of a father appears no more onerous to manage than Atlas's burden of the world. It is doubtful that "Aeneas and his cohorts," for whom Sartre declares himself the sole defender, are any more aware of their "plight" or interested in extricating themselves from it than most of the proletarians (for whom Sartre would write all his life) cared about his intricate arguments in their support. Yet, defend them he will, throughout his work, as he did any oppressed subject.[27]

Ethical Weight

Paternity, as a visceral bond, constitutes an important element in the formation of imagery in all of Sartre's writing. He chose to express both his condemnation of paternity in *The Words* and his ethical propositions of *Being and Nothingness* by means of allegories that blend varying intensities of the same two elements: weight and man. Eventually, in *Being and Nothingness,* Sartre harnessed the energetic lightness of the subject's radical freedom by bringing the weight of universal responsibility to bear upon it, thus creating the Atlas figure crucial to his anticipated ethics. In *The Words,* two opposite configurations present themselves concurrently yet exclusively of one another: on the one hand, what Sartre considers a norm of present-day existence in which offspring labor under the moral weight of their genitors and, on the other, rare exceptions to the norm where the fatherless experience their freedom as weightlessness—being exempt from paternal burden. In the Virgilian version of the episode that inspired Sartre, Aeneas took Anchises on his shoulders to save him from the conflagration of Troy. Filial duty motivated Virgil's Aeneas and his Anchises represented only a temporary burden, emblematic of the execution of that virtue. By exaggerating his classical source, Sartre creates the two extreme configurations that incorporate the fundamental ethical question of responsibility, while maintaining the tension necessary for polemicizing about paternity.

Though both the ontology and the autobiography use allegories of relative human weights to approach the problem of ethical imbalance (the source of immorality), their suggested solutions are diametrically opposed. While *Being and Nothingness* begins with an incredibly light and free subject and concludes by proposing to emburden him with a weight proper to creating his ethical being, the 1960 tale of childhood attests to the damage that a like burden causes the subject, condemns the imposition of that burden, yet admits to the futility of any struggle against it. The former seeks subjective equilibrium in the form of ethical ballast ("I carry the weight of the entire world") as the only way that man can cease his flight into bad faith and realize that he is "responsible for the world and for himself insofar as [this is his] manner of being" (1943, 612). In the latter text's rift between the two radically different forms of reproduction—*to make* versus *to have* children—Sartre would envision the possibility of a not-yet-created norm in which fathers survive to exercise a fatherhood that does not hinder their children, and, reciprocally, one in which children assume responsibility for their parents even though it is a heavy burden to carry.[28] This would, in any case, elucidate the hint of nostalgia in Sartre's voice when speaking of his dead father in *The Words*.

Besides their use of essentially identical allegories, both works are concerned with the constitution of being. *Being and Nothingness* examines the initial moment of man on philosophical and psychological premises, while *The Words* studies nascent being within a historically specific sociological context. As with most of Sartre's work, the eschatological horizon of these texts is ethical. These points of contact indicate that the allegorical passages upon which I have concentrated address the same question. Between the proposition of universal responsibility in the form of an encumbrance and the problematic relationship of fathers and sons, there exists an interchangeability of which Sartre rarely speaks but which nurtures the entirety of his ethical thought. Upon viewing Sartre's oeuvre in this manner, one is tempted to claim that the sum and substance of Sartre's repeated stories of fathers and sons—rehearsals for a solution to their strife—are, if not tantamount to the elaboration of an ethics, the closest thing we have to it.

Paternity and filiality intertwine in the problematic constitution of being as an ethical subject. The purpose of Sartre's exaggerated rendition of the Aeneas-Anchises episode was to condemn paternity. But once had not been enough. Sartre had vented his outrage against the most basic oppression to which man is subjected. More is at stake than a condemnation when Sartre works on paternity elsewhere. The vital equilibrium of an ethical relation is sought in the midst of the mortal dangers of family strife.

The Condemned of Altona: Worst Case Scenario

Whoever chose *condemned* to translate *séquestrés* in the title of Sartre's 1958 play was dead right.[29] Just as Sartre's Aeneas was condemned to enslavement by an exaggeratedly burdensome father, so are each of the characters in *The Condemned of Altona*. Here, the genitor of whom Sartre conceives wields the power of a demiurge. As if he represented every manifestation of the paternal phenomenon, Sartre calls him, simply, the Father. Three of his subordinates are his children, Frantz, Leni, and Werner and a fourth, Johanna (Werner's wife) nonetheless succumbs to the authority of this father figure. The Father embodies Sartre's most disastrous visions of how the rotten bond of paternity, condemned in *The Words*, may manifest itself. For Frantz, the mere fact of being a son, especially of *this* father, is already a damnation. The Father's greatest regret is that Frantz, his most gifted child, did not follow in his footsteps. Herein lies the central irony of Sartre's play, for in spite of his best efforts, and contrary to what the Father thinks, Frantz perpetuates and indeed perfects (albeit through different channels) the ego-centered desires that motivate the paterfamilias.

The Father wished Frantz to become a successful capitalist, succeeding him at the helm of a shipping empire. Frantz turned out, instead, to be the basest of modern Germany's pariahs: a vicious SS officer. Still under the sway of some of the tenets of Stalinism,[30] Sartre, in 1958, invites us to confuse or conflate the economic and political alternatives of the capitalist with those of the fascist. Hence, the treacherous Father seems unaware of what has occurred since the birth of his favorite son and, as if history has played a trick on him, seems baffled by the results of his fatherly handiwork: "I made you a monarch, [but] today that means good-for-nothing" (1960b, 362). His amazement derives from a refusal to see that the crimes of his fascist son mimic and even have their source in the white-collar crimes of a capitalist like himself.

Because Frantz is a casualty of paternity, Sartre's sympathies are clearly with him, even though the pariah's evil has crystallized in the existence of a Nazi. Situated years after his crimes as "the butcher of Smolensk," the series of episodes represented in the play finds Frantz in the throes of a struggle with a phantasmagorical adversary that he is yet unable to clearly identify.[31] Through an identification with the historical and moral dilemma of what action to take in Nazified Germany, we, as spectators, come to understand Frantz's struggle to be an attempt to exorcize his father's malignant influence. But by abstracting and generalizing this nefarious paternity into a collective suffering, Frantz rationalizes his choice and remains no better than an aberration of the Father. Frantz perceived the father-son configuration through the unmistakable images omnipresent in Sartre's work: like the Aeneas in *The Words*, Frantz is "bestraddled" by his destiny (1960b, 356), but unlike Poulou, he is blind to the source of his suffering and therefore remains powerless. The play's father-son reunion culminating in the final act's murder-suicide makes plain that between them rots the source of Frantz's existence: the gangrenous umbilical cord of the paternal bond. Theirs incorporates the struggle Sartre described in *The Words* as the period of Poulou and Jean-Baptiste's competitive moves toward death, punctuated by feints and motivated by the hope that the rival would succumb first. This time, however, both individuals tied by the bond have refused to give way and resolution descends upon the stage in a climactic liquidation facilitated by an automotive projectile.[32]

In spite of the heinous crimes his Nazi protagonist has single-handedly perpetrated, Sartre compels us to compassion for Frantz because, in those acts, he was the unwitting instrument of an oppressive paternity that pursued him even into the recesses of his years in seclusion (*séquestration*). Cynically feigning vainglory, he says to his sister-in-law, Johanna, "You know, he made me into quite a machine . . . and the machine still works" (1960b, 286). Even before his birth, the Father's grip clutched him in a vise of will to mold him into what he wanted, recalling Sartre's injunction against having or possessing a child: "I am chosen, nine months before my birth" (177).[33] The immoral slant of Frantz's existence was predetermined by his being *had*, even if specific manifestations of that immorality were yet to be decided in the historical context of Nazi Germany: "I'm a torturer because you're a stool pigeon" (341). By laying plans for his son to become a capitalist boss, the Father figures prominently in the Sartrean gallery of *salauds*.[34] Frantz would have become a *salaud* too if he had passively followed his father and invested his "talents" in a family (and its capitalist enterprise) rather than with the fascists.[35] Far from being an apology for fascism, the power of Sartre's play derives from his insistence on showing the capitalist father as a *salaud* while necessarily imputing that moral destiny to a Nazi torturer.

The Father's paternal force is even felt by those not genetically descended from him, but who, through marriage, come to be sequestered under his roof. Though stronger in character than her husband, Werner, Johanna nevertheless falls under the fatherly spell. In Gerlach's opening paternalistic gesture, Johanna symbolically experiences the weight of the Father to which she will ultimately fall victim.[36] As he enters a room, she halfheartedly rises in ambiguous deference. "But the Father crosses the room with a lively step and makes her sit down by placing his hands on her shoulders" (1960b, 24). The anatomical location of this downward thrust is a somatic reminder to the audience that all of the play's characters labor under the Father's weight in precisely the same manner as Sartre's Aeneas did.[37]

Festering even during the years when everyone except his sister thought Frantz dead, Werner's resentment of his older brother is not the source but the expression of his existential suffering: he too is smothered by the Anchises of capitalism. Perhaps because of his timorous passivity, Werner feels his oppression differently than Frantz. Once Gerlach became convinced that Frantz was dead, he proceeded to groom this second-best (because second-born) son for the role of company boss. He turned him into a hapless cat's paw—a state of being that Werner describes as feeling like a "flowerpot" (1960b, 31). Earlier in his career, Sartre had already discovered the usefulness of this odd metaphor in depicting another son of a boss, Lucien Fleurier (who will be discussed extensively in Part 3). The excessive weight of paternal oppression on Werner breeds a total powerlessness to take charge of anything: instead of carrying, he is carried like a "flowerpot." As his father says to him, with the exception of his own funeral arrangements, "I'll take care of everything [*Je me charge de tout*]" (26)—literally, "I'll take charge of everything."

Father Gerlach destroys all of his children, but none more definitively than Frantz. "Look what he has made me into!" (170)—a cry coming from some human turned monster at the hand of a Dr. Frankenstein. But somehow, strangely, the weight that comes with this mutation does not repel Frantz. His pitiful attempt to come to terms with having been a chip off the Gerlach block consists of seeking desperately for a burden of moral responsibility. In one of the few scenes where he drops his ironic tone, Frantz expresses sincere amazement at his father's insensitivity and his lightness of ethical being: "Father, you scare me: the sufferings of others don't make you suffer enough" (75). Such disingenuous forthrightness is perhaps a bit weird coming from the mouth of a Nazi torturer, but this is Sartre's extremist way of demonstrating his moral preference for a son over a father. In *The Condemned of Altona,* the corrupt offspring is still capable of compassion for the suffering of mankind even though he was an executioner of that suffering. Whereas Frantz is painfully cognizant of the responsibility linking him to his acts,[38] the Father is totally dispassionate about the ruthlessness that facilitated his ascension to a position of economic power. If there is any resolution to the play, it is at the very end, when Gerlach loses some of his insensitivity about the crimes of paternity he has perpetrated against Frantz.[39] But before that, having learned that he is dying of cancer, he becomes monomaniacal about the future of his shipping company. The lifelong wish of a bourgeois paterfamilias is kindled once again: with his eldest son Frantz rediscovered, he wants him to take over the business and shoulder his rightful (bequeathed) responsibility. He dismisses, as misguided naïveté, Frantz's desperate quest for an altogether heavier burden located outside the home economy (*oikos*). The weighty responsibility that Frantz desperately lures himself into thinking he can still shoulder is precisely the universal responsibility that Sartre depicted in *Being and Nothingness.* But with the Father relentlessly riding him, Frantz's accession to the ethical state of being ballasted by a weight is barred.

Although Frantz is the only character literally "locked away," the play's title bears the plural noun, *séquestrés,* as if a *No Exit* scenario were to ensue. And one does. Attempting to ward off a split inheritance, Gerlach blackmails his vassals into swearing that they will never leave the house. But with no armed guard to prevent eventual escapes, the old man, if put to the test, would have proven a paltry enforcer of his interdiction. The only way this detention can be guaranteed is by the uncanny strictures woven by the bond of paternity. Since all *four* Gerlach "offspring" sustain the damage of the fatherly oppression (thus qualifying for our sympathy), some criterion must be at work, prompting us, if not to elevate Frantz, at least to empathize with him in particular. If Frantz is not to be considered a *salaud,* as Sartre portrays the Father to be, then how can we overlook his audacity at committing crimes more monstrous than those of his genitor? Within the "situation" created from his inability to escape the weight of the father, the subject becomes what his father wanted: a monster. Frantz's evil springs from that of the Father: "I'm a torturer because you're a stool pigeon." It is inspired by the Other and it escapes his control. Or, as Sartre would argue in the case of Jean Genet, Frantz is as morally unreliable and unpredictable as a "Saint Genet"—that incarnation of both evil and virtue produced by a monstrous collective fatherhood that backfired, and who undermines that very society or patriarchal instance.[40] The duplicity of Frantz's position as both fascist and son of a "good" family is, however, an even more tragic one than Genet's because he actually has perpetrated heinous crimes and therefore cannot escape guilt.

The Condemned of Altona takes its place, along with *The Words,* among Sartrean recriminations of paternity. But like the autobiography, this worst case scenario of fatherhood hints, in the same breath, at a way out of the impasse of the paternity it condemns. With a father, Frantz was destined to have his freedom quashed and to inherit evil: either the masked evil of a capitalist *salaud* like his father or what his father would consider the "perverted" professed evil of the Nazi torturer. Fatherless, Frantz could have *chosen* a road to freedom and not *been chosen* ("I am chosen nine months before my birth"). What makes *The Condemned of Altona* a tragedy of paternity is not the evil deeds recollected at every turn of the plot: Frantz's tragedy lies rather in this son's tenuous but tenacious hope that he can still shake the father and thereby become fully responsible for his own acts. Frantz's tragedy consists of the futile hope of acquiring an ethical weight under whose unethical counterpart he suffered to the end.

The Story of Mr. Flowerpot

The Condemned of Altona presented a son at the crucial moment of his life. Frantz had attempted to overcome the guilt for his crimes by disguising their significance to himself during his voluntary sequestration. The cathartic taping of messages to a "tribunal of crabs" enabled him to come out of hiding, confront his father one last time, and reveal to the audience that the burden of guilt fell not on him but on the bond of paternity, just as Sartre argued in *The Words*. In Sartre's 1939 short story, "The Childhood of a Boss" (1981, 314–88), he made a less direct attack on the iniquity of paternity. At first appearing similar to Poulou's case in *The Words*, and as a prototype for both Werner *and* Frantz, Lucien Fleurier turns out to be different from both characters. All three are sons of business tycoons. The story encompasses a much broader time span than that of the 1957 play: like *The Words* it covers the protagonist's entire childhood. In the play, the hallucinations, the talk about the past and its reenactments are the only sources of knowledge we have concerning the development of the characters. "The Childhood of a Boss" reveals the diachronic evolution of Lucien. This difference in narrative time underscores, on the one hand, the immutability of the shattered state of Frantz von Gerlach's being and, on the other, the lability, or wild changeability, that makes a son like Lucien Fleurier every bit as much a *salaud* as the Father.[41]

Only in the very last pages of the story does Lucien come around to the destiny of a boss that his father mapped out for him. Lucien's existence, from infancy through adolescence, is a mixture of velleity (which Sartre, of course, mocks) and the kind of rebelliousness which he would commend. After an early bout with scarlet fever, Lucien adopted the habit of playing at being an orphan (1981, 317). This was a kind of playacting that Poulou, thanks to his "break of a lifetime," carried over into his adult life as Jean-Paul Sartre identifying with Jean Genet and other "orphans" like Jean Genet, André Gorz, and so on. Lucien, proceeding a bit deeper into revery, imagines that "he had been picked up by thieves who wanted to make a pickpocket out of him" (317). This fiction recalls the scenario of being labeled a thief that Sartre will invent to dramatize the turning-point in Genet's childhood.[42] Be that as it may, there can be no doubt as to whom, between the writer (himself or Genet) and the boss (Lucien) Sartre holds in higher esteem: whether or not there actually ever was a "vertiginous word" of *voleur* aimed at the foster child, Genet actually did become a thief while Lucien can only dream of being an orphan and a pickpocket.

Determined, however, to show that even the most despicable of individuals are potential ethical beings, Sartre occasionally endows little Lucien with a precocious capacity for discriminating within himself between bad faith and authentic behavior.[43] But because he is laden with paternal onus, Lucien always regresses from this moral semilucidity into the familiar pattern of bad faith:

> he thought all through the night that there must be a real Lucien who walked, talked and really loved his parents, except once the morning came, he forgot everything and started pretending to be Lucien all over again. (1981, 322)

His ultimate choice will be to submit to paternal pressures by introjecting his capitalist father's law. He will thus play to the hilt at being a boss, making a definitive choice of bad faith.

Though in *The Words* Sartre distinguishes between a praxis of paternity *(faire)* and an appropriation of offspring (*avoir*), according his consent only to the former, his invented and abhorred fathers use this same verb when describing their plans for molding their sons.

For these *salauds*, "to make a child" (*faire un enfant*) is not only to impregnate a genetrix, it is to weigh down heavily on those sons once they hatch to be sure that they become *sub-jects* ("thrown under") as they were preconceived ("chosen" before birth). Similar to the Father's proclamation to Frantz that he *made* him to be a monarch, in the first lesson of his apprenticeship as boss, Lucien learns that he was *made* to fill a very specific role:

> Once . . . Papa took Lucien on his knees and explained to him what a boss was. Lucien wanted to know how Papa talked to the workers when he was at the factory and Papa showed him how to do it and his voice was so changed. "Will I become a boss too?" asked Lucien. "Of course, my little man, that's why I *made* you." "And who will I lead?" "Well, when I die, you'll be the boss of my factory and you'll lead my workers." (1981, 325; italics added)

Because Sartre wishes to concentrate on satirizing a few favorite targets like surrealism and psychoanalysis in "The Childhood of a Boss," Lucien's assuming his role as little master is deferred until the final page: "He was too sensitive to make into a boss [yet] but not to make into a martyr" (335). Just before the existential inflection between *reading* and *writing* in *The Words,*[44] Sartre, too, considered himself the martyr of his father's absence, as inferred from the passage where he condemned paternity:

> In a word, I could neither draw from myself the imperative mandate which would have justified my presence on this earth nor recognize anyone's right to deliver me. I took up my horseback patrols, nonchalantly, I lolled in the midst of battle . . . an indolent martyr . . . lacking a czar, a God or simply a father. (1964a, 114)

Unlike the dubious Sartrean hero, Jean "Saint" Genet, martyrdom finally deters Lucien from his revolt when playing at it threatens to require that he engage in homosexual acts. To avoid an impending "fall" through a deflowering objectionable to his bourgeois upbringing, Lucien intones a rosary, each bead of which is another paternal ancestor: "He remembered that the Fleurier's, from father to son, were industrial bosses for four generations: 'Whatever they can say, the family exists!' And he reflected upon the Fleurier's moral health" (1981, 359).

Young Lucien is a strange blend of several familiar Sartrean fictions: "a good little boy, polite and hardworking" as we imagine Frantz's younger brother Werner might have been or as Sartre will characterize the plodding obedience of an Achille Flaubert. But Lucien is also "so wretchedly indifferent to everything" (326), a trait he would share with Mathieu in *The Age of Reason* and the "family idiot" Gustave, Achille's younger brother. Sartre's descriptions of this almost vegetative apathy are amazingly analogous to the attributes of the author of *Madame Bovary* as a young man: in "a kind of sleepiness, he answered questions indolently [*mollement*], with a finger always up his nose" (321).[45] An adult observer of Lucien comments that "even games didn't seem to interest him much. Sometimes he is turbulent, even violent, but he gets bored quickly" (326). Besides characteristics tying Lucien into a network of other fictional creations, we must not ignore the undeniable resemblance to the portrait of Poulou in *The Words.* Sartre's signature marks Lucien's youthful accomplishments: "Lucien, who had got a 15 out of 20 for his paper on Ethics and Science, had thought about writing a *Treatise on Nothingness*" (334).

In *The Words,* Sartre wrote that he was stricken with anxiety as a youth when he noticed that certain adults counted so much for others that, when they were absent from a group, everyone felt their absence as a fundamental lack (1964a, 79). We have already explored the lightness of being sensed by a subject delivered into radical freedom. Both this lack and this lightness are feelings Lucien experiences and, thus, shares with his creator:

> Nobody saw Lucien. Nobody heard him. He jumped to his feet and had the impression that his movements encountered no resistance, not even that of gravity. . . . it was as if he existed in a vacuum. . . . it was more than silence: it was nothingness. (1981, 361–62)

Unable to live up to Poulou's standards, but also unlike Frantz and Werner who resist assuming their predetermined place in the world,

Lucien, in his apparently definitive stage of development, welcomes this insertion into the ruling class:

> Well before his birth, his place in the sun was marked. . . . Already, well before his father's marriage, he was *expected*. If he came into this world, it was to occupy that place: "I exist, he thought, because I have the right to exist." . . . he had a flashing and glorious vision of his destiny. (387)

Lucien capitulates and enters the fold, submitting to the father's preconceived plan and to the weight that is ready to enforce his insertion into a proper place.[46]

"Who am I? . . . My name's Lucien Fleurier but that's just a name" (333). Lucien experiences the archetypally Sartrean difficulty of knowing for certain who he is. His problems with self-identity are exacerbated by that deceptively imposing label passed down to him—almost inscribed in his flesh—by his father. "Lucien Fleurier" proves to be more than "just a name." Following Freud's description of superego formation, Jacques Lacan claims that the primordial law governing the decidability of identity is the introjected name of the father.[47] Lucien senses that one's *being* should be a burden for which one is responsible. However, he is incapable of imagining this burden in any other form than as the name inherited from the genitor, dragging him down: "there were labels that would be hung onto you one fine day and you'd have to carry them your whole life" (356). But perhaps Lucien's patronymic burden is illusory. A certain frivolity in the weightlessness of Lucien's being is underscored when the narrator sarcastically employs a derivative of his *inherited* label, "flowerpot," to metaphorically designate his being. Through a pitiful series of revolts he undertakes, especially in his association with the caricaturized surrealist "shepherd," Berger, Lucien "Flowerpot" Fleurier is transported (just as Werner von Gerlach was) through youth to his destiny of a retreat into passivity, letting himself be pushed gently into his corner of life's garden where he can dispense with carrying anything more important than the family name.

If there is an ethical difference between Frantz and Lucien it is that Frantz remained stubbornly (though absurdly) resistant to the inevitable destiny of becoming as unscrupulous as the Father. Lucien, on the other hand, turns out to be a willing follower of his father's plans.[48] Instead of pushing his wretchedly ineffectual adolescent revolts to the limit and attempting to reject the weight of his father, his nonconformism ends up horrifying him and he takes refuge in the niche the paterfamilias carved out for him. The final full stop punctuating the end of the 1939 story is not a dot but the Hitlerian moustache that Sartre has Lucien grow.

The Flies and Prosthetic Act

The Condemned of Altona and "The Childhood of a Boss" recount how monsters of immorality are created by fathers forcing sons to sustain a nefarious weight of paternity. As he did with the "new" Aeneas imagined in 1964, Sartre empathizes with Frantz, the Nazi who comes to recognize responsibility for his crimes. Yet he spews parodic venom at Lucien, a crypto-fascist. The iniquitous relation that produces any of these sons was indicted and condemned by a "son" who boasted of his own fortune at not having a father. Paternal deadweight is viewed in each of these works as the most destructive force affecting the budding subject. A pattern of condemning paternity would seem discernible whenever Sartre's narrator speaks from the position of a son.

The Flies (1943) disrupts this pattern. The play's point of view is again that of a son. But paternity, albeit indirectly, is condoned. At the time of Orestes' return to Argos, Agamemnon is dead, having been murdered by Aegisthus, the usurper of both Orestes' father's throne and the conjugal bed. This legendary father-son configuration duplicates, to a certain extent, that of the Sartre family: with the father dead, paternal deadweight is *absent*. If we compare the play with the theses on paternity expounded in *The Words* and if one thinks of Sartre's reaction in that text to being fatherless, it is extremely odd that Orestes is so profoundly unhappy with his unlimited freedom. He seems to suffer from a lack of ethical ballast in his existence. In fact, he seeks, through the act of avenging his father's death, a weightiness that would make his being complete. I will argue that the weight-giving act, the preparations for which make up the action of the entire play, constitutes a substitute for the missing father in the form of a burden of guilt. This, in turn, should cast some fruitful doubts on the certainty with which Sartre condemned paternity in *The Words* and point to the inflection needed to introduce my discussion of "endorsed paternity" in Part 4.[49]

Orestes, "a young man liberated from all servitude and from all beliefs, without family, without a homeland, without religion and without a trade, free for any commitment" (1960c, 26) possesses a radical freedom identical to Poulou's.[50] But Orestes' *experience* of radical freedom is radically different from Sartre's: "What a superb absence my soul is" (26), he laments. The spiritual freedom his preceptor has trained him for is a vacuous promise of fulfilled life rather than a gift of plenitude. The *preparation* for commitment puts Orestes in a state of eternal suspense, where he knows implicitly that no real commitment is meant to ensue. The similarity of Mathieu's existential predicament in *The Age of Reason* to Orestes' paralysis within freedom in *The Flies* is uncanny: "moreover," Sartre writes, he is "a superior man, capable of teaching philosophy in a great university city" (26). The case of Orestes is an illustration that radical freedom is not fun but flawed: absolute freedom *condemns* Orestes to a total detachment from intercourse with others and he describes this dislocation from his peers as a weightless floating above the ground: "you left me the freedom of those threads [*fils*][51] that the wind tears from spider webs and which float ten feet off the ground. I weigh no more than a thread and I live in the air" (26). Whereas in his autobiography Sartre considers such freedom a rare and precious gift, Orestes' voice expresses nothing but skepticism. Here, it is because the "invisible genitor" remains the preeminent object of Orestes' ruminations that he can envision deliverance from an unsatisfactory present situation. Unlike *The Words,* the chance of a lifetime in *The Flies* is an act of vengeance that can restore Orestes' father as a moral burden and Orestes takes stock in that chance. But his existential dissatisfaction will not be calmed until the final scenes, in which his father's murder is avenged.

Sartre's condemnation of paternity instructs us that absolute freedom is to be cherished and safeguarded above all else. What happened to that position? Like the ethical subject described at the end of *Being and Nothingness,* "there are men who are born committed," Orestes tells us, but because he has yet to commit his act of vengeance in the name of his father he yet lacks being. He understands with vivid imagery, however, what it means for others to be committed: "they were thrown on a road at the end of which there was an act which awaited them—*their* act" (1960c, 26). Weightless and now fatherless, Orestes ruefully ponders the relative weight of his committed peers "[who] march along, their bare feet pressing down on the earth, getting scratched on the gravel" (26). He imagines that, paradoxically "as a child," he must have been one of these consequential and committed beings. If he had remained so,

> the city gates would have been my playthings, I would have thrust myself against them. They would have creaked without giving way and my arms would have learned their resistance. (27)[52]

Orestes longs for and regrets his lack of a certain gravity imposed upon him by the authority figure—a gravity that actually would have attenuated his unlimited freedom, a weight that would have driven him to feel the bite of the earth's rough surface, a weight allowing for his foundation in ethical existence.

Orestes experiences his gift of absolute freedom as a deficiency instead of "the chance of a lifetime." His existence lacks something without which he, as man, is not fully human. "I am too light. I must," he tells Electra, "emburden myself with a very heavy crime" (71). Electra's role as a sounding board for Orestes' ruminations has led some critics to consider Sartre's version of this brother-sister relationship as exaggeratedly intimate, implying that incest was Orestes' primary goal. The lightness of originary freedom, however, requires the intervention of a weight of responsibility (not one of mere guilt for immorality) in order to complete the representation of total ethical being. Orestes will seek to impose upon himself a guilt of altogether greater magnitude through the act of avenging his father.

By the time the act of retaliation has been executed upon Aegisthus, Orestes is hailing his (and Electra's) newfound freedom in tones markedly more positive than those witnessed at the rather lugubrious beginning of the play. Ecstatic outbursts as "It's not dark. It's the dawn. We're free, Electra" (91) would suggest that, although they had been calling it freedom, the existential quality of being that

Orestes and his preceptor theorized about in his youth bore no resemblance to "true" freedom. Postvengeance freedom is a sort of rebirth for Orestes and takes its place among the many conversions in Sartre's work. He fervently believes that his act of justice is tantamount not to incest but to a sort of self-midwifery. In fact, he takes his sister as witness once again, conveying to her his feeling of having engendered and delivered the two of them. "I feel as if I helped you to be born and that I've just been born with you" (91).

Orestes' conversion to being laden with purposefulness resonates with the problematic notion of *ens causa sui* that was part of Sartre's thought since the 1940s. In *Being and Nothingness,* he warned that because "self-created being" required the impossible synthesis of the for-itself with the in-itself, it is doomed to remaining a vain desire. However, Orestes' "rebirth" would seem to indicate the miraculous possibility of attaining that ultimate desire of the human subject. What distinguishes Orestes in his newfound and responsible freedom from his prevengeance, free-floating state is the weight factor. In elated amazement, Orestes describes his new freedom thus: "I am free, Electra, and freedom has crashed down upon me like lightning" (91).[53]

Electra has not fathomed the propitious gravity of Orestes' conversion from an existence in absolute freedom into one of ballasted freedom. Apparently more glorious than what Hugo undertook in *Dirty Hands,* Orestes' hand-sullying act has metamorphosed him into something of the ethical Atlas promoted in *Being and Nothingness.*

> I have committed my act, Electra, and that act was good. I shall carry it upon my shoulders *as a ferryman carries passengers.* I will *carry it to the other shore.* And the heavier it is, the more joyous I will be, for *it is my freedom.* (1960c, 91–92; italics added)

A guilt-emburdened Orestes has waxed lyrical and what has led him to such high-flown rhetoric is his newly discovered weight. The correlation between Orestes' guilt-ridden fresh existence and the situation of an ethical Atlas with a moral burden to bear is perhaps predictable, given the contemporaneity of the texts (both appeared in 1943). Less predictable is how, through the occurrences of the image of a ferryman (*passeur d'eau*) shouldering such ethical weight, a crucial link exists between the Atlas-world dyad in *Being and Nothingness* and that of Aeneas-Anchises in *The Words*. Burdenless Poulou, it will be recalled, was free to "move from shore to shore," while pathetic *true* sons remained paralyzed under paternal weight. Here, on the contrary, Orestes requires such a burden in order to make such river crossings.

"And the heavier it is to carry, the happier I will be, for it is my freedom [*Et plus il sera lourd à porter, plus je me réjouirai, car ma liberté c'est lui*]." The antecedents of the pronouns *il* and *lui* are, of course, *mon acte*, but would it be so farfetched to interpret them as recalling the father, Agamemnon? For, indeed, the act that Orestes takes upon his shoulders is an act of vengeance carried out in the name of the father. Symbolically, then, and with the dead Agamemnon calling for vengeance, Orestes, as weightless being, has equated the comfort of a future freedom with a symbolic Agamemnon as burden of filial vengeance. In his final address to the people of Argos, Orestes enumerates abstractions in which his father, now dead, has been brought back to life as this introjected weight: "Your faults and your remorse, your nightly anguish and Aegisthus's crime, all of it is mine, I take all of it upon myself." (1960c, 120)

The condemnation of paternity in *The Words* confirms a "posterity" for the ethical Atlas allegory from *Being and Nothingness*. Writing about paternity is an exercise that aids Sartre in determining how to make universal responsibility a viable basis for ethics. By returning to paternity in a variety of texts, then, Sartre does not so much convince us that paternity is a hopelessly iniquitous relation, as he argued in *The Words*. Rather, he establishes it as the locus of a utopian intersubjectivity. In defending Aeneas and his cohorts, Sartre displayed both unfilial hubris and, contradictorily, a suspicious will to vicariously experience the weight of those sons' fathers. The act of vengeance carried out by Orestes, for which he willingly recognizes and endorses responsibility, proves to be a prosthesis—an introjected substitute—for his dead father. *The Flies* thus demonstrates that underlying Sartre's wild enthusiasm for unfettered freedom lies a nostalgia for responsibility as *embodied* in the missing father. Thus the problematization of Sartre's unilateral condemnation of paternity is complete. As with most every other notion Sartre stressed, what at first appears to be unity and totality becomes transgressive multiplicity.

Notes

1. Virgil, *Vergil's Aeneid in the Dryden Translation,* ed. Howard Clark (University Park: Pennsylvania State University Press, 1989), ll. 706–9.

2. Sartre legally adopted Arlette El Kaïm in March 1965 (1981, lxxxvi); see also Annie Cohen-Solal, *Sartre: 1905–1980* (Paris: Gallimard, 1985).

3. It is necessary to treat Poulou as critics of Proust's *Searching for Lost Time* treat Marcel, that is, as an individual discrete from Sartre. Poulou was the nickname Sartre's mother, Anne-Marie Mancy (formerly Sartre and née Schweitzer) gave him.

4. Typically, the subject's father inseminates the mother irresponsibly: conception is viewed as a blunder. If the child is conceived "on the run," the assumption is that it will be cared for just as little after it is born.

5. *Paterfamilias* is the term (which has taken on pejorative connotations in the last hundred years) that Sartre chose to designate bourgeois fathers. The word becomes common coinage in *The Family Idiot* (Jean-Paul Sartre, *L'Idiot de la famille* [Paris: Gallimard, 1971–72]). In light of Sartre's particular usage of the term *ens causa sui,* under Roman law, a head of household was not the only paterfamilias, but also any person, of either sex, and of any age who was sui juris and free from parental control.

6. Sartre's early awareness of the Biblical resonances in his parents' first names is discussed in Robert Harvey, "Sartre/Cinema: Spectator/Art Which Is Not One," *Cinema Journal* 30, no.2 (1991): 43–59.

7. This "risk of death" is a characteristic experience of the nascent for-itself in *Being and Nothingness.*

8. The experience Sartre recounts of his childhood is a prototype for the situation of "loser wins" (*qui perd gagne*) that became increasingly central toward the end of his career. It appears prominently in *The Condemned of Altona* (Jean-Paul Sartre, *Les Séquestrés d'Altona* [Paris: Gallimard, 1960]). Cf. pt. 3, bk. 2 in *The Family Idiot* entitled "The Crisis Envisioned as a Positive Strategy . . . or 'Loser Wins' as a Conversion to Optimism."

9. As if his father's death did not come soon enough, Sartre indulges, nearly sixty years later, in the disturbing sarcasm we have seen. Each member of the family trio wasted away until "upon my father's death, Anne-Marie and I awoke from a shared nightmare: I recovered" (1964a, 17). If Anne-Marie's husband's lengthy illness was a debilitating experience for *her,* this maidenly mother's nightmare consisted of the thought that her darling Poulou might perish. When that nightmare ended for both of them, Poulou's life began.

10. The title of this section is taken from a groundbreaking essay on the relationship between psychoanalysis and philosophy with regard to Sartre's work in François George, *Deux études sur Sartre* (Paris: Christian Bourgois, 1976), 239–79.

11. See, for example, Sartre's "Childhood of a Boss" (1939), where psychoanalysis and surrealism are pilloried (Jean-Paul Sartre, "L'Enfance d'un chef," in *Oeuvres romanesques* [Paris: Gallimard, 1981], 314–88). For a study on Sartre's ambiguous relation with psychoanalysis, which closely parallels his attitude toward surrealism, see Michel Beaujour, "Sartre and Surrealism," *Yale French Studies* 30 (1964): 86–95; William Plank, *Sartre and Surrealism* (Ann Arbor: UMI Research Press, 1981).

12. Sartre wrote a first draft of his work on Flaubert in 1955.

13. Sigmund Freud, *The Ego and the Id* (1923) in *The Standard Edition of the Complete Psychological Works of Sigmund Freud,* ed. James Strachey (London: Hogarth Press, 1973–74), 19:1–59.

14. See "Compulsion de répétition" in Jean Laplanche and J.-B. Pontalis, *Vocabulaire de la psychanalyse* (Paris: Presses Universitaires de France, 1967), 86–89.

15. Both of these hypotheses are alternately proposed in Josette Pacaly's exhaustive (and perhaps inevitably reductive) Freudian study of Sartre's work (*Sartre au miroir* [Paris: Klincksieck, 1980]). Freud, in any case, would never, even in his wildest speculations, attribute to a nursling the acute awareness of the potential for competition for a mother's affection that Sartre attributes to Poulou.

16. Sartre assures us that, although his maternal grandfather, Karl Schweitzer, took over the fatherly position, he was, by that time, too old a man to become the burdensome influence that Sartre condemns.

17. Sartre uses the term *orphelin de père* frequently in his work, most often to designate those of his male subjects with whom he himself feels fatherly affinities, e.g., Jean Genet.

18. A fascinating passage about his shuttling between high and low positions in observing others, between alternately viewing others from above and below, refers to his "irresistable lightness" (1964a, 54).

19. "Au moment où j'ai repris *Les Mots* . . . vers 1963, j'ai demandé à un ami psychanalyste, Pontalis, s'il voulait entreprendre une analyse avec moi. Il a estimé qu'étant donné les relations que nous avions depuis vingt ans, ça lui était impossible" (Jean-Paul Sartre, *Situations, X* [Paris: Gallimard, 1976], 146).

20. Virgil, *Aeneid,* esp. ll. 723–24: " . . . on my bending back, / The welcome load of my dear father take."

21. The formation of which takes place, said Freud, by the gradual identification with the father, an interiorization or even an introjection of the father's law. See, inter alia, "Intériorisation" (Laplanche and Pontalis 1967, 206).

22. "From my window I can see a road-mender on the road and a gardener

working in a garden. Between them there is a wall with bits of broken glass on top protecting the bourgeois property . . . I can see them without being seen and my position and this passive view of them at work situates me in relation to them" (1960a, 100). See also my discussion of "Erostratus" in chap. 3.

23. For Sartre's most extensive comments about hope, see his "L'espoir, maintenant," *Le Nouvel Observateur* 800 (10–16 March 1980), 801 (17–23 March 1980), and 802 (24–30 March 1980). This is, however, a highly disputed document, many Sartre faithfuls considering it to be a complete distortion of Sartre's thought at the hands of Benny Lévy. See, inter alia, Olivier Todd, *Un fils rebelle* (Paris: Grasset, 1981), 14–15.

24. This discussion makes up the chapter entitled "Faire et avoir: la possession" (1943, 635–61).

25. Jean-Paul Sartre, "Une idée fondamentale de la phénoménologie de Husserl: l'intentionnalité" (1939) in *Situations, I* (Paris: Gallimard, 1947), 38–42.

26. According to Contat and Rybalka (*Les Ecrits de Sartre* [Paris: Gallimard, 1970], 385), Sartre drafted most of the text in 1954 and it was revised and refined in early 1963.

27. One might rightfully suspect that Sartre's intercession as *paternal* savior of stifled sons is another form of surrogate fatherhood.

28. Sartre's formulation of the for-itself's responsibility speaks of this utopia (1943, 612).

29. Published in 1960, the play was written during the time in which the *Critique* was being composed. Sartre hatched the idea for the play in 1958 and it was supposed to be put on in that year. *Les Séquestrés* premiered in 1959.

30. Although Sartre published "Le Fantôme de Staline" in early 1957 in *Les Temps modernes,* condemning the Soviet invasion of Hungary, this argument, which holds back on condemning *all* forms of totalitarianism, is a residue of Sartre's period of militancy for the Communist Party (Jean-Paul Sartre, *Situations, VII* [Paris: Gallimard, 1965], 144–307).

31. This nightmarish allegorical enemy takes the form of a tribunal of crabs. Sartre had mescaline administered to himself in 1935 and was the subject of frightening hallucinations that featured crustaceans (Simone de Beauvoir, *La Force de l'âge* [Paris: Gallimard, 1960], 240–41).

32. Frantz takes his father for a car ride along Hamburg harbor, steering the Porsche off into the water and killing both of them. There is a fascinating correlation, mediated by these watery circumstances and the parent-child relationship, among *The Condemned of Altona, No Exit,* and *Nekrassov* (see chap. 6).

33. The notion that we are *chosen* (by someone else) rather than *choosing* (by/for ourselves) is to be found in *The Words, Being and Nothingness, Baudelaire,* etc. Sartre stresses the scandal of forced passivity by the use of the

passive form of a verb directly juxtaposing it with the active form: "But I never choose . . . I am chosen."

34. See Roquentin's visit to the Bouville Museum: Jean-Paul Sartre, *La Nausée* (1938) in *Oeuvres romanesques* (Paris: Gallimard, 1981), 98–113. Sartre's books often include such rogues' galleries of right-thinkers.

35. And so, Gerlach belatedly tries to do something makeshift with Werner. As the latter points out with the resentment of a second-born son, which will have an echo in the Gustave portrayed in *The Family Idiot,* Gerlach spared nothing in fashioning Frantz in his image (1960b, 28). Resentment, it will be recalled, was the motivation for Poulou's infantile aggression against Jean-Baptiste; perhaps it is the principal emotion in all second-best rivals. But Gerlach's heavy-handed attempt at modeling a successor by means of omnipotent fatherhood was destined to go awry: instead of a *salaud,* like himself, he, in a certain sense, produced a true bastard (*bâtard*). And, as Francis Jeanson and others have shown, the bastard is just the kind of character Sartre favors. Sartre's sympathies go to the *frank* torturer, not to the weasely stool pigeon, Gerlach.

36. With *The Condemned of Altona* in mind, one could define paternalism as a benevolent despotism combining oppressive superiority with a semblance of good intentions.

37. This vassalization of subordinate family members receives Sartre's full consideration in *The Family Idiot.*

38. In this respect, he inherits the sensitivity for weighty responsibility from his prototype, Orestes.

39. *The Father:* I beg your forgiveness.
Frantz: You're asking *me* for forgiveness? . . . For what?
The Father: For you. (Pause) Parents are assholes [*des cons*]. (1960b, 360)

40. See chapter 9.

41. If we recall that, in *The Words* and *Being and Nothingness,* the free subject is uniquely valorized by his freedom of mobility, then the "shiftiness" of Lucien (which gives rise to Sartre's satire of him) produces a contradiction, hence my use of the term *lability.*

42. In the chapter entitled, "Un mot vertigineux," 1952.

43. A precocious authenticity for which Poulou was also noted: "He thought to himself that he had had enough of playing at being Lucien" (1981, 318).

44. "Reading" and "Writing" are the titles Sartre gives the two parts of his autobiography. They delineate his transition or conversion from passivity to activity and, thus, constitute another version of his valorization of *faire* over *avoir.* For the best study of structure and meaning in *The Words,* see Philippe Lejeune, "L'ordre du récit dans *Les Mots* de Sartre," in *Le Pacte autobiographique* (Paris: Seuil, 1975), 197–243.

45. That this last gesture is an all-too-obvious pose in the squabble with

Freudianism is granted (finger in nose = sword in sheath = penis in vagina); it is Lucien's similarity to the two contrasted brothers that I am establishing. For a reading of Sartre's usages of *mou, molle, mollement,* see chap. 5.

46. For the full impact that Sartre lends to the word *proper,* see chap. 5.

47. Jacques Lacan, *Ecrits* (Paris: Seuil, 1966), 812–13.

48. The irony of the leader being a follower is another form of the "loser wins" doctrine that pervades Sartre's writings.

49. In a language anticipating my later reading of political texts, where paternity plays an unexpected role (chap. 7), we might say that the offspring's point of view is employed by Sartre to articulate the condemnation of paternity as a relation of production whose product is bound to be defective.

50. Identical also to that of André Gorz, one of Sartre's protégés. See André Gorz, *Fondements pour une morale,* (Paris: Galilée, 1977).

51. Was Sartre thinking of sons or a son (*fils*) as well as of threads (*fils*)?

52. This same turgid language is used in *The Age of Reason* in the language of Mathieu's imaginary to describe his "true" being. See chaps. 4 and 5.

53. The same thunderbolt (*foudre*) of freedom struck down the protagonist of *Bariona, ou le fils du tonnerre* ("son of thunder") and converted him to paternity (see chap. 6).

CHAPTER 3

Fathers Rejecting Sons: Paternity Refused

> Qui, apprenant qu'il est père d'un
> enfant, n'a pas été pris d'une
> sueur froide, et puis d'une colère
> froide, et aussi d'un écoeurement
> et d'une haine?
>
> —Henri Michaux[1]

So forceful did Sartre want his condemnation of paternity to be that he did not restrict himself to rejecting the relationship merely from the point of view of sons, as in the examples discussed in the last chapter. In Sartre's portrayals, paternity is also refused from the perspective of those after whom the bond was named: fathers reject sons. In his saga novel, *The Roads to Freedom* (1945–47), Sartre's narrative voice once again focuses on a male character, but oddly, as we shall see, that voice does not consistently surge forth from this confused fictional individual. As *The Age of Reason* (the first volume) opens, Mathieu Delarue learns that his lover has become pregnant. Every aspect of the story that unfolds in this part of the trilogy revolves around Mathieu's desperate efforts to refuse paternity. Yet in the context of the present reassessment of Sartre's work as a whole, this apparent corroboration of an emphatic stand against the father-son relationship undermines the consistency of his position rather than sealing the fate of the already questionable bond.

For the young free-thinkers seemingly poised for the advent of something like existentialism, café-crawling through St.-Germain in post-Liberation euphoria, and even for a serious reading public in France avid for ideas that would foreshadow a new world, 1945 was the first in a series of bumper years for publications by Sartre, who was emerging as their apostle. *No Exit* appeared in March, *The Age of Reason* and *The Reprieve,* the first two volumes of *The Roads to Freedom,* in September. On 15 October the first issue of *Les Temps modernes* caught the eye of the intelligentsia and soon the journal was taking their world by storm.[2] In the midst of Sartre's increasingly public presence through the written word and along with his unprecedented involvement in politics over the next few years,[3] the "pope of existentialism" was making a supreme effort to elaborate the ethics he had promised in 1943, at the end of *Being and Nothingness.*[4] But that project never came to fruition and some time in 1949 Sartre set aside the planned ethics in order to busy himself with what he judged to be more pressing matters in the realm of politics. He felt that the world was not ready to show him the path for its own ethics as long as a political solution to inequalities, colonialism, and social injustice had not been instituted.[5]

Meditation on ethics, however, stood firm in Sartre's mind: as soon as he stopped writing the treatise, he began work on *Saint Genet,* which is primarily concerned with ethical questions. This subterranean moral reflection simply insinuates its way into his literary discourses, becoming their fiber whenever Sartre's philosophical rumination meets an ethical obstruction. *The Age of Reason* plays a key role, here, because it is one of the several texts in which he deals explicitly with issues surrounding paternity. Sartre's first novel after *Nausea* (1938), *The Age of Reason* is the only one where the main character is placed in the position of potential fatherhood. By Sartre's own admission, the trajectory of father-to-be Mathieu Delarue parallels that of Sartre. Although such "leads" must be followed with caution, one that involves the abhorred relation of paternity is bound to shed light on the psychology of a philosopher who, at the precise moment he was writing *The Age of Reason,* was on the verge of developing an ethics that he was ultimately unable to bring to fruition. *The*

Age of Reason is quite possibly the most disturbed of Sartre's texts: advancing positions only to retract them, the narrative voice inhabiting one character then another. Much of the hesitant quality of *The Age of Reason* may be attributable to Sartre's rather awkward position of taking the *defense* of a potential father and writing from *that* perspective rather than on behalf of sons as he usually does. Until this novel, Sartre's work had really not rendered any debate about paternity explicit. And it had certainly never related family matters to questions of ethics. However, in the footsteps of André Gide, there could be no doubt that, for Sartre, being an integrally free subject signified the rejection of the family in all of its manifestations.[6]

To signify "the man on the street" or "Everyman," the French use the phrase *l'homme de la rue*. Accordingly, what is going to happen to Mathieu Delarue in *The Age of Reason* is universally applicable. By the surname he has selected for Mathieu, Sartre stresses that, unlike Roquentin for example, this character is the rule and not the exception.[7] Mathieu *Delarue* is not just a lycée philosophy professor but (like the "whoever" [*qui*] in this chapter's epigraph borrowed from Henri Michaux) every male who has ever learned unexpectedly that he is to become the father of a child. Mathieu not only could be Sartre, he is in the position of any free subject faced with a decision of crucial ethical importance.

The Burden of Fatherhood

From the street, where he walks about in anxious aimlessness in the opening scene, Mathieu enters the dank apartment of his mistress, Marcelle, only to learn that their careful contraceptive program of seven years has failed. Thus begins the story of impending paternity as lived from the point of view of an unwilling father-to-be. Mathieu's first road to the supposed freedom (ironically referred to in the saga novel's title) is one that takes him without further ado back out to the street on a quest for abortion money.[8] Of a dubious nature given the illegality of abortion in France at the time and the fact that it is far from clear that Marcelle shuns parenthood along with him, Mathieu's monetary quest is the thread around which the novel's events and insights cluster.

An existential smugness about Mathieu, nurtured in the sanctum of radical freedom, gets disrupted by this unexpected news from Marcelle that she is expecting. As a "sequel" to the legend of Poulou, the ideal of freedom Mathieu had adhered to up to that moment had required him to remain detached from others, even within otherwise strong affective relationships. He was convinced that any emotional dependence would threaten the complacent, freewheeling availability that he had cultivated and that had been his sole serious preoccupation (1981, 446). For this reason he also firmly rejected the institution of family, stating in terms reminiscent of Gidean polemical revolts: "you're never rid of the family. It's like smallpox: you get it when you're a kid and it scars you for life" (510).[9] Mathieu views the impending child as an impediment that would ground his high-flying freedom definitively. The consequences of keeping a child, of assuming fatherhood, had always been one of his worst nightmares.

With the same vehement imagery that Sartre deployed in deploring the unbearable weightiness of fathers in *The Words,* Mathieu of *The Age of Reason* refuses paternity, rejecting the *superimposition* of a child upon his life. To this potential father wishing to remain a free subject, the prospect of an offspring appears to be a moral burden every bit as immoral as the paternal deadweight imposed on sons. However, none of the narrative instances in which one might identify Sartre assume an unequivocal stance either approving or disapproving of Mathieu's approach to the dilemma. The alternations set off by the disruption of Mathieu's life and reflected in the undecidability of the text itself would seem to echo Sartre's own ambivalence about paternity.

A False Sense of Freedom

We might infer from the global title, *The Roads to Freedom,* that the author plans to illustrate Mathieu's attainment of freedom after having chosen one of various paths leading to it. Instead, Sartre offers us the adventures of an individual who already thinks he is free but who is, in fact, condemned to an endless series of tentative directions that never lead him to any sense of certainty about gaining anything.

Despite his declarations to the contrary, Mathieu never behaves like a free subject. He is morbidly beholden to the opinions of others and is a prisoner of his own confused conscience.

The material object of the quest guiding Mathieu is funds sufficient for an abortion that, as yet unfathomed by him, Marcelle has begun to "unwant." As Marcelle proceeds to abjure her previous agreement with him providing that under such circumstances they would abort the pregnancy, she is gripped by an inner struggle (whose progress is left for the reader to imagine), moving her steadily toward an acceptance of motherhood. Marcelle's coming to terms with having a child and its relation to other similar decisions by women in Sartre's work has been explored very little by scholars. Such a study would have to include, among others, Marcelle and Sarah (*The Age of Reason*), Sarah (*Bariona*), and Estelle (*No Exit*). In any case, this ultimate choice, to welcome her child in face of the pact with Mathieu, is one line of action open to Marcelle with regard to an unwanted pregnancy. Thus, in putting an end to her vacillation by deciding she wants the child, she "unwants" the abortion. Mathieu's grim search for abortion funds, on the other hand, will prove fruitless because, by the time he finally does scrape the money together, Marcelle will have made her own unobstructed free choice, having long before decided to marry their mutual friend, Daniel.

Profound lessons for Mathieu intervene, however, during his quest—lessons that modify his conception of himself and seem to prepare a groundwork for ethical freedom at some later point in his life. His farcical failure to expediently resolve what he views as nothing more than an annoying biological mishap allows a progressive moral panic to invade him, sinking him into morbid reflections on his own childhood, on the potential child he has engendered, and on pregnancy, embryos, and parenthood. This morbidity, touched off by the crisis at hand, is rife with associative extensions of his nauseated reaction to women as specifically embodied by Marcelle.[10] From the moment Mathieu refuses paternity, Sartre, in turn, seems to lose all control over the general plan of his saga novel, letting it become so diffused in style and argument that Mathieu's implicitly promised discovery of responsible freedom is endlessly deferred. Like Penelope's tapestry, the novel is woven toward ethical resolution, only to be unravelled just before reaching it.

The Clean and the Dirty

> Do you know what I think? I think that you're sterilizing yourself a bit. . . . Everything is clean and proper [*net et propre*] with you: everything smells of fresh laundry. It's as if you'd autoclaved yourself. The only thing is, it all lacks dark spots. There's nothing superfluous, nothing fuzzy or fishy left in it. (1981, 402)

With these words calling for a bit of dirt, the acceptance of a bit of imperfection in life, Marcelle challenges Mathieu's chosen manner of existence. With a single vague invective, a single dirty word—"shit!" (405)—Mathieu sums up his reaction to the news of Marcelle's pregnancy. Considering Marcelle's rather lucid assessment of his spotlessly designed and supposedly free existence, *shit* is an expletive impeccably appropriate to Mathieu's attitude and marks the turning point, in his inner self, between a former disdainful distancing from human reproduction and a growing obsessive preoccupation with the feminine. Sartre then thematizes the feminine around the woman's biological role in bringing the reproductive process to a tangible reality.

Even before Mathieu emitted his one-syllable ejaculation, as it were, summarizing his hapless repugnance at "those things" (410) (i.e., pregnancies), Sartre's transcription of Mathieu's thoughts had already been providing the reader with a far from flattering appraisal of his mistress. Apart from her "stern" or "hard mouth" (404) out of which emerges an "abrupt and masculine voice" (397), all the other adjectives describing Marcelle evoke a humid, sickeningly sweet world of flabby uselessness. She is "fat" and her "breasts heavy" (396). Her body, whose "flesh is plump and a bit worn out" (404) lending her the "air of a stout Levantine" (398), emits a "dull odor" (397). When her voice does not come off as manly, she "coos" like a portly pigeon (401). These epithets, which echo Sartre's lurid descriptions of "the viscous" in the final pages of *Being and Nothingness* (1943, 661–78), form the qualitative foundation of Mathieu's refusal of paternity. They rise up from a deep-seated repugnance at the feminine and reproduction.

If Mathieu was aesthetically less than enchanted with Marcelle before her pregnancy, he now comes to perceive his lover as hardly more sophisticated than a hen clucking with pride at the sheer pleasure of egg laying (512). Mathieu views his very being as having lost an original wholeness when his own body impregnated Marcelle, and this thought redoubles his fundamental revulsion at women. The revelation that he now concretely consitutes the progenitor of another potential being—his own offspring—disturbs and contaminates his abstract and narcissistic musings about potential *ideal* man. "For God's sake, what a filthy mess! [*quelle saleté*]" (406). Mathieu's fears about the effects the impending child will have on his existence well up and spill forth verbally, revealing in the narrative voice the depth of his disgust at the anatomical details of procreation. Dirt has encroached on Mathieu's existence in the form of a repulsive embryo that he feels he must quickly and quietly eradicate: "Before a week's gone by, everything will be taken care of [*tout sera réglé*]" (409). In contrast, to reinforce the sordidness in Mathieu's abortion plans, Sartre has him first visit Sarah in his search for a loan. Sarah's spouse, Gomez, a man of action reminiscent of Malraux's revolutionaries (though less sensitive even than a Garine or a Kyo), has abandoned her and their young son, Pablo, to go off and fight in the Spanish Civil War. Sarah recounts to Mathieu how once, before the birth of Pablo and in compliance with Gomez's wishes, she agreed to an abortion that she has always regretted.[11] Mathieu immediately feels cornered, taking Sarah's confession as an indirect moral judgment against him, and he flees, too ashamed to advance his request for money.

With panic exacerbating hallucination and sinking him deeper into confusion about how he could have "made such a balls of things,"[12] Mathieu issues forth with a whole symphony of unsavory epithets designating the unborn child. All references, spoken or not, to the fetus he himself has fathered are eventually reduced to the minimalist and distancing pronoun *ça*.[13] Sartre is masterful in making embryogeny the leitmotiv in a wide range of metaphors describing everyday situations for this increasingly obsessional accidental father. When Daniel, Mathieu's masochistic, closet homosexual friend, decides to marry Marcelle, a new bond is created between him and Mathieu that the latter thinks of as a "filthy and flaccid [*mou*] bond like an umbilical cord" (563).

Who Is the *Salaud*?

In virtually every Sartrean creation there must be a *salaud*. And so the careless, feckless fecundator, Mathieu, who thinks he has abortion written all over his face (436) pounds the streets in unwitting desperation, clinging to the hope of finding the sum that will eradicate the impediment to his freedom. After the disconcerting visit with Sarah, Mathieu's quest brings him to his brother, Jacques.

Roquentin's unforgettable visit to the Bouville Museum suggests that, by Sartre's standards, the mere fact that Jacques successfully practices the profession of attorney makes him a dirty bastard—a *salaud*.[14] There are just some social functions that make anyone who fills them automatically and irretrievably reprehensible, relegating them to the Sartrean category of *salaud*. This encounter between the two "opposed" brothers is crucial as an illustration of how Sartre himself subtly problematizes certain concepts like the *salaud*, which otherwise might be thought to be immutable. Rather than valorize the vaguely Leftist intellectual, Mathieu, over and above his conventional and rather reactionary brother, the scene heightens our suspicion that Mathieu is actually more morally deficient than Jacques.

In his necessity of soliciting a loan from an individual he considers despicable, Mathieu sets aside his sibling hatred and plays a game of cynicism and feigned civility. Under all other circumstances, his disdain for Jacques would, if we believe the narrator, be devastating; here it is held at bay and is hardly apparent. On the other hand, Jacques' paternalism and supercilious reprobation immediately cut through Mathieu's stilted mask of congeniality. From the moment that the subject of unwanted pregnancy is broached, it is clear that, swollen with a sense of moralistic mission, Jacques will ultimately refuse Mathieu the loan: "you're the one who has always spit on the family and now you're using our family ties to hit me up. You know, you wouldn't come to me if I weren't your brother" (502). In no time, Jacques' mock innocence exasperates Mathieu, leading him to weaken his own position and unveil the immorality of his being: "'Did you want a child?' He was egging me on by pretending not to understand. 'No, it was an accident'" (503). Mathieu displays a draconian attitude with respect to such "accidents" that, juxtaposed with Jacques' moralism, reveals him as the real *salaud:* "I don't want a child. One happens to come along. I eradicate it: that's all" (506). Mathieu is convinced that, by rejecting the responsibility of a father, he will preserve some pre-ethical, not-yet-total freedom. As we predicted in reading other Sartrean texts, the rejection of responsibility in *The Roads to Freedom* confirms the immorality of the subject.

Somewhat surprisingly, Mathieu does not dismiss Jacques' words outright and remains of two minds about his brother's condescending and pharisaical lesson. As distressing as he finds it to bear an upbraiding by a family-anchored peer, Jacques' remonstrations cut through Mathieu's hypocrisy and weakness, touching a raw truth that Marcelle had also pin-pointed but that, for reasons to be examined in the next chapter, Mathieu ignored completely. In terms that resonate with the quandary that plagued Orestes and Frantz about how to acquire the proper weight of being, Jacques thrusts before Mathieu the most likely explanation for his quest: "you want to get rid of the child because you don't want to accept all the consequences of your acts" (506). Whereas Frantz and Orestes were painfully conscious of the deficiency in moral responsibility characterizing their lives, Mathieu will remain eternally refractory to that awareness. His ontological inertia irascible, he obstinately turns his back on what Marcelle, for her part, convinced herself was "the most beautiful adventure in the world" (402). As he did with Marcelle's observations, Mathieu will relegate Jacques' paradoxically precise comment about his irresponsibility to quasi-oblivion and the problematic of weight proper to total being will remain intangible throughout *The Roads to Freedom.*

Act/Gesture/Action

We reach the end of this hefty first volume of *The Roads to Freedom,* the *Bildungsroman* of a late bloomer, with the distinct feeling that Mathieu has gained nothing. After having had considerable time to reflect upon what was happening to his being (or more precisely, what was *not* happening to his being), Mathieu sums up his existence to this point with some uncharacteristic lucidity: "I yawned, I read, I made love: all these things marked me! Each of my gestures instigated, well beyond, in the future, a little obstinate expectancy [*une petite attente obstinée*] which would mature. Those expectancies were *me*" (599). A mere gesture, Mathieu thinks, not an act,[15] a manifestation of fake rather than authentic commitment, copulation had (just like reading in the quotation) been an empty activity for Mathieu. Neither was an activity carrying any weight and each inspired in Mathieu the same bored yawn. Despite its blasé tone, this assessment conceals an almost hysterical fear of inseminating a woman, common to many of Sartre's male characters. However, a primal fear of loss, theorized by Freud as castration complex, proves insufficient for explaining Sartrean impregnation anxiety.

In a moment of sexual "carelessness," Marcelle became pregnant. The *mark* of an *act,* something indelible finally did happen to Mathieu. Yet this indelible mark was produced purely by chance or by what Mathieu repeatedly calls "bad luck." What Mathieu had always expected out of his program for free existence was that *he* would be the cause of a committed act. However, in this case, the act that marked occurred fortuitously, proving that a propelling act inherent to human experience and out of the control of the willful subject consciously carrying out action, is the cause of being.

Instead of embracing this indelible concrete mark that he had longed for, Mathieu proceeds, in bad faith, to search for a remedy to his unpleasant situation. He seeks to erase the mark. He continues to think that the responsible action that would lend weight to his being still lies somewhere in the future. In the quoted passage about yawning, reading and making love being equally insignificant, Mathieu tells himself what Jacques and Marcelle had already tried to drive home to him. But he no more listens to what he himself now is saying than he did to his brother and his lover: the "little obstinate expectancy" is no nebulous abstract concept that might require a lifetime of reflection to grasp. This expectancy is him. It is a reproduction of his partial being. It is another chance at total being—perhaps his "last chance," as the projected final volume of the saga novel was to be entitled.[16] The "little obstinate expectancy" is analogous to that repulsive but necessary "quality of being" of which Sartre spoke in the final pages of *Being and Nothingness.*[17] The expectancy for which Mathieu obstinately refuses to recognize his paternity is nothing more and nothing less than the child he engendered.

"I don't know what I'd give to commit an irremediable act" (728),

Mathieu laments as *The Age of Reason* comes to a close. But the "irremediable act" that he thinks he has yet to commit is the "indelible mark" he has just pondered. That act has already been inscribed in history and Marcelle is going to give birth to it in the next few months. Blind to recognizing this, Mathieu takes one more blind stab at commitment. Vaguely repulsed at Daniel's choice of homosexual martyrdom in deciding to marry Marcelle, Mathieu phones her in desperation. He is answered by silence, "loses his head" and screams that he wants to marry her (724). She "barks" an incoherent answer and crashes down the phone. Thus, his last, half-hearted act of commitment is violently unmasked as one more mere gesture. Daniel, on the other hand, who assures Mathieu that "[he] isn't marrying [Marcelle] as a gesture" (724) has understood that the weight-carrying *act* in this twisted family drama is centered on the recognition of and responsibility for the child as potential total human and not on the admittedly irresponsible, accidental gesture that set the biological phenomenon into motion.

Mathieu's rejection of paternity, for the purpose of safeguarding radical freedom, engenders neither his happiness nor his ethical being. The panic that beset him when he thought he would have to endorse the paternity of his child was only temporary: by the end of *The Age of Reason,* a calm of sorts has returned to him. But the chimeric charm of radical freedom is shattered. His momentary existential breakdown has demonstrated the extent to which the stability of an existence in radical freedom is illusory. Mathieu wonders, with the same vague anxiety he displayed in the opening scenes, whether he will still "be like this" in the years to come. Sartre then grants him a "reprieve" (the English title of the second volume) from such weighty considerations. In the third installment, *Troubled Sleep,* Mathieu does commit an act—or so he calls it. But, like his "abandonment" of Marcelle "for nothing" (729), this putative act turns out to be just another weightless gesture. The anxiety that had gripped him in envisioning an unchanging existence and uncommitted manhood proves to have foundation. This scene, which we will examine next, provides the impetus for taking a completely different look at *The Roads to Freedom* and considering it as much a text Sartre wrote "against itself" as one recounting events within the confines of the conventional narrative tradition. An altogether un-Sartrean *acceptance* of paternal responsibility lies implicit at every turn without the author actually explicitly taking that stand that would, perhaps, have placed him in an untenable contradiction. Sartre, not knowing quite whether or not he should revive Mathieu after his suicidal swan song, shelves the saga novel after drafting a fourth volume.

Meanwhile, as the bond of paternity continues to rot, as the words of *The Words* will predict, Sartre's ethics remains uncharted territory. Is the diseased model for intersubjectivity curable or is it a lost cause? The "distance" between the unequivocal rejection of paternity in *The Words* and the nostalgia for a father in *The Flies* reveals Sartre's ambivalence about a position where sons always reject fathers, while Mathieu embodies the simply unacceptable results obtained from imagining the consequences of fathers rejecting their potential sons. To the extent that we may speak of an "unconscious" of a written text, as many poststructuralist critics have done, then it is that surface of *The Roads to Freedom* that will form the material for the close reading in the next chapter.[18] It will enable us to enter onto the experimental space in literature at the service of Sartre's philosophical problems. While his ethics may have remained uncharted territory, it does not follow that it was unexplored or that Sartre's resources were depleted: I therefore suggest that something resembling a "symptomatic reading"[19] of the novel illuminates the cleavages in which ethical relationships between humans may be possible by revealing and making sense of the strained contiguity with the feminine of Mathieu and perhaps of his creator, Sartre.

Notes

1. "Who, upon learning that he is the father of a child, has not broken into a cold sweat, followed by cold anger, then disgust, then hatred?" (my translation).

2. For a detailed sociological study (heavily influenced by Pierre Bourdieu) of *Les Temps modernes* and its prominent place in postwar French intellectual life, see Anna Boschetti, *The Intellectual Enterprise: Sartre and "Les Temps modernes,"* trans. Richard C. McCleary (Evanston, Ill.: Northwestern University Press, 1988).

3. Sartre's early political career is discussed in several works, amongst them Michel-Antoine Burnier, *Les Existentialistes et la politique* (Paris: Gallimard, 1966) and Mark Poster, *Existential Marxism in Postwar France* (Princeton,

N.J.: Princeton University Press, 1975). Sartre's most important forays onto the political scene are the inauguration of *Les Temps modernes* under his directorship in 1945 and his involvement in the dissident left-wing political formation called the Rassemblement démocratique révolutionnaire with David Rousset, Georges Altman, and others. For a further discussion of Sartre's early political involvement, see chap. 6.

4. In the last lines of *Being and Nothingness* we read: "We shall devote a subsequent study to the domain of ethics" (1943, 692). The results of Sartre's incomplete ethical reflections during this postwar period are published as Jean-Paul Sartre, *Cahiers pour une morale* (Paris: Gallimard, 1983).

5. See Simone de Beauvoir, *La Force des choses* (Paris: Gallimard, 1963), 1:277.

6. With regard to the family, Sartre is a direct inheritor of the sentiments of André Gide as expressed in the vituperations of such novels as *Les Nourritures terrestres* (1897) and *Les Faux-monnayeurs* (1925). See my discussion of their relation in chap. 8.

7. Although it should be added that Roquentin (whose name Sartre chose purportedly for its "comically symbolic" value) shares certain character traits, which are embedded in his name, with the hero of the saga novel: *rocantin*, a noun lost in French today, at one time meant "a ridiculous old man who pretends to be young" (1981, 1674).

8. The narrative of *The Age of Reason* is structured as a medieval epic, where a knight errant sets out on a quest whose road is punctuated by various tests of courage.

9. As Sartre was not the first to put forth such theses, it would be just as erroneous to think that his preface to André Gorz's *The Traitor*, entitled "Of Rats and Men" (1958), was, as one scholar put it, Sartre's "first major hostile statement on the family." See Douglas Collins, *Sartre as Biographer* (Cambridge, Mass.: Harvard University Press, 1980), 111.

10. Psychocritics have extensively studied the bizarre aspects of Sartre's relation to women. See Josette Pacaly, *Sartre au miroir* (Paris: Klincksieck, 1980).

11. Less well known than Sartre's relative perspicacity on matters concerning anti-Semitism, particularly in *Anti-Semite and Jew*, is this derogatory remark gleaned from the pages of the saga novel (Marcelle says to Mathieu): "If you ask Sarah, [the abortionist]'ll be a kike for sure" (1981, 408); cf. Jean-Paul Sartre, *Réflexions sur la question juive* (Paris: Paul Morihien, 1946).

12. The slang term Mathieu repeatedly uses for his gaff is *connerie*, which derives from *con*, connoting a stupid person. *Con* and the family of related words in various Latin-based languages originally denoted female genitalia and still do.

13. As the *Grand Robert* dictionary explains, the demonstrative pronoun may express an amused refusal (*Pas de ça!*) or refer, in a demeaning tone, to a person (*Ça, ce n'est pas un homme!*). Prudishly and colloquially, it designates

the sex act. Of course as a noun, *ça* is the French psychoanalytic term corresponding to Freud's notion of the id.

14. Like bad faith, an essential category in Sartre's thought, *salaud* has had a variety of translations ("swine," "son of a bitch," etc.). In order to further problematize Sartre's diametrical moral opposition between the *salaud* and the *bâtard*, I will translate both as *bastard*, being careful to show, when necessary, which term I refer to by using square brackets.

15. As Ingrid Joubert has observed in her excellent *Aliénation et liberté dans "Les Chemins de la liberté"* (Paris: Didier, 1973), 242; see also Denis Hollier, "The Handbook of the Intellectual," *Raritan* 1, no.2 (1981): 73–88.

16. The definitive history of the plans for this fourth volume and its ultimate incompletion may be found in Michel Contat and George Bauer's notes to the fragments published in the Pléiade (Sartre 1981, 2136–38).

17. We will see (in chap. 5) that the viscous is not a quality of *things*. Things, or being-in-itself, are in opposition to humans, or being-for-itself. The viscous is the feminine—by definition also being-for-itself but in practice excluded by Sartre from "legitimate" ontological status.

18. In evoking the notions of "writing against oneself" and "unconscious text" I am thinking of and, indeed, indebted to the work of Jacques Derrida as analyzed in "The Rhetoric of Blindness," Paul de Man, *Blindness and Insight* (Minneapolis: University of Minnesota Press, 1971), 102–41.

19. Although many of his analyses have proven groundless, one of the most fruitful notions to come out of the speculative thought of Louis Althusser is that of the "symptomatic reading," *Lire "Le Capital"* (Paris: Maspéro, 1969), 106ff.

PART THREE

BEING ENGULFED BY PATERNITY

The novels comprising *The Roads to Freedom*, especially *The Age of Reason*, are pivotal texts for attributing to paternity the role of ambivalent metaphor that Sartre would then apply to his ethical thought. Without the altogether undecided attitude toward women evinced in these novels it would be impossible to argue that the theme of paternity could possess a complexity sufficiently subtle for it to form the basis of an area of philosophy that Sartre found impossible to formulate fully in the discourse of that discipline. Without Mathieu Delarue's ambiguity and the doggedness with which the narrator seems bent on unravelling it, it would be impossible to assert that when being becomes engulfed by paternity, the male subject—the only gender Sartre really ever consciously wrote about—begins to find a way to attain ethical being.

The Age of Reason locates Mathieu at the moment of his most critical personal choice. Before the narrative began he had, by accident, impregnated Marcelle. Having thus become a *biological* father, the choice remained to him whether or not to recognize and accept paternity. This decision, which one way or the other would cause an unprecedented upheaval in his existence, is one of crucial ethical import. To become or not to become a father finally signifies, in Mathieu's case, to become moral or to remain free for no reason.

In the preceding chapter I examined Mathieu's overt response to the choice before him. We saw that, as might be expected from a Sartrean male, his decision was to attempt a rejection of paternity. Rather than the overt argument describing existential stasis, however, we will now consider the text in what might be called its "organicity," scrutinizing its texture, analyzing linguistic associations and shifts springing from Mathieu's subconscious, as presented in the narrator's voice. I intend to concentrate on the fictional *monologue intérieur* created for Mathieu, rather than on the series of consciously aborted actions. In doing so, we will gradually see Sartre betraying himself as a closet advocate of paternity and as a man intrigued by women not simply as objects of a male sexual desire complicated by anxiety, but also insofar as women, given their unique relationship to children, could be considered innately more capable than men of interacting with others in an ethical manner.

CHAPTER 4

The Unbearable Lightness of Being

In the second chapter I showed Orestes and Frantz embodying the pain that humans endure when the absence of another human, for whom one is responsible, causes "lightness of being." In his saga novel, Sartre focuses his and our attention on this same lack of proper weight. We soon learn that the lightness of being of Mathieu Delarue becomes particularly unbearable when he refuses paternity.

Mathieu has always suffered from an existential malady that he calls "being free for nothing (for no reason)" (*je suis libre pour rien*).[1] Sartre's device for making sure he has a grip on the reader is to create a suspense, through two-and-a-half of the saga novel's three volumes, about whether Mathieu still has a chance of doing something to remedy this deficiency in freedom. If committed action is indeed the key factor for correcting Mathieu's problem with nothingness, certainly the novel's historical setting of 1939 Europe would seem to provide Sartre's hero with only too many *causi belli* from which to choose. At the end of the first part of *Troubled Sleep*, when Mathieu makes a final exit from the uncompleted work, Sartre devises a smoke screen for real action.[2] Mathieu is at his moment of truth,[3] and Sartre, bringing dramatic tension to a climax, wants it to appear that Mathieu finally reaches a solution to his dilemma of existential meaninglessness, or, as I call it here, his weightless freedom. We are supposed to be lured into assuming that, in this final scene, Mathieu breaks the vicious cycle of waiting, of leaving himself available in that passive and ineffectual sort of way for a miraculous mandate for action.[4] Given the scene's extreme violence, one might suspect that just such a dramatic shift must indeed be taking place. Pursued by German troops, Mathieu's small beleaguered patrol of soldiers holes up in a village belfry. He witnesses blood and gore at close range for the first time in his life. As the group's total annihilation becomes imminent, Mathieu opens fire in a blind rage, sniping indiscriminately at the enemy soldiers below. Then, in a dense shower of bullets from the advancing Germans, the episode culminates with Mathieu holding forth heroically, yet facing certain death. What more "Sartrean" circumstances could one imagine for Mathieu to at long last "dirty his hands" than in war against the Third Reich?[5] Yet something just doesn't coincide with Sartrean *engagement,* a commitment with its sociopolitical consequences laid bare for all to admire. Something about the automatism with which Mathieu proceeds seems in disharmony with the idealistic purity of commitment. Oddly, as he is firing his weapon, Mathieu busies himself mentally by lending to each bullet an attribution for some aborted chance to commit himself in the past.

> He made his way to the parapet and stood there firing. This was revenge on a big scale. Each shot avenged some old scruple. "One for Lola whom I didn't dare to rob; one for Marcelle whom I should have ditched; one for Odette whom I didn't want to screw. This one for the books I never dared to write, this one for the trips I never made, this one for all the guys in general that I wanted to hate and tried instead to understand." He fired away and the Tables of the Law were blown to smithereens—thou shalt love thy neighbor as thyself—bang! in that bugger's face—thou shalt not kill—bang! at that mealy mouth over there. He was firing on his Fellow Man, on Virtue, on the World. Freedom is Terror. The city hall was ablaze, his head was

> ablaze. Bullets were whizzing round him free as the air. "The world is going up in smoke, and me with it." He fired. He looked at his watch: fourteen minutes and thirty seconds. Nothing more to ask for now except one half-minute. Just time enough to fire at that smart looking officer running toward the church, at all the Beauty of the Earth, at the street, at the flowers, at the gardens, at everything he had loved. Beauty took an obscene dive and Mathieu went on firing. He fired. He was cleansed. He was all-powerful. He was free. (1981, 1344)

To be sure, this shooting spree has all the characteristics of a supremely cathartic moment. Mathieu displays an ecstasy one might easily associate with a religious conversion.[6] The scene drips with the kind of satisfaction real commitment might bring.[7] But the magnitude of Mathieu's sense of gratification can in no way derive from a politically tolerable or even commendable extermination of World War II villains even though those murders would be pardonable for their having sprung from the choice of a just cause. The heaving cadence of Sartre's style and the transference involved in personifying and allegorizing each bullet clearly shows that Mathieu's sole purpose in shooting is to evacuate nervous tension.

By meticulously itemizing the objects of his frustration, then exploding them symbolically as bullets, his act becomes one of pure psychic discharge. After this mental potlatch, it will matter little whether he has actually died or not because the scene is a paroxysmal display of Mathieu's death instinct and not of a life-giving, ethical commitment. In the tableau preceding this one,[8] Mathieu had called life quits in words that leave no doubt that Thanatos (and not Atlas) is hard at work in the belfry. Having reached the top of the stairs, he says to himself:

> Screw it all. Too bad for those down below, too bad for everybody. No more remorse, reservations, or restrictions . . . . I've decided that *death has always been the secret meaning of my life,* that I've lived in order to die. I'm going to die to bear witness to the fact that it's impossible to live . . . (1981, 1323; italics added)

For "impossible to live" one may just as easily substitute "impossible to locate the secret of responsible freedom," to take responsibility for my acts by placing them symbolically like a burden on my shoulders as in the Atlas ideal outlined in *Being and Nothingness.* Unlimited freedom, the type of freedom Mathieu cultivated, ultimately to his profound frustration, is unbearably light.

Esprit de Survol

Even if at one time it might have been Sartre's intention, Mathieu's massacre of Nazis can in no way be considered to represent some initiation rite ushering Mathieu into "full humanity" through commitment.[9] On the contrary, the episode is just another demonstration, as violently dramatic as it might be, of the lycée philosophy professor's failure to devote himself to anything at all. The ultimate futility of this act and its ethical emptiness becomes clearer when we note the uncanny similarities between the belfry scene and circumstances in two other texts by Sartre where failure at commitment coincidentally involves killing someone with a gun. Rather than noble acts of commitment, the situations I will now examine induce their protagonists to reactionary measures.

Mathieu's shooting spree is, in many ways, a near replication of the conceit of Sartre's 1938 short story, "Erostratus," in which Paul Hilbert, a man with an acute inferiority complex, dreams of becoming a modern-day incarnation of the ancient incendiary whose name is Sartre's title.[10] Both Mathieu and Hilbert position themselves in perches high above the street, making their future victims who move about below more vulnerable to observation and attack. Hilbert gathers the courage to commit his act by spying, day after day, on passers-by from his apartment window.[11] As Sartre explained in *The Words,* this is also an activity that he enjoyed engaging in as a young boy.[12] Later, in *The Family Idiot,* taking an "ultimate standpoint" (*esprit de survol*) becomes a category of human behavior.[13] When positioned in their elevated places, both Mathieu and Hilbert experience a deceptively exhilarating "lightness of being."[14] Ironically in both cases, those who began as the real or projected victims of their violence ultimately triumph over *them:* Hilbert is stopped short of his terrorist act and packed off to an asylum and Mathieu goes missing in action in a cloud of gunsmoke produced by representatives of the Wehrmacht.

With all of Mathieu's intentions and gestures failing to measure up to the standard of true action, parallels also emerge between the saga novel and *Dirty Hands,* Sartre's 1948 play about a bourgeois intellectual who has joined the Communist Party. We are led to believe that Hugo plans to carry out orders from a Stalinist group within the Party to assassinate the Trotsky-like party leader, Hoerderer. But this act of commitment through murder disguises the veritable motive of jealousy when he suspects an affair between Hoerderer and Jessica. Setting aside the historical issue of the animosity against Sartre that his play stirred up among Communist stalwarts, committing irreversible and destructive acts for morally reprehensible motives is the most powerful debate *Dirty Hands* inspires. Hugo, like Orestes and Hilbert, refers to murder as both a liberating and weight-giving act.[15] Because the weight of being is a much more explicit theme in *Dirty Hands* than it is in *The Roads to Freedom,* the play helps to elucidate some of the ambiguous gestures in the novel. Sartre was writing the play while work on the novel was starting to stall. The problems of finishing the latter inevitably spilled over into the former, which Sartre was able to write quickly and easily. Thus, Mathieu's cathartic rituals, from his verbal outbursts against reproduction to the massacring of German soldiers, are apparently (like Hugo's assassination of Hoerderer) mere pretexts for responsibility and action that carry no more weight than the "political" murder.

Historical Moment, Fatherly Foment

In *Being and Nothingness,* Sartre wrote that freedom *and* responsibility—the two qualities that total man would embody—render inescapable his being situated in, even thrust into, the political and the historical. He is always free and responsible within a specific historical framework. Conversely, and in accordance with the premise of overwhelming responsibility, the framework is also of his making: he creates it and is accountable for its contours.

> . . . totally, free, indiscernible from the period for which I have chosen to be the meaning, as deeply responsible for war as if I had myself declared it, incapable of living out anything without incorporating it into *my* situation . . . , I must be without remorse or regrets just as I am without excuses. For *from the moment of my surging forth into being, I carry the weight of the world all by myself.* . . . (1943, 614; Sartre stresses *my;* the remaining italics are added)

Just as universal responsibility implies that an exact correspondence exists between me and the world illustrated by my carrying the responsibility for others on my shoulders, so must there be a one-to-one correspondence between the projected, planned, tentative motives for my actions and the actual materialization of those actions. If Hugo's plan consisted of killing Hoerderer for political motives but he ends up killing him out of jealousy, all the time insisting that it was still a political assassination, then he is not only guilty of bad faith but he falls short of Sartre's most stringent ethical criteria for consistency. In the terms laid out in the Atlas model from *Being and Nothingness,* responsibility for action has failed to fall squarely on Hugo's shoulders when his projected and actual motives are out of synchronization with each other. When this occurs, the subject's action will not provide him with the proper weight for his ethical being. This is why Hugo's act ultimately aborts and why Mathieu's sniper episode is similarly off target with respect to his search for the weight-giving act. Neither ends nor means should take priority one over the other, according to Sartre's ethical thought: a moral foundation springing from a hierarchy of motives behind *both* means and ends forms the basis of action.

Within the realm of possibilities that Sartre made available to Mathieu, the only act that could have provided him with the kind of ethical weight he sought was the adoption of responsibility for the child Marcelle carries. Having become complacent in the assumption that the biological intent, as it were, of coitus was being effectively circumvented when he and Marcelle made love, he grew to ignore that biological reality. Yet even a recalcitrant and confused Mathieu came to partial realization of the validity of the resolution that Marcelle prompted him to adopt. When he rehearsed an acceptance of paternity by toying with the idea that to somehow convince himself to marry Marcelle would be the consummate act of freedom left to him, he was at least ventriloquizing the validity of Marcelle's suggested resolution: "to will myself to be what I am is the only freedom left to me. My only freedom consists in willing myself to marry Marcelle" (1981, 633). And although Mathieu never recognizes, never endorses the paternity of their child, Marcelle elaborately prepared him for that weight-lending task—a preparation that is present in Sartre's text. Marcelle's latent influence over Mathieu is the literary manifestation of an atypical Sartre—one who allows exceptionally for a feminine voice to be heard through his narrative voice. Just as Mathieu was blind to the eventuality of Marcelle's pregnancy, so he misses his opportunity to endorse paternity at her behest. Both were too close to him; both were too obvious. Although it is a commonplace in literature, at least since the Book of Genesis, to find a woman placed in the position of mediator for a transcendence enacted by a male character, it is unusual within Sartre's corpus, where the feminine is almost always rejected or presented in a negative light. Sartre, in the 1940s, is trying out the practice of mediating ethical being by means of a feminine voice.

These are the contours of the un-Sartrean reading of *The Roads to Freedom* that I propose both in this chapter and in the next. By attempting to show how obvious an endorsement of paternity should have been to Mathieu, by saying that Marcelle (in a certain sense) prepared him for the task, I am maintaining that, in this novel at least, Sartre wrote simultaneously *for and against* paternity and that, while the tenor of his novel is that of a rejection of paternity, the texture of its language conveys paternity's validation.

Woman as Weak Superego

At first Mathieu was clear in his understanding of the purpose of his quest for abortion money. Once the pregnancy was terminated, the status quo of his relationship with Marcelle would be reestablished and his personal freedom once again safeguarded against intrusions. Originally they had made a bilateral pact similar to the one that Sartre and Beauvoir devised to guarantee the "authenticity" and "immutability" of their relationship. Marcelle and Mathieu vowed to communicate everything to each other and, should ever a procreational "accident" occur, Marcelle agreed to submit to an abortion. The fundamental contradiction between the clauses of these agreements apparently escaped the couple. While a vow of openness implies unconditional intimacy, the agreement to remain childless is not only motivated by a fear of compulsory commitment, but it sets practical limits to sexual intimacy, albeit at a time when contraception was a less than foolproof enterprise. In the first conversation between Marcelle and Mathieu, the relative lack of communication between them is striking. Marcelle has obviously not been energetic enough in explaining herself to Mathieu up until this juncture, while Mathieu hardly listens to her until his freedom is threatened by the pregnancy.

In the first, oddly hesitant pages of *Civilization and Its Discontents,* Freud describes the notorious "'oceanic' feeling" (57–67).[16] He discusses, with evasive condescension, a feeling "of limitlessness and of bond with the universe" (68) from which he, Freud, takes a personal distance, attributing it only to "people in whose mental life [the] primary ego-feeling has persisted" (68), to those who "seek something like the restoration of *limitless narcissism*" (72; italics added), in other words, to those whose ego identification continues to derive primarily from desire for the mother's breast (67). It would seem that prolonging unlimited narcissism, which Freud obviously considers a retrogressive tendency toward the mother, works in direct opposition to the civilizing forces of the introjected father as source and embodiment of the law—the forces that create the superego.

The unlimited narcissism to which Mathieu is prone, like that of young children as Freud goes on to describe them, causes him to be virtually blind in all of his relations with others. His astonishment at the news of Marcelle's pregnancy is only a preliminary indication of this blindness. Throughout *The Age of Reason,* he systematically misjudges Marcelle's feelings and, to the very end of his role in the novel in *Troubled Sleep* in the belfry scene he maintains the delusion that *he* abandoned *her* when in fact she gave up on him to build a new life for herself long before he was capable of making a clear decision. He also clings to an ancillary relationship with the neurotic student,

Ivich, for which there is not and probably never was any hope. When he learns of the impending marriage between Marcelle and his homosexual friend, Daniel, he is still frantically searching for abortion money and is stunned.[17] By the end of *The Age of Reason,* still feeling only slightly ridiculous, still not quite fathoming that it is long since over with Marcelle, he only vaguely recognizes the obsolescence of his abortion quest.

Mathieu is aware that his system for guaranteeing personal freedom is flawed. The willful blindness of France and other nations with regard to impending war in 1939 Europe serves as a historical analogy for Mathieu's narcissistic freedom and the blindness it causes. Just as Chamberlain and Daladier's hopes for peace soon proved illusory and even absurd, Mathieu, abandoned by everyone, feeling "free for nothing," finally recognizes that his embattled and impotent situation might, indeed, never change: "in two, three, four years . . . will I still be like this?" (1981, 726). His reflex to turn to Marcelle for consolation is irrepressible. But she, disgusted like everyone else, has left him.

> And he was suddenly seized by the desire to speak to Marcelle about it. She was the only one to whom he could speak about his life, his fears, his hopes. But then he remembered that he would never see her again and his desire, suspended in air, unnamed, slowly metamorphosed into a kind of anguish: he was alone. (726)

This loneliness in abandonment forces him, in desperation, to recollect, but only confusedly, some of the first words we hear Marcelle pronounce about him. He realizes, though he still does nothing about it, that while he never *listened* to Marcelle, he *heard* her quite well. The difference between listening and hearing accounts for how Mathieu could completely ignore Marcelle's first analysis of him, failing to put it to practice, and yet preserve those words at an almost irretrievable level of consciousness. The fact that Mathieu is now perhaps oblivious to Marcelle's exact words does not diminish their profound impact. We, as readers, experience their repercussions at the level of Mathieu's narratized memory and in the thematic structure of his subconscious that is unfolded before us. In Freudian terms, Mathieu introjected Marcelle's words, thus forming a weak superego.[18] What the narrator said of him at the beginning remains true to the last:

> Marcelle's consciousness was still back there . . . and Mathieu hadn't left it: he too was back there in that pink bedroom, naked and defenseless before that heavy transparency that was more unsettling than a look. (1981, 409)

"Marcelle's consciousness" (*la conscience de Marcelle*) is a purposely ambiguous expression. In a fleeting moment before deciding on how we want to understand the phrase, Sartre allows us to float between "[Mathieu's] awareness of Marcelle" and "Marcelle's consciousness"—both valid translations of *la conscience de Marcelle* in this context. This possible undecidability in meaning is corroborated by the next part of the quote, which could (because of the ambiguity of *la conscience de Marcelle*) again be translated either as "Mathieu had never left *her*" or as "Mathieu had never left *it*," that is, her consciousness. Perhaps Sartre intends to have us understand that Mathieu inhabits her consciousness, that he (in a way) dwells within her. Finally, the imagery that Sartre imputes to Mathieu in describing Marcelle's consciousness, "that heavy transparency," although something that "unsettles" Mathieu, resembles the very ideals that he (and Sartre) sought in life: "transparency" evokes the ideal of uncensored communication between beings and "heaviness," the necessity of completing freedom by ballasting it with responsibility, and finally the noun and adjective reunited connoting "the viscous."

As we saw, Mathieu's recollection of Marcelle's words at the end of *The Age of Reason* occurs at a symbolically transcribed level in the belfry potlatch. In order to measure the extent to which he *heard* Marcelle we must retrace Mathieu's own memory paths and go back to Marcelle's early remonstrations, emphasizing the themes that later inspired the verbal transcription of his thought processes.

> Do you know what I think? I think that you're *sterilizing yourself* a bit. . . . everything is *clean and proper* with you: everything smells of *fresh laundry* [*blanchissage*]. It's as if you'd autoclaved yourself. The only thing is, *it lacks dark*

> *spots.* There's *nothing superfluous, nothing fuzzy* or *fishy* left in it. It's torrid. (402; italics added)[19]

Marcelle observed further that, as a result of Mathieu's "limitless narcissism," he emptied himself of substance. Every effort he makes in his quest runs counter to the meaningful freedom he is trying to achieve in his existence.

> It's all in order to free yourself *from* yourself. To contemplate yourself, to judge yourself, that's your favorite attitude. When you observe yourself, you're convinced that you're not what you see—that you're nothing. At bottom, that's your ideal: *to be nothing.* (403; italics added)

Each of the accusations Marcelle levels at Mathieu corresponds to an eventual obsessional theme in his stream of consciousness to which we, as readers, bear constant witness. Marcelle's character evaluation is a canon containing the elements of Mathieu's "weak superego." Marcelle has stepped in where the father typically would be in Freud's famous theory of superego development. But equipped with that introjected psychic material from a woman, Mathieu does nothing about his dilemma.

Mathieu's internalization of Marcelle's criticism, forcing his thoughts and later obsessions about reproduction to comply with it, is not bereft of theoretical foundation. Freud hypothesized in *The Ego and the Id* that the superego evolves essentially from "word-presentations" or "verbal residues" whose content, in turn, derive primarily from auditory perceptions.[20] The following example from Sartre's narrative will show how the weak superego that Mathieu acquired was formed very much in this manner. Marcelle, still analyzing Mathieu, says: "Your life is full of *missed chances* [*occasions manquées*]"; "You're so rarely *tuned in* [*être dans le coup*] to what's going on" (401); "[the idea of] finding out you've been had makes you so jittery that you'd turn down the most beautiful *adventure* in the world" (402; all italics added). Immediately following these comments comes Marcelle's announcement portending traumatic developments for both of them. In their discussion about the unexpected turn of events, Marcelle remains conciliatory and, despite her misgivings about terminating the pregnancy, manages to muster some enthusiasm over information she herself has obtained about a cheap abortionist. Meanwhile, Mathieu's psyche has already set itself to hard work expropriating the expression "missed chances" from what he has just heard from Marcelle and *converting* it into an ironic aside about the "deal" or "bargain" (another meaning of *occasion*) on an abortion, which really should not be "passed up" (*manquée*):

> "She only asks 400 francs. You know, I've heard that's an absurdly low price," Marcelle suddenly said in a reasonable tone of voice.
>
> "Yeh, I can see," said Mathieu bitterly, "in short, it's a bargain." (1981, 406)

The semantic slippage that has occurred here, facilitating Mathieu's internalization of the law, may be divided into two stages. First, Marcelle's use of the figure of "missed chances" in order to call Mathieu's manner of existence into question: the mechanism that regulates his life consists in his systematically letting opportunities drift away whenever they arise. In the second moment, Mathieu attempts to deflect the intensity of this judgment from himself by projecting it onto the hypothetical abortion that he sarcastically refers to as "a deal of a lifetime." Mathieu's internalization of Marcelle's ominous words that warn that he is doomed to miss chances has, however, been initiated. And now, as he mulls over his contraceptive slipup, she predicts that he will miss even a chance at "the most beautiful adventure in the world"—obviously not a suicidal mission against Nazis.

An examination of Mathieu's psyche, at the conscious and subconscious levels, should demonstrate that it adheres to "verbal residues" not from a paterfamilias, as Freud predicted, but from a *woman*—Marcelle becoming a weak authority figure. The narrative voice provides us with the elements of Mathieu's thinking in microscopic detail. The network of Mathieu's obsessions, while pointing the way to a missed endorsement of paternity, at the same time exposes the reasons why that solution proved impossible for him and, thus, illuminates Sartre's own continuing struggle to formulate a model for ethical intersubjectivity. The crucial role of *The Age of Reason* in Sartre's work is in the author's having used the voice of a woman rather than that of a man for the formation of a superego.

Being or Nothingness

As Proust, Joyce, Céline, or any number of other modernists show in those writings where remembering and forgetting play such integral parts, when we try to represent some modicum of meaning in our existence, we more often than not begin by using our faculty of memory to establish historical and causal distinctions between events. Willy-nilly, we attempt to sort out from apparent chaos those events perceived as having certain ego-grounded purposefulness. Marcelle's analysis of Mathieu turns on this attempt to distinguish between events—dismissing many and valorizing a few. As we have seen thus far, the words *opportunity* (*occasion*), *chance* or *luck* (*chance*), *adventure*, *accident*, and, of course, *coup* (with its multiplicity of meanings and idiomatic applications)[21] figure prominently in that analysis.[22] From the moment Marcelle pronounces these words, Mathieu's psyche becomes haunted by them. They are the source of a vague but constant sense of guilt in him, as if (as in the functioning of his superego) they were the injunctions of an authority figure. Marcelle's words and the intersections between their meanings have a palpable influence in setting into motion the vicissitudes of Mathieu's mind.

Those intersections are also essential to understanding the transformations that occur in Marcelle and Daniel, prompting them to form, against all likelihood, a couple. Whereas Mathieu remains unable to unravel meanings in events and words and eventually take control of his life, Daniel and Marcelle resolve the various dilemmas of their troubled existences by recourse to the institution of marriage. And perhaps their solution is not as unconventional and abject as it appears through Mathieu's eyes. Mathieu's knowledge of Daniel's homosexuality incites the former to protest, "you're just marrying her to be a martyr." "So what?" (1981, 725) Daniel replies, acquiescing to Mathieu's observation that masochism, indeed, motivates his decision to get married. But for Daniel, masochism functions in *favor* of the preservation of life: in a twisted way, it is his life instinct. Before he found purpose through marriage with Marcelle, he had to think of himself as a future martyr. He had to project himself into the future as a monument to husbandhood.[23] Later, in *The Reprieve,* Daniel will hope for war so that mass conflict would accomplish the job of suicide he could not muster the courage to carry out at his own hands.

> And he thought: "If only the war would come!" She'd be widowed with the child and six hundred thousand francs in cash. Not to speak of the memories she'd have of an incomparable husband. (772)

Before the chance for a new life, Daniel convinced himself he was suicidal in order, paradoxically, to survive. Marriage with Marcelle replaces that sterile compulsion to repeat the death drive with a purpose projected onto others. "I'm not marrying her as a gesture. Besides, what she wants most is the kid" (724).

Having realized that she wanted to keep her child all along, but finding it difficult to contemplate doing it alone, Marcelle, for her part, seizes an opportunity she perceives in Daniel's proposal to provide the child with a father. Before Mathieu's announcement to Daniel that Marcelle is pregnant (493), which sets off Daniel's campaign to encourage her to keep the baby, Marcelle already subconsciously wanted it: "[her] body, flowering absurdly, was made for maternity. But men had decided differently" (465). Without anyone else's support, she would perhaps have resigned herself, once again, to a man's decision, gotten an abortion, and relegated the pregnancy to the same category of nonevents that she criticized Mathieu for cultivating: "Another missed opportunity!" (465). As if the two were made for each other, the vocabulary of Daniel's encouragement seems to spring from Marcelle's subconscious: "if you had this kid, maybe it would be a disaster, but maybe it would be a stroke of good fortune [*chance*]" (566). In this empowerment of a woman to overcome paternalistic fathers making decisions for her, we glimpse an uncharacteristically feminist Sartre.

Both Daniel and Marcelle thus convert an accident—the product of chance—into purposeful opportunity. From the positive consequences of Daniel's choice to become a surrogate father, there can be no doubt that endorsement of paternity is the path to ethical existence that awaited whomever in the story had the courage to embark upon it. The chance encounter of Mathieu's sperm and Marcelle's ovum—"your accident," as Daniel calls it[24]—has provided Daniel with the opportunity of a lifetime. Luridly and incongruously (thus effectually), a passage describing one of Daniel's homosexual trysts illustrates this new purpose in life in imagery that again links ontological "weight" and paternity. Pinning his lover to a bed, Daniel marvels at how Ralph is "crushed under this weight of a real man, of a paterfamilias" (1981, 689). The remark can be construed in two ways (as indeed it should be in order to preserve the essential duality and mutuality in the ethical relation). Ralph, we learn, is married and has children. He is thus, according to Sartrean allegory, already weighed down by family responsibilities, whereas Daniel is not yet thus emburdened. We might wonder why, then, the image appears precisely when it is this true father who is *literally* crushed under the body of a surrogate father-to-be. The childless Daniel has already made his decision to ask Marcelle to marry him—an act that will bring along with it the guardianship of a child, an act that will thus emburden him with the same ethical responsibilities already present in Ralph. Daniel, anticipating his soon-to-be-acquired weight of being, can think of himself already as crushing Ralph.

In this context, Daniel's discovery of the crushing weight that he shares with his lover would make no sense at all without our knowledge of the same imagery being invoked in *Being and Nothingness* and in *The Words*. In the former, once again, Sartre compared ethical being to an Atlas shouldering the responsibilities of the whole world, while his autobiography singles out paternity as the most "iniquitous" of all interpersonal relationships and illustrates this claim with an allegorical scene in which a father's weight eternally overwhelms his son. Through the highly unusual scene of homosexual ecstasy between two fathers, Sartre wants to ensure that we are reminded of the ethical weight inscribed in the parent-child relation, no matter where in society that relation occurs. Daniel realizes that becoming even a surrogate father lends weight to his being.

It is often thought that Sartre's portrayal of humans in *Being and Nothingness* is quite simply (if not simplistically) reducible to an existence in pure negation, amounting to nothingness.[25] Indeed, my study thus far would appear to reinforce that negative assessment through the fictional example of Mathieu's existence. Unlike Daniel and Marcelle, who manage to convert chance or accident into opportunity or purpose, thus lending ballast to their existence, all events are uniformly fortuitous to Mathieu and his being remains unbearably light. Heidegger's adverbial construction that Derrida made a commonplace is particularly apt here because all of Mathieu's "opportunities" [*occasions*] for commitment are *always already* "missed" [*manquées*]. *Occasion*, in Mathieu's world, becomes inseparable from *manquée*. Opportunity can never be present: something that is *manqué* is longed for, but often only in the unattainable way of being longed for nostalgically because it is something already passed by or buried in the past. It is always already too late for the opportunity that's *manquée: tu me manques*, literally "you lack from me, from my existence," the French expression that throws all beginning students off by its logic, syntactically opposite to English, which simply means "I miss you," but strongly conveys this radically originary lack. Opportunity is always felt as a lack: *un manque* is a gap one might desire to fill in one's future or that one might regret not having filled in one's past. According to Mathieu, there is no future. As far as he is concerned, opportunites harbor no potentiality, no germ of a future wholeness.[26] What he chooses to ignore, however, is that his discrepancy from being, the flaw in his perfect existence, lies in his having created, unwittingly, an opportunity and a future for himself that could, in fact, save him from pure negation and nothingness.

That Amorphic Age of Reason

Mathieu's inability to distinguish between chance and opportunity establishes, if not a precedent, at least a pretext for reading the entire economy of his psyche as a series of blurred distinctions.

—Whose life is closed tight like a shell? Marcelle's or Mathieu's?

Mathieu likens entering the stifling atmosphere of Marcelle's apartment to being closed into a shell (1981, 396). Yet later, when he realizes that he has constructed a life of phony freedom, the abject shell image boomerangs: he associates his own state with the secretion of a shell (599–600).

—Is abortion "metaphysical" or infanticidal?

Persistent in Western countries that legalized abortion in the 1970s and that now contemplate rescinding that right, this debate becomes muddled in Mathieu's conversation with Jacques. Jacques first accuses Mathieu of being an infanticide, then retreats into irony when faced with Mathieu's verbal challenge, observing with detachment, "I agree, abortion isn't infanticide, it's 'metaphysical' murder." But then Mathieu himself as much as affirms the abortion-infanticide equation by saying "I don't want a child. One happens to come along. I eradicate it: that's all" (505–6).

—Has Mathieu refused paternity definitively or is there a chance he might still endorse it?

For a while, Mathieu plays a game of telling himself that he's "screwed" (*foutu*) if he endorses paternity and saved if he rejects it (497ff.). This paradigm appears to fall apart in an astounding outburst where the prospect of paternity brings on the problem of carrying weight (versus being carried): "Screwed, I'm completely screwed. I used to carry the days on my back, passing them from one side of the river to the other. Today they carry me" (799).[27]

—Is freedom heavy or light?

Mathieu says to Brunet, "My freedom? It weighs down on me" (525). But Daniel, before commitment to Marcelle, is described as "not touching the ground, [as] flying with the joy of feeling diabolical" (558).

But of all of the blurred distinctions in Sartre's work, Mathieu's age, whose theme is announced by the first volume's title, is the most complex. If, in *Saint Genet* (1952), Sartre took up Diderot's playful paradox "Est-il bon? Est-il méchant?" in discussing the ethical ambivalence of Jean Genet,[28] both the indeterminacy of Mathieu's age and the ethical implications of *The Age of Reason* could well be expressed by asking about the bumbling protagonist: "Is he old or is he young?"

Whatever their opinions about him as a moral being, the secondary characters perceive Mathieu's age as an anomaly. Boris, in blind reverence for his mentor, is convinced that Mathieu's age is perfectly appropriated to his being: "there were guys like Mathieu who were made to be thirty-five because they had never had a childhood" (425).[29] Boris has idealized Mathieu to the point of considering even his own childhood (which, for the moment, he still has to live with), as a negligible part of life: to him and perhaps to Mathieu himself, Mathieu was like an adult trapped in the body of a child. Yet without a childhood of some sort, what sense remains in using the expression *the age of reason* and how does it pertain to Mathieu? The term is a legacy of canon law. The teachings of the founder of the Jesuit Order, Ignatius de Loyola, led the Catholic Church to consider seven years to be the average age at which children supposedly have acquired most of their ability to reason—hence the age of reason. According to Boris, Mathieu has always been thirty-five, so at first glance it does not seem to make much sense to attribute the maturity of a seven-year-old to him. This rather scrupulous line of investigation would be superfluous were it not corroborated by another character with an altogether different point of view on Mathieu's intangible age. While lecturing Mathieu about the disorder of his life, his brother Jacques seems more than a bit unsure about what age to attribute to him.[30]

> "*You have reached the age of reason*, my poor Mathieu," said he, in a tone of pity and warning. "But you try to dodge that fact too, you try to pretend you're younger than you are. Well, perhaps I'm doing you an injustice. Perhaps *you haven't in fact reached the age of reason*, it's really a moral age . . . perhaps I've got there sooner than you have." (1981, 508; italics added)

Then, as in that final breath of life, the death rattle, *The Age of Reason* ends with its deceptive simplicity: "[Mathieu] was done with his youth. . . . He yawned again as he repeated to himself: 'It's true, it's really true—I've reached the age of reason'" (729). One might easily be led to the conclusion that a kind of age equilibrium has been attained, that Mathieu is really at long last satisfied with his stage of maturity (if not with anything else). Even if no one else thinks so, Mathieu seems to believe that he has finally reached the milestone promised in Sartre's title. Perhaps even Sartre thought so in writing that ending. No impression could be more false, however, for Mathieu is no different, developmentally, than the day he acknowledged the truth in Marcelle's remark that, at thirty-four, he was "out of touch with the present" (*ne pas être dans le coup*). It is worth observing here that Sartre, at age thirty-four (i.e., 1939—the same year in which the action of *The Age of Reason* takes place) did not yet feel himself "in the thick of it" either.[31] There is, thus, perhaps more than enough justification in promoting the confusion between Mathieu and Jean-Paul.

Mathieu cannot yet have finished his youth because he still has not committed himself to anything. And as the narrator repeatedly explains, Mathieu's eternal "availability" (*disponibilité*) or "waiting" (*attente*) implies that he is still entrenched in a sort of latent state of being.

> . . . his sole concern had been to keep himself available. For an act. . . . he always felt as though he were somewhere else, that *he was not yet fully born*. (1981, 445–46; italics added)

So, by the end of *The Age of Reason*, none of that has changed at all. While an admiring Boris might contend that Mathieu *has always been* that perfect thirty-five, now that he actually *is* thirty-five, Mathieu feels his being is located elsewhere. Not yet altogether born, ontological and ethical Mathieu is an embryonic notion, a theoretical being. Boris's adulatory remark is not completely off-base though, since this thirty-five-year period of latency also, paradoxically, causes Mathieu to feel exaggeratedly old: "that's what existence means," Mathieu thinks to himself, "draining one's own self dry without feeling thirst. For thirty-four years I've been sipping at myself and I'm old" (443). Throughout *The Roads to Freedom* Mathieu rehashes the contradictory complaints of being either past his prime or embryonic.[32]

Sometimes, as if suffering from a dual personality, Mathieu pits one extreme of his borderline being against the other. Trying to force himself to do what he believes to be morally right with respect to Marcelle, for example, the "child" in him tries to make an "adult" decision: "He clenched his fists and, addressing himself with all the gravity of a big person, a bourgeois, a man of the world, a paterfamilias, said, 'I *want* to marry Marcelle.' " But abhorrence at this prospect prompts the "mature" Mathieu to immediately take over and dismiss the "childish" one: "Pah! These were mere words, a childish, empty choice . . ." (633–34).

Any claim that Mathieu ever reached an equilibrium known as the age of reason is false. He no more escapes the undecidability of existence, represented by his elusive age, than he commits himself by slaughtering Germans. The web of confusion over Mathieu's age is crucial to understanding how his weak superego prodded him (ineffectually) toward an endorsement of paternity.

> I sit and bathe in a wave of
> nostalgia for an age yet to come.
> —Pete Shelley[33]

The kernel of Sartre's ethical thought and its inseparability from paternity is at the crux of *The Age of Reason*'s apparent stasis. What does it mean for Mathieu to be the subject of, to be subjected to, "the age of reason"? What does it mean for him and others to insist that he has attained that age qualification and yet for that age to be in no way an accurate assessment of his existential (i.e., ontological and ethical) maturity? To put it simply, is Mathieu young or old? And more precisely, is he *too* young or *too* old?

From the evidence in the novel, it is as valid to respond that he is *both* too young and too old at the same time as it is to respond that he is *alternately* one and then the other. But such an indefinite answer does not advance us. Mathieu's age schizophrenia must spring from something more complex than a simple binary temporal discrepancy with self in the form of his actual age. We may focus with greater precision on this apparently incoherent being called *Mathieu* by taking an even closer look at the passage where he tries to coax himself into marrying Marcelle.

Mathieu's approach to the question of matrimony is composed, as we saw, of two movements, in each of which a dominant and a repressed (or subjugated) agent is at work. In the first movement, the voice of a child, equipped with the amplified vitality of a "big person," threatens to disrupt Mathieu's complacent waiting by attempting to compel him to an act abhorrent to the adult in him. In the second movement, the authoritarian voice of a "mature" man vetoes the infantile one, thereby reaffirming Mathieu's status quo of passive availability. This suggests that the vicissitudes inherent in determining Mathieu's age (or being) are not ascribable to the poles of a single binary system of exaggerated age attributes (i.e., "too old" or "too young"): they are, in fact, the products of two such binary systems which may be expressed in a simple diagram inspired by linear algebraic matrix theory. We first attribute to the epithets *old* and *young* both concrete and abstract connotations: *old man* and *child* (concrete); *feebleness* and *vitality* (abstract). These four elements can then be arranged in a two-by-two matrix that formally illustrates the system subtending Mathieu's age and whose contours constitute the saga novel itself. The concrete connotations will form the rationale for one diagonal of the matrix, while the abstract connotations govern the other.

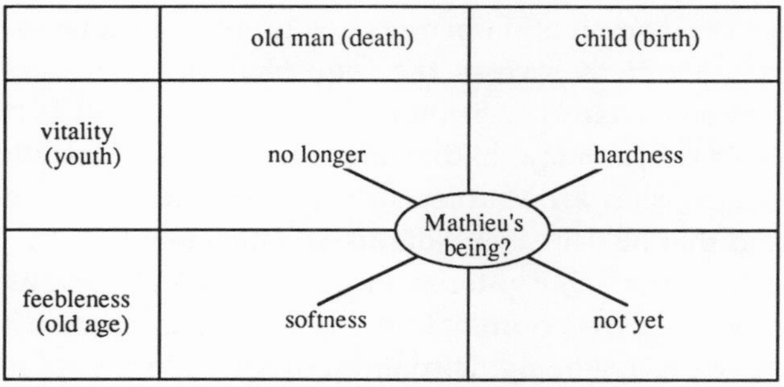

old man (death)
child (birth)
vitality (youth)
feebleness (old age)
no longer
hardness
Mathieu's being?
softness
not yet

Summary of Mathieu's *age-being*

In order to bring out this structure, to not permit the reader to ignore it, Sartre amplifies the products of Mathieu's phantasmic activity with the result that each of these four elements tend toward their most extreme manifestations. Thus, in most representations of himself as an old man, Mathieu will feel or appear to be near death, while the childlike qualities of his personality—the child in him—tends to retain the characteristics of an embryo.[34] Youthful vitality will be made all the more impressive by appearing as a potential whose energy has not even begun to be tapped. Feebleness may diminish into complete debility, stagnation, or impotence.

As in any two-by-two matrix, there are four products (domains), each with its particular *properties*. In addition, I call the relationships existing between these four products *functions*. By describing these properties, the different parts of Mathieu's heretofore shattered being can be organized into one coherent system. The functions that interconnect them enable us to circumscribe the mystery of the supposed "nothingness" at the crux of his being. Mathieu's endorsement of paternity (of which I assert the existence as a potentiality at the kernel of being) is the key to elucidating the central, albeit ambiguous, role that Sartre forecast for the bond of paternity in his ethical thought.

Using this matrix, the product of youthful vitality coupled with an "aging" professor is the public image that Mathieu energetically cultivated and tried to maintain in order to compensate for his lack of commitment. It is the easiest Mathieu for us to recognize. As we enter the story, however, those who observe him are beginning to notice that this combination betrays a vain, incongruous, and rather ridiculous attempt to reverse the inevitable aging process. To his contemporaries—Marcelle, Brunet, Jacques[35]—Mathieu is beginning to resemble a ridiculously childish old man. At first, Marcelle still has enough compassion for Mathieu to warn him that he is "no longer with it" and that his "life is full of missed chances." But the next day, when he visits the self-righteous Jacques for a loan, Mathieu walks into a no-holds-barred humiliation whose insults are anticipated in our matrix of his age-being. Disdainful of this "old irresponsible student" (509), Jacques tells his *younger* brother that he may think he "looks younger than he is" (508), however,

> "Look at yourself in the face: you are thirty-four years old, you are getting slightly bald . . . you're no longer a young buck; bohemian life doesn't suit you at all." (509)

Back at his apartment the same afternoon, Mathieu receives a visit from Brunet who, although even more estranged from him than Marcelle, remains nevertheless a compassionate friend. He would never humiliate Mathieu as Jacques perversely does. No such humiliation is needed, though, in order to reveal Mathieu's strategies of compensation for age(-being) failings: his admiration for the self-assured and committed Brunet betrays him. Suggesting that he, Brunet, and Daniel should see each other more often, Mathieu says: "it seems to me that we'd age less quickly if we could get together from time to time, just the three of us" (517). But this *we* is pure projection and he and Brunet both know it. Mathieu is the only one of the group of cronies who needs the occasional infusion of authentic existence that he is proposing because he is the only one desperately trying to maintain youth artificially by hanging onto whatever bit of that quality he might have possessed in the past. This is the domain of what is no longer in the matrix of his age-being, the domain of what a person may long for but which will never return.

The inverse of this relation, copresent in Mathieu's being, is the child overcome with weakness. Jacques, as we saw before, told Mathieu that he hadn't yet reached the age of reason. A depressing enough verdict to hear, but Mathieu takes it one step further by confessing honestly to himself, "I haven't yet been born" (446). Thus, when he recapitulates his conversation with Brunet by reasoning that "Brunet was right to say I'm an old child" (610), he is, in essence, admitting that he is a latency too weak, too wanting in energy to be born—a decrepit embryo. As "old child," Mathieu's *potential for being* never harnesses enough energy to trigger the long-awaited *inception of being*. He is condemned to the condition of that which is endlessly *not yet*.

From Metaphysics to Sexuality

The phrases "Mathieu, you are no longer . . ." and "Mathieu, you are not yet . . ." reverberate in the addressee's mind. Thematized into temporal commentaries, Mathieu internalizes these two fundamental criticisms that govern the parts of his shattered being. As polarized opposites pulling against each other in the economy of his age-being, both criticisms become character traits resisting stasis and hypostasis. Mathieu never considers himself altogether dead or irreversibly stillborn. Childish old Mathieu always hopes to have one more chance at commitment, refusing to believe that he is ethically washed up, while the weary child in him longs for some external impetus that would finally break the thirty-five-year wait and propel him from latency into real being.[36] Mathieu's allergy to any type of voluntarism inspires Marcelle's warning that he is sterilizing himself (402). He waits for intercession from the world around him to provide his "last chance." Mathieu rightly suspects that a coherent identity is situated somewhere *between* the four aberrations of his age-being. But this coherent, unified "Mathieu" appears to him as a hiatus or lack rather than as the linchpin that holds it together. Mathieu's pessimism about the possibility of attaining full humanity closely matches some of the nuances of the for-itself in its vain quest for ontological plenitude according to its tale told in *Being and Nothingness,* particularly in Sartre's several descriptions of man as *hole in being.* As some commentators have argued (and this applies to many of Sartre's well-known philosophical metaphors), describing one's being in such language means that a fear of feminization has encroached upon one's consciousness.[37] As Marcelle said, "your ideal: to be nothing" (403).[38] Unified being remains as compelling to Mathieu as it is incomprehensible. Split between incommensurable poles, he longs for coherence but shuns a unified being obtained at the cost of finding out something he would rather not know. Between the *no longer* and the *not yet,* Mathieu seems content to remain in an impossibly utopian mode of "nostalgia for an age yet to come."

While Mathieu's ideal may be "to be nothing," his *being* is not nothing. Yet the place where his being lies seems as daunting as the vast and mysteriously feminine "hole in being" haunting the pages of *Being and Nothingness.* I have implied that Mathieu's hesitation before responsibility and total being is, in fact, a fear of the feminine, abstracted and disguised as metaphysics, and that it conforms closely to Sartre's own descriptions of the "psychology" of the for-itself when confronted with the viscous. This, in turn, is similar to Freud's ruminations in *Civilization and Its Discontents* on the "oceanic feeling." Many feminists have analyzed this passage in the 1929 text, most of them taxing the author for what they interpret to be his resistance to approaching the "pre-Oedipal" child because that stage is supposedly much more closely linked to the mother and, therefore, to women in general.[39] Along with Freud's repeated claims of his own impenetrability to the "oceanic feeling," one can detect in his style a certain fascination tinged with apprehension for "these almost intangible quantities" (Freud 1973–74, 72) inseparable from the feminine. Something like the "oceanic feeling" also arrests Mathieu's compulsive self-knowledge as he comes face to face with the dark hole where his being lies.

The ontological no-man's-land where Mathieu's consciousness resists venturing is, in fact, the locus of his total being. Although metaphysical descriptions of this being are absent from *The Roads to Freedom,* it is traversed in our illustration of Mathieu's age-being by the functions of Mathieu's shattered ego components which, in their exaggerated differences, *do* comprise the narrative material for the novel. With that material, we are able to apprehend Mathieu's unified being. The *no longer/not yet* polarity, corresponding to Mathieu's "being-for-others," is a "Mathieu" of which he himself has acquired an uneasy comprehension. He did not repress this avatar of being even though it caused him to seem ridiculous or aberrant to his friends and to himself. He often thought about how he appeared to others and discussed it with them. He acknowledged his "being-for-others." Mathieu seemed comfortable enough with a split self as long as he felt it was only an abstract being. However, the properties of the *hardness/softness* polarity we will examine in the next chapter are physical and specifically sexual properties and these are areas of being that Mathieu would rather not explore.

Every shred of textual evidence we will use to illustrate the next chapter is recoverable either from Mathieu's subconscious or from the voice of the unnamed narrator—both of which, being his creations, correspond to Sartre's "legitimate" position in the text. Yet this legitimate authorial presence in the narration is occupied by a woman's voice: the voice of the mother. The further we approach Mathieu's being through a *fictitious* primary process created by Sartre, the closer we come to cross-examining Sartre himself about his ambiguous positions on paternity. Although Mathieu becomes engulfed by paternity, as he became overwhelmed by the "oceanic feeling" and the feminine—an engulfment that puts him face to face with responsibility in the inevitable confrontation that Sartre put into theoretical and allegorical terms in *Being and Nothingness*—he fails to "convert" to paternity and, therefore, fails to attain his goal of total being.

Notes

1. "The truth is that I've abandoned Marcelle *for nothing*" (1981, 727). Mathieu thinks that abandoning Marcelle (which he deludes himself into believing he has accomplished) guarantees his freedom.

2. Jean-Paul Sartre, *La Mort dans l'âme* (1949) in *Oeuvres romanesques* (Paris: Gallimard, 1981), 1135–57.

3. Although there is no bullfight in Sartre's novel, tauromachy, as illustrative of life's struggles and, in particular those of the artist, pervaded continental art and literature in the 1930s and 1940s (e.g., Michel Leiris, André Masson, Pablo Picasso, Ernest Hemingway).

4. The feeling of being mandated is one with which Sartre tells us he was familiar early in his own life. As a youth, the writer-to-be felt that, by divine right, he was meant to become the Victor Hugo of the twentieth century (1964a, 114 and 145).

5. The gesture alluded to in the title of Sartre's 1948 play signifies, of course, committed action.

6. Conversion is an integral part of Sartre's ethical thought.

7. This catclysmic scene is the concretization of one of Mathieu's sexual phantasms in which he connects the indelible memory of Marcelle's pregnancy to his anticipation of personal involvement in the war. "'Draftable': Mathieu got small and round; Marcelle was waiting for him with her legs spread. Marcelle was a bean toss game and when Mathieu was all curled up like a ball, Jacques threw him and he fell into a black hole streaked by missiles, he fell into war . . ." (898). Any actions of Mathieu at war are displacements of the action he refused to take with respect to Marcelle and the child she bears.

8. Perhaps in imitation of cinema, with which Sartre and Beauvoir were enamored in the 1930s, *Troubled Sleep* is divided into *tableaux* instead of chapters. See Simone de Beauvoir, *La Force de l'âge* (Paris: Gallimard, 1960), 58–59.

9. Sartre went to great lengths to find a way to bring Mathieu back to life. The project of finishing this saga novel seemed to retreat into a progressively deeper impasse as time went on. After *Troubled Sleep,* he abandoned the cycle altogether in 1949, in the midst of the incomplete "Last Chance" (published in Sartre 1981, 1585–54). It is, however, possible to suppose that, at an early stage, Sartre intended this scene to be that of Mathieu's "baptism" into committed existence. But his later difficulties in finishing perhaps derive from his conviction that commitment for Mathieu was ultimately incongruous.

10. Written in 1936, "Erostratus" is the third short story in *The Wall* (Jean-

Paul Sartre, "Erostrate" [1939] in *Oeuvres romanesques* [Paris: Gallimard, 1981], 262–78). Erostratus was an Ephesian who, in order to immortalize his name, set fire to the famous temple of Artemis in 356 B.C. He was burned to death and any mention of his name was prohibited under penalty of death.

11. "On a seventh story balcony is where I should have spent my whole life" (1981, 262); the first line of "Erostratus" reads: "One must observe humans from above" (262).

12. Sartre assumed the same "ultimate standpoint" to observe the phenomenon of "duality and the third party" in the *Critique of Dialectical Reason* (see chap. 2, n. 23).

13. Hazel Barnes calls *l'esprit de survol* "the overview or bird's-eye view," defining it, in accordance with Sartre in *The Family Idiot*, as an attitude of the imagination enabling Flaubert to "look down at the entire human species, scoff at its paltry goals and easy satisfactions, deride its unenlightened suffering, and feel that by detaching himself from all of it, he escaped his own denunciation. Meanwhile he was not above the desire to injure those who might otherwise be content." Hazel E. Barnes, *Sartre and Flaubert* (Chicago: University of Chicago Press, 1981), 50–51. Note that a form of "ultimate standpoint" is the overarching theme of Albert Camus' *La Chute* (Paris: Gallimard, 1956) as well.

14. From this position of lightness, Hilbert wants to seek and lend weight to his name by his act. He is impressed by the notion that, while the name of the architect in the legend (see n. 10) is forgotten, the name of the building's arsonist is not (1981, 269). "I only needed one hour in order to delight [*jouir*] [in my crime], to feel its *crushing weight*" (273; italics added).

15. "Being free is weird: it makes you dizzy" (1948, 16); a comrade warns him: "It's entirely probable that you will carry the responsibility for [Hoerderer's] death" (135); as he aims a pistol at Hoerderer, he shouts, "You delivered me" (226).

16. Note the care Freud takes to distance the experience of this feeling from himself by the use of scare-quotes. See Sigmund Freud, *Civilization and Its Discontents* (1930) in *The Standard Edition of the Complete Psychological Works of Sigmund Freud* (London: Hogarth Press, 1973–74) 21:57–146. He almost overemphasizes his having borrowed the adjective from his perhaps more sensitive correspondent, Romain Rolland.

17. "Daniel said negligently, 'I'm marrying her. We're keeping the child.' Mathieu took a cigarette and lit it. His skull was vibrating like a bell" (1981, 719).

18. Marcelle is already psychologically estranged from Mathieu and, thus, her analysis is somewhat half-hearted. She is, after all, not his father. Nevertheless, there are indications of the value Mathieu places on her as an "authority figure." For example, this exchange: "'If I lied to myself, I'd have the impression I was lying to you at the same time. That would be unbearable to me.' 'Yes,' said Marcelle, but she didn't look very convinced. 'You don't

look very convinced.' 'Yes I am,' she said indolently [*mollement*]" (1981, 402) One effect of her lackluster responses to him is the weakness of his superego.

19. Hoerderer reproaches Hugo in similar terms: "How you cling to your purity, pal! How scared you are to dirty your hands. . . . Doing nothing, staying immobile, keeping your elbows close to your body, wearing gloves. My hands are dirty . . . up to the elbows" (1948, 193).

20. See chap. 2, n. 14.

21. A few of which are "stroke (of luck)" [*coup de chance*], "(to receive a) blow" (either physical or moral) [*recevoir un coup*], *être ou ne pas être dans le coup,* right down to derogatory usages like "thrust of the dick" [*coup de queue*], the expression that Mathieu employs to depreciate the physiological phenomenon that started the whole story off.

22. Cf. another passage comparing the terms *accident* and *chance* in Sartre 1943, 613 and 615.

23. Sartre sees Genet and Flaubert as having made themselves into monuments; see chap. 10.

24. "Accident" is what Mathieu calls it, too (1981, 503). He is terrified by the randomness at the origin of conception.

25. Vincent Descombes criticizes Sartre for dwelling far too much on *nothingness* and attributing very little *positive being* to man in his brilliantly clear, well-argued, and highly useful *Le même et l'autre* (Paris: Minuit, 1979), 64–70.

26. In a pitiful attempt to convince his friend, Brunet, a "man of action" whom he admires, that he hasn't missed any opportunities, he toys with the idea that opportunities don't exist at all. When Brunet concedes dryly, "If you're saving yourself for a better opportunity, that's your right," Mathieu replies, "I thought to myself . . . that it would never come about or would happen too late or that maybe *there aren't any* opportunities" (1981, 526). Disgusted, Brunet gets up and leaves.

27. Note the new inflection given to the ferryman image: this almost exactly repeats the image I discussed in chap. 2, which Sartre used in his condemnation of paternity in *The Words.*

28. Denis Diderot, *Est-il bon? Est-il méchant?* (1781) in *Oeuvres* (Paris: Gallimard, 1951), 1297–1372. See, inter alia, the chapter entitled "Le couple éternel du criminel et de la sainte" in Sartre 1952, 76–133.

29. Hoerderer (*Dirty Hands*) has experienced the same development: "Youth, I don't know what it is: I went directly from childhood to maturity [*l'âge d'homme*]" (1948, 132). Boris gives Mathieu's age as thirty-five, while Marcelle gave thirty-four. For more information on these and other textual discrepancies concerning Mathieu's age, see Sartre 1981, 1943 n. 1. Denis Hollier pursues an enlightening discussion on chronological discrepancies in *Nausea* in his *Politics of Prose: Essay on Sartre,* trans. Jeffrey Mehlmann (Minneapolis: University of Minnesota Press, 1986), 75–83.

30. The disorder of Mathieu's life contrasts with the rather reactionary order of his brother's. "Jacques was very proud of his youth; it was his moral

guarantee, it allowed him to defend the cause of order with a good conscience" (1981, 508).

31. Cf. Simone de Beauvoir, *La Force de l'âge* (Paris: Gallimard, 1960) and Annie Cohen-Solal, *Sartre: 1905–1980* (Paris: Gallimard, 1985). The subtitle to Hollier's book in French, "Sartre et l'an quarante," suggests, among other things, that Sartre's experience as prisoner of war in 1940 finally changed all that, plunging the "aging" philosopher into the reality of the human collective.

32. Other references: "too old" (395, 404, 442); "embryonic" (444, 446, 798).

33. Pete Shelley, "Nostalgia," *Love Bites* (The Buzzcocks), IRS Records, 1978.

34. Like the real child he has sired, the child within Mathieu (his childishness) is not just metaphorical but literal: he carries (*pherein*) the offspring with him and it carries him in that it controls part of his consciousness. Thus we see the Christopher-Christ configuration described in chap. 1 being applied.

35. Mathieu has two other contemporaries: Lola and Sarah. Sarah is one of several secondary Sartrean characters favorable to maternity; she is described as someone for whom "life is sacred" (1981, 433). See chap. 6 and the discussion of another Sarah, Bariona's wife.

Mon vieux, a colloquial term of endearment, loses some of its banality in light of our discussion of the ridiculously childish old Mathieu. Marcelle frequently calls Mathieu "mon (pauvre) vieux," showing her compassion for him while revealing to him the weakness of his public self. Brunet's fraternal "vieux social-traître" (517) has the same effect (i.e., "vieux" = what Mathieu *is;* "social-traître" = what he perhaps once hoped he *was*); Brunet also calls him "mon pauvre vieux" (517).

36. The word *wait* (*attente*) is one of the most frequently repeated nouns in the novel.

37. Toril Moi, "Existentialism and Feminism," *Oxford Literary Review* 8, nos. 1–2 (1986): 88–95.

38. Benny Lévy, who as Sartre's last secretary was close to him at a time when he was again rethinking his ethics, puns in speaking of Sartre's writings that *n'être rien* ("to be nothing") always implies a *naître rien* ("to be born nothing"). This is perhaps one way of interpreting how the collapse of the abortion-infanticide distinction became transformed into an ontological crisis for Mathieu.

39. For a résumé and bibliographic information on these feminist discussions of Freud, see Jonathan Culler, *On Deconstruction* (Ithaca, N.Y.: Cornell University Press, 1982), 167–75; for a discussion of feminists and *Civilization and its Discontents* specifically, see Alice Yaeger-Kaplan, *Reproductions of Banality* (Minneapolis: University of Minnesota Press, 1986), 12ff.

CHAPTER 5

The Voice of the (M)other

> Vous découvrez que c'est là, en
> elle, que se fomente la maladie de
> la mort, que c'est cette forme
> devant vous déployée qui décrète la
> maladie de la mort.
>
> —Marguerite Duras[1]

By the end of the ontological meanderings in *Being and Nothingness* (1943), Sartre has navigated us beyond the descriptions of the for-itself's bodily life in everyday experience: he has readied us for our long-awaited landing in the harbor of ethics. Yet Sartre is never far from carnal desire and puzzlement at how our body plugs into the world. The treatise's last chapter, entitled "On Quality as a Revelation of Being" (1943, 661–78), proves to be an increasingly lurid account of the means by which an unmistakably feminine *slime* may afford the (masculine) for-itself the euphoric experience of total being. In a last stab at describing an ideal embodiment of ontological totality, Sartre's famous surrogate in this odyssey of the for-itself, Pierre, corporeally enters a netherworld in which he knows full well that *le visqueux* ("slime," or "the viscous") will emperil his monolithic existentialist freedom. Yet, risking his life, Pierre cuts deeply into this voracious "quality of being," the final metaphor for the Other in *Being and Nothingness,* and reemerges unscathed by coital contact with the dark side of being. But rather than recapture his stolen being by figuratively killing or ingesting the Other in the manner that the Sartrean for-itself usually proceeds, Pierre leaves "the viscous" as an ever-thriving threat.

Collected letters and autobiographies being intimate writings addressed to third parties are intended to convey their message in confessional, rather familiar language. Yet because the addressor is before all else conscious of the future "presence" of his addressee, various forms of distortion and censorship invariably intercede. Sartre's *Lettres au Castor* and *The Words,* although fascinatingly frank, limit their revelations about their author's innermost desires and fears by virtue of the properties of discourse I have just mentioned. For this reason, I think that Serge Doubrovsky was right when he stated that the weirdest aspect of Sartre's philosophical writings is that they contain more information about Sartrean eroticism than either his or Beauvoir's fiction, or even their intimate writings.[2]

The third part of *Being and Nothingness,* which is about "being-for-others," teaches me that to know myself objectively, I must first pass through the other. An extension of Husserl's theory of intentionality in consciousness, Sartre's strange notion that the for-itself penetrates, then escapes, the other is crucial to his ethical thought. In ethical terms, this sort of initiation rite implies a submission (bolstered by the preservation of autonomous existence) to the will of the Other. Referring to sexuality in Sartre's ontology, Alphonso Lingus writes: "I must make contact with alien subjectivity in order to reach my own being, but contact can only be the capture and negation of my freedom."[3] In "On Quality," Sartre claims that an operation he terms "the psychoanalysis of *things*" (note that this is not a psychoanalysis of human subjects) can reveal to us the modalities of our quest for ontological totality. To illustrate his hypothesis, he takes an example, chosing one quality and one quality only—the viscous. He then proceeds to recount, in meticulous detail, that he got the whole idea of talking about slime from reading Gaston Bachelard's *Water and Dreams.*[4] This explanation is, however, no more than a process of denying his own fascination with this type of substance—a denial whose purpose is to have us believe that *le visqueux* is really only a "quality" (one of many) and not the metaphor he favors for *Woman.*

What is intriguing in this bizarre little chapter that brings *Being and Nothingness* to a close is how Sartre has his surrogate, Pierre, decide to perform that "synthetic fusion of the for-itself and the in-itself" (1943, 691) to which he says we all aspire when he is in the intimate company of a feminine substance. What does Sartre mean by emphasizing the for-itself's survival following passage through such an obviously feminine medium as *le visqueux*? To what should we attribute this strange virtual connection between eroticism and ontology (a connection everywhere present and nowhere explained)? To address these issues, we should again examine Mathieu's ontological crisis as presented in *The Age of Reason;* that crisis is enmeshed with the biological and psychological crisis stemming from Mathieu's problems with sexuality. By conducting a close thematic reading of the novel and comparing it to Sartre's ontology, I hope to shed some light on the relations between sexuality, reproduction, and ethics in Sartre's thought.

> Cette cote n'était-elle pas plutôt
> un *côté* d'Adam?
> —Emmanuel Levinas[5]

Mathieu lives in a mode of "nostalgia for an age yet to come." He cultivates an illusory hope that committed existence awaits him in a brighter future that that demiurge, the narrator, tells him has already passed him by. Being passive and uncommitted, his present is the part of his existence about which he seems least concerned. Now, however, that present is engulfed by the less than pleasant biological reality of a regrettable night from the past when the rosy future that he caressed like a fetish was indelibly altered by careless ejaculation.

> [H]is consciousness was annihilated . . . his present . . . was the stale future [*vieil avenir*] of those days gone by. *He* was the one they had been waiting for for twenty years. *He* was that worn out man [*homme fatigué*] that a hardened child [*enfant dur*] had ordered to bring his hopes to fruition. Whether those childish oaths were to remain childish forever or become the first indications of a destiny depended solely on him. (1981, 623)

The narrator's voice offers several such remembrances that surge up from Mathieu's subconscious and in which two figures interact: the tough child that he used to be and the rapidly aging, weary man that he feels he has become.[6] Sartre equates youthful vitality with images of physical hardness, while a mental and physical softening, characteristic of a feeble old man (or, worse yet, a woman) signals ontological debility. Mathieu's being seems to be located, despite his resistance to the idea, somewhere within the antithetical imagery of softness and hardness—more precisely, between what Sartre considers the essential characteristics of the feminine and the masculine.

Mathieu wakes up unrested, his eyes in a sorry state. This ocular discomfort psychosomatically triggers a recollection of more youthful days.

> Mathieu had opened his eyes. They felt soft and doughy in their sockets. . . . Mornings had been different in the old days: real beginnings. The alarm clock would go off and Mathieu would jump out of bed, *his eyes hard,*[7] feeling refreshed as if roused by the sound of a bugle. (1981, 798)

The mammalian placenta and the eye of higher animals: both are tissue sacks whose firmness endures as long as their walls remain unviolated. Once that barrier is breached and their volume of fluid escapes, only a flaccid membrane remains. Mathieu draws a correlation between the anticipated rupture of Marcelle's placenta with hallucinations about putting an eye out with a sharp instrument. Vision, a sense that is relegated to a secondary role in many of Sartre's writings, assumes the same privileged place in Mathieu's primary process that it does in the theories on "the gaze" (*le regard*) in Sartre's ontology.[8]

Not unexpectedly, a politically committed character like Brunet possesses the youthful hardness that Mathieu can only envy in others at an ever-widening distance. The firmness and vigor, radiating from Brunet's very fiber, strike awe in Mathieu: "[he] was enormous and solid" (432); "he could no more be budged than a boulder" (435); "[Mathieu] felt the clench of Brunet's hand on his shoulder" (436); "Brunet climbed the stairs with surprising suppleness" (437); he is "indifferent and solid, weighty and massive" (517). This sturdiness contrasts Mathieu's half-baked flabbiness. While Brunet looks him over "with an air of hardness," Mathieu sits passively like "a big naked guy made of bread dough" (436). In the presence of Brunet's massive and solid grandeur, even Mathieu's posture betrays pathetic limpness: "Mathieu stood before Brunet not knowing what to do with himself [*les bras ballants*]" (517). Brunet is obviously valorized for his political commitment and descriptively rewarded by images of phallic toughness. Yet, in a later volume of Sartre's saga novel, the more ambiguous and cynical activist, Schneider-Vicarios, takes center-stage. This suggests, as in many other instances, Sartre's subversion of his own convictions—both political and sexual.

Sartre is fond of translating the dialectic of hardness and softness that governs Mathieu's subconscious into images from the bakery oven, an example that we have already seen in the "doughiness" of Mathieu's eyes. In another phantasmic memory of his past as a tough little boy, Mathieu recalls having been "a little headstrong uprising [*surgissement*] who had burst through the earth's crust" (444). If we juxtapose the image of this larval being who mustered the energy to crack through the outer shell of a maternal terrestrial globe with the description of Mathieu's doughy eyes, we find another version of his confusion of abortion and blinding. The physically powerful and willful infant is in diametrical opposition to the inert hunk of existential dough Mathieu has become.[9]

What Goes Up Must Come Down

Rationalizing a life-style that Marcelle is increasingly intent on criticizing, Mathieu thinks to himself: "the freedom I'm telling her about is a healthy man's freedom" (404). Similarly, the narrator attempts to valorize vitality by referring to it as an intrinsically masculine quality, emphasizing the flabbiness (*mollesse*) of Marcelle's physique as well as the lifelessness (*mollesse*) of her verbal responses. It is as if the narrator, in order to preserve a patriarchal image of virility, has forgotten that it is the dullness and emptiness of Mathieu's existence that constitute the main leitmotiv in the story. If there is anything lacking in consistency, it is Mathieu's purportedly unassailable freedom. On the other hand, by taking responsibility for her child, by exercising sociological choice to a degree that Mathieu can only passively envy, Marcelle ends up much less soft than Mathieu wished to convince himself she was. In attempting to valorize masculinity, the stream, as it were, of Mathieu's consciousness becomes indistinguishable from an otherwise aloof (thus traditional) narrative voice.[10]

At the deepest level of the novel's narrative (i.e., where Mathieu's voice seems indistinguishable from Sartre's autodiegesis), erection and limpness—the polarized physical states of the male organ—govern the elemental valence of Mathieu's imagination. Mathieu's observations of positive male characters are expressed, with no irony intended, in unabashedly phallic terminology. This terminology resembles Sartre's perception of freedom, commitment, and their quintessential manifestation, writing, all three of which relate in one way or another to an unavowed admiration for the penile erection.[11] Whether idealizing the tough child he was or observing Brunet, Mathieu admires the quality of hardness and denigrates the quality of softness. His present existential langour only reminds him of the flaccidness which is, to his dismay, the usual state of the penis—the state his was in following the ejaculation that impregnated Marcelle.

Underlying this obsession with genital dialectic is a fear of the feminine. But, taking us well beyond physical or even psychological considerations, Mathieu's dread cannot be considered the classic Freudian fear of castration. His realization that his very being is as flaccid as a drooping male organ nauseates him. The possibility that femininity inhabits his being is so horrific that he represses the thought. This ontological femininity is only discernible in the ambivalent narrative voice between Sartre and Mathieu. Mathieu's attempts to disguise his femininity to himself are apparent in the transference that governs his allusions to Marcelle's physical and moral *mollesse.* By accentuating her supposedly feminine qualities, he attempts to deny the possibility of his own less than determinate ontological status. This attempt is a failure.

While Marcelle ends up one of the most phallic characters in the whole work, she does so only in contrast with Mathieu.[12] In fact, she possesses, as we shall see, less a masculine than a *hybrid* being. Dwelling on Marcelle's hard features and "masculine" gestures, Mathieu/the narrator/Sartre makes a virago out of her in order to mask sexual ambivalence. When she shares a photo of herself at eighteen with Mathieu, he thinks: "a skinny girl with a boyish haircut who looked hard as she laughed" (1981, 396).[13] Whenever she stopped smiling, there was either a "hard crease . . . at the corner of her mouth" (403),[14] or her face would take on "a reasonable and masculine expression" (398). As an older woman, she is often "tough" and "aggressive" (403), but her "masculine gestures" (395) seemed never more virile to Mathieu than in their first encounter (397).

If one were to try to locate the most "feminine" element of this scene it would be Mathieu's penis, "that guilty flower," as he himself thinks of it, "resting cosily [*douillettement*] between his thighs" (406).[15] Thus, read with the hard/soft or masculine/feminine polarity in mind, the novel introduces Marcelle as the woman with masculine traits, juxtaposed with Mathieu, the embodiment of manhood turned feminine. And it is the revelation of Marcelle's pregnancy that unmasks the true state of Mathieu's existence as emblematized by a "feminized" phallus.

Undecidablility, Androgyny: Toward Total Being

To see the *The Age of Reason* as a demonstration of simple reversals in culturally assigned gendered attributes would be seriously superficial and, in the end, erroneous. Mathieu is no more entirely feminized than Marcelle is totally masculine. The novel's vicissitudes in gender specificity are indicative, however, of Sartre's own curiosity and even aspirations for ontological androgyny or, perhaps, even sexual "betweenness."[16] These aspects are evident in a remarkable scene where an absolute confusion of traditional sexual roles occurs.

The night before Mathieu and Marcelle's final encounter, Mathieu had, on a dare by Ivich, stabbed the palm of his hand with a knife (610).[17] Sartre has taken the habitually masculine Marcelle and, in this instance, put heavy make-up and her best dressing gown on her. She is unusually "motherly" in response to Mathieu's wound.

> Mathieu's hand rested inert between her two burning hands. The wound was repulsive with its black, juicy scab. Marcelle slowly raised this hand to her face. She stared at

> it fixedly and then, all of a sudden, in a burst of humility, pressed her lips to the gash. "What's with her?" [Mathieu] wondered. He drew her up against him and kissed her on the ear. (698)

This passage contains far too many lurid details for it to simply be the product of fanciful writing. Like the panting that accompanies erotic excitation, the sentences become shorter or simpler in syntax. Sartre carefully orchestrated the event in the three movements of (1) Marcelle's kiss, (2) Mathieu's suppressed reaction to it, and (3) Mathieu's kiss in return. In the first long sentence, evenly measured by regular punctuation, Marcelle's series of actions takes place "slowly" (*lentement*) at first, then "all of a sudden" (*tout à coup*) comes her kiss. Apparently dumbfounded, Mathieu's subconscious intervenes in the text with an abrupt question. Then his two-part response falls into place, "drawing up" (*attirer*) and "kissing" (*embrasser*) Marcelle, restoring equilibrium to this piece of murky prose through virile mastery.

The play of genital imagery underlying the physical attributes Sartre actually names in the passage is even more interesting. Thus we may, without undue exaggeration, consider Mathieu's gashed hand as a violently "feminized" male organ resting in uneasy passivity between the nurturing hands of a "masculine" woman. His wounded prehensile member has assumed a position analogous to that of his "guilty" lanceolate one as it rested cozily between his thighs in the opening scene. Substituted for his penis, Mathieu's hand becomes a doubly feminized organ: not only is it "inert," but the "black, juicy scab" covering its self-inflicted and "repulsive [stab] wound" (*plaie répugnante*) attests to Mathieu's repugnance at female anatomy, which nothing in the narrative voice contests. At the scene's paroxysmal moment, Marcelle kisses this androgynous organ (a limp phallus whose wound's equip it for the occasion with vulval labia) with what amounts to her own androgynous organ: the mothering lips (*elle appuya ses lèvres*) of a virago's face.[18] Mathieu, in utter confusion, musters an equally ambiguous gesture: pulling her toward him with an energy uncharacteristic of him, he returns the kiss on yet another less than conventional bodily orifice—the ear.

The Erosion of Masculinity

Mathieu's being is located between the polar opposites of a hard child and a soft old man, between a turgid and a flaccid masculinity, and ultimately between the masculine and the feminine. Mathieu does not wish to face this truth and Sartre seems not to wish it to be explicit in his novel. Indeed, Sartre's inability to finish *The Roads to Freedom* saga can be traced to this ontological undecidability.

In a chapter from her book *This Sex Which Is Not One,* entitled "The 'Mechanics' of Fluids," Luce Irigaray poses the question of how the power of scientific ideology can be maintained after the discovery of the role of fluids in the formation and destruction of solids.[19] This question is directly related to the biological fact that the male erection requires the marshalling of fluids to a restricted region of tissue. The organ returns to limpness when, for whatever psychological or physical cause, those fluids ebb and disperse. Now, in the collective psychology of Western consciousness, liquids are eminently feminine substances, as Freud's remarks about the "oceanic feeling" in *Civilization and Its Discontents* attest. Irigaray bases her challenge to the tenets of dominant culture on the hypothesis that, because the "mechanics of fluids" is responsible for both maintaining and subverting the penile erection, the same mechanics that have contingently maintained phallocentric ideology also have the potential for subverting it. Conversely, that ideology was founded to downplay the "mechanics of fluids" and to preserve patriarchy. Because the application of fluid is, in the case of male erection, to "a form with consistency" (Irigaray 1977, 108), the subversive use of fluids remains within the dominion, and therefore control of, the ideology one wishes to surpass. The true feminine—"that which exceeds form, like the female genitalia [or the female sex: *le sexe féminin*]—[is] necessarily relegated to a position below or above the established system" (109).

Within the boundaries of Irigaray's analysis, another "excess" beyond "form" is seminal fluid. In fact, Irigaray herself takes note of this substance that, because it is a "substance of excess," must be, by her own definition, a feminine one. But because semen also dwells in the male body, Irigaray speculates that it may hold the secret of a *masculinity beyond phallocentrism.*[20] Is it not, after all, the ejaculation of semen that initiates the gradual resoftening process of the male organ? According to Irigaray, the voice of "excess" is woman. But her language, which she calls *fluid-speak* (*ça parle "fluide"*), cannot be understood within the form of phallocentric culture. This is to say that neither the proponents nor the victims of Western ideology can understand it. In Irigaray's rather convoluted, Lacan-influenced language:

> Nevertheless, woman, it speaks [*la femme, ça parle*]. But not "same," not "identical to self." . . . It speaks "fluid." . . . *And learning how to listen otherwise than conventionally* [*en bonne(s) forme(s)*] *is necessary for understanding* [*entendre*] *what it says.* It's continuous, compressible, dilatable, viscous, conductible, diffusable. . . . (109; italics in original)

Imagining Marcelle in this capacity is easy: she is both the "slimy" (*visqueux*) repository of Mathieu's seminal fluid (his own slimy "excess": that which is beyond his "form") and the verbal "conduit," the internalized addressor, or disseminator, who confronts Mathieu with an explanation of what he really is. But readers familiar with Sartre's generalized abhorrence of slimy substances will find it equally easy to foresee how hopelessly refractory Mathieu will remain to such "fluid-speak."

"Only once in seven years," laments Mathieu, aghast at his sexual oafishness (1981, 409). For seven years, Mathieu had presumably avoided impregnating Marcelle by practicing coitus interruptus. Until that mishap, Mathieu's genital contact with Marcelle always took place with a full erection. Ejaculating inside Marcelle's body has triggered not only the immediate crisis of potential fatherhood but also the ontological crisis that Mathieu never resolved. The accidental semen spillage subverts Mathieu's belief in phallic ideals and erodes his self-image. From the moment Mathieu "forgot himself inside [Marcelle] like a child wets its bed,"[21] it had seemed to him that he had been cheated out of his masculinity: "he had been had. 'A kid! Here I thought I was giving her pleasure; instead I got her pregnant [*je lui ai fait un gosse*]" (411).

Staying hard was also tantamount to providing Marcelle with erotic gratification. Maintaining the illusion of a pure masculinity involved unfailing skill at coitus interruptus, which precludes direct contact between a postejaculation, softening penis and the viscous entrance of the womb. The revelation of her pregnancy bothers him less than the thought that his intervaginal ejaculation and his consequently "feminized" penis might be emblematic of an even less honorable failure to satisfy Marcelle "like a man." Timely withdrawal safeguards phallic pride. But at present, Mathieu can only think of his penis as "a satisfied and peremptory nudity" (407). Contraceptive failure, on the other hand, implies a feminization that collapses the edifice of Mathieu's phallic world, the organ becoming a "guilty flower" (406). Impregnation brings on the flood tides of his fundamental crisis of being. The expression "making a child" or "getting someone pregnant" (*faire un enfant*), which in the French of the 1930s and 1940s was employed euphemistically to signify sexual intercourse, has returned to its literal meaning for Mathieu: the distinction between the libidinal and the procreative functions of coition has been irretrievably blurred.

rien (980, *ren non* "nulle chose"; 1050, n.f., "chose" encore au xvi s.) II. N.m. (1406) . . . 2. Cour. Un rien: peu de chose, chose futile . . . Fam. Comme un rien: très facilement . . . 3. Un rien de . . . : un petit peu de . . . (Cf. Une goutte, une miette)

—*Le Petit Robert*

If it be asked what this *nothing* is that founds freedom, we shall answer that it cannot be described since it *is not*.

—*Being and Nothingness*

This *nothing* will weigh upon your soul like a mountain.

—*The Flies*

Rien, meaning *nothing,* is like several other negative adverbs in French in that it originally designated a thing (albeit a thing of nearly negligible size): a tiny something that, for all its minuteness, was somehow extremely precious to the person uttering the word. "Freedom," Sartre writes, "is not *a* being, it is *the* being of man . . . his nothingness of being" (1943, 495). The most important Sartrean concept, freedom, or the being of man, is founded on a *nothing*. But *a* nothing is not nothing. It is an infinitesimal something: a precious crumb (*miette*) of bread, a drop (*goutte*) teeming with spermatozoa, a microscopic ovum. Yet Sartre ultimately found freedom impossible to describe "since it *is not.*" Mathieu "forgot himself," allowing what Irigaray would call that infinitesimal amount of fluid excess of himself to get lodged where he could no longer dispose of it properly, that is, dispose of it as he wished. In doing so, he fathomed nothing (*ne rien comprendre, n'y entendre goutte*), Mathieu was totally in the dark (*n'y voir goutte*).

Marcelle's observation of Mathieu's obsession with what is proper and clean cannot be stressed enough in light of what Irigaray writes about "fluid-speak," the language of women that resists comprehension. Despite her minor role in *The Age of Reason,* Marcelle speaks fluid.

> Woman never speaks identity [*ne parle jamais pareil*]. . . . And she isn't listened to unless one wants to risk losing one's sense of propriety [or, of cleanliness: *le sens (du) propre*]. That's where the resistances to this voice overflowing the "subject" come from. (Irigaray 1977, 110–11)

Mathieu believed, just as he did in his sexual practices, that freedom required keeping everything clean and proper, keeping things out of the shadows, by a continual process of "self-sterilization." But he does not hear this truth about himself until Marcelle's assessment, given in her elusive "fluid-speak":

> "you're sterilizing yourself . . . everything is clean and proper with you: everything smells of clean laundry. . . . The only thing is, it lacks dark spots. There's nothing superfluous [*rien d'inutile*], nothing fuzzy [*rien d'hésitant*] or fishy [*rien de louche*] left in it." (1981, 402)

Marcelle thus gave voice to Mathieu's silent terror of everything dirty, dank, or dark. She is calling for and extolling excess, warning him that the very thing his being lacks is a "bit of superfluity" or "uselessness" (*rien d'inutile*), this "bit of fishiness" (*rien de louche*) a paradigmatic representative of which her body is presently gestating.

Upon learning that something "dirty" had taken place and unable to deny biological reality,[22] Mathieu proceeded to repudiate the fluid nothing of himself that had become united with the "filthy" and dark reaches of Marcelle's womb,[23] thereby rejecting the very total being he lacked and had been seeking all along.

"Woman cannot hear herself/be heard/be understood/get along [*s'entendre*]," writes Irigaray (1977, 110). If we bracket the parenthesized *du* in *le sens (du) propre* cited earlier, then listening to woman's voice also requires losing the literal meaning of words. Her "fluid-speak" is unfathomable to those who remain within the false security of dominant ideology. In Mathieu's case, "this voice that exceeds/overflows the subject" would have restored the "literal meaning" (*sens propre*) of his semen (the fluid nothing that overflowed from the subject), while destroying the literal meaning of his phallic ideological beliefs. While Mathieu never loses his "sense of cleanliness," it would seem that Sartre has had him fulfill what Irigaray would later consider a basic requirement for listening to woman: all of the "neat" distinctions that enabled him to bolster his phallocentric notion of freedom collapsed once he found out Marcelle was pregnant. The meanings that follow the letter or the law of the originals,[24] the "literal meanings" of his most trusted concepts, became hopelessly confused with their metaphorical manifestations. And, because Sartre's philosophy is always put in figurative language, the literal became indecipherable from the metaphysical.

Mathieu's most complex subconscious metaphor for the placenta is not "bubble [*bulle, enflure*]" (another sac and a common enough term for pregnancy in colloquial French), but rather a "little vitreous tide" (*une petite marée vitreuse,* 410). The polyvalence of the semantic choice of *marée* is in its combining the idea of *flux* (the means by which his sperm was conveyed to Marcelle's ovum) with a reminder of the eye in the windowlike quality of fluid connoted by the word *vitreous*.[25] The fluxional movement of a tide also equates the seminal fluid that had to enter the womb with its "translation" into the amniotic fluid making up the baby's support system.

News of the pregnancy makes Mathieu want to vomit (406)—a fluid function usually noted in pregnant women, not in their inseminators. Thinking of the fetus as a photographic image of himself developing in the by-product of his semen, Mathieu shrugs "the rest is just work carried out in a darkened room in a bit of gelatin" (411). He likens the embryo to an eye, that anatomical camera obscura, the only organ filled with vitreous humor, a gelatinous substance. Marcelle's "fluid-speak" is ever-present in Mathieu's subconscious. His imagery approaches absolute repulsion at the feminine when he describes the embryo as a "blister" (*cloque*): he is undoubtedly unable to forget about the repulsive "cloaca" (*cloaque*) where the whole "dubious" (*louche*) process is taking place. Both *cloque* and *cloaque,* with only a letter difference between them, occur prominently and several times in the text. *Cloaca,* meaning sewer, came to our modern vernaculars from the Roman waste disposal system called the Cloaca Maxima. The term is used in biology in reference to birds, reptiles, amphibians, and some fish who are equipped with a common cavity for urinary, fecal, and generative functions. The larval being that Mathieu once was broke through the earth's crust in a manner analogous to the way these cloacal animals are born by hatching from shells. An analysis of this aspect of *The Age of Reason* could obviously be pursued in conjunction with the "cloacal theory" in Freudian psychoanalysis, designating the young child's putative belief that a woman possesses only one orifice serving both vaginal and anal functions.[26]

But again, it is not at all clear that Mathieu is yet born, ethically or even ontologically. Baffled and trying to ready himself for almost any change, Mathieu sums things up: "'My life'—a weird object without beginning or end and yet not infinite surrounded him" (600). Marcelle had described his life bereft of real freedom as "self-sterilization." In the passage from which the quoted line is taken, the narrator will name this yet intact and "weird object" as nothing more or less than a "shell" (*coquille*)—a flawless one with no irregularities, no "excesses" with respect to the "form." In desperation, Mathieu will consider marrying Marcelle—an action that would have marred that shell's perfection: "What to do? Shatter the shell? That's easy to say. Besides, what would be left? *A little gummy, viscous thing* [*une petite gomme visqueuse*]" (600). What would have been left of Mathieu after marrying Marcelle, after accepting fatherhood, after chucking his false freedom and manhood? The answer: a very suspiciously semenlike substance. The voice of his feminine superego reverberates in these passages, but weakly: the viscous is too "improper" for its meaning to penetrate and be heeded.

The "fishy" or "dubious" (*louche*) stickiness of viscous substances permeates the imagery of *The Roads to Freedom.* Loss of literal meanings (of senses, propriety, cleanliness) imputable to *the viscous* is not limited to Mathieu, but affects the saga novel's other characters indiscriminately. While Mathieu suffers from morning sickness, Marcelle vomits a liquid resembling sperm.[27] Daniel's subconscious, perhaps because it actually represents that of the author, is virtually indistinguishable from Mathieu's in its captivated disgust at the "feminine" and the sliminess it exudes.[28] Even something as banal as a narrative description of the weather conveys the same quality of vaguely feminine viscousness: "Summer: the air was tepid and thick [*touffu*]" (430).[29] Irigaray writes that "fluid . . . is unstable by nature" (1977, 110). Is it possible that Sartre, too, like Mathieu, and in a possible vindication of Irigaray's original theory, "lost his senses" over the viscous? To what extent is the viscous responsible for Sartre appearing to endorse, through the voice of Marcelle, something so contrary to Sartrean individuality as parenthood, when his logical maneuver would be to reject it? And what does slime have to do with man's "lack of being"?

Slime Time

The moment has come to give new direction to reading "On Quality as Revelation of Being," the last chapter of *Being and Nothingness.* Just as we can dismiss Sartre's imputation of the choice of slimy substances upon Bachelard as pure denial,[30] we must take his use of first person pronouns throughout the chapter at face value: "I, me, mine" *means Sartre.* Recall that his purpose is to demonstrate how man can get his own being to reveal itself to him through the "[existential] psychoanalysis of *things*" (1943, 661). In fact, what happens in these rather astounding few pages is that the viscous psychoanalyzes Sartre.[31]

If, for Irigaray, "a *viscous substance* is an aberrant liquid," what is it for Sartre? No less than the "great universal symbolic network by which we translate everything repugnant to us" (1943, 667). Even presymbolic children, those who have not yet mastered spoken language, already intuitively understand the viscous as something resembling a philosophical category, associating everything they consider "soft" or "base" to it (667). But while slimy substances, intrinsically linked to the feminine, are fundamentally offensive to Sartre, they exercise an irresistible attraction upon him: "the viscous teaches me its virtues as *leech sucking at me* [*ventouse qui m'aspire*]" (668; italics in original). This is precisely the image that Mathieu's imagination conjured up each time his observation of Sarah's little boy, Pablo, caused him to think about the pregnancy of which he was the author.[32] And Marcelle's thoughts about the *quality* of pregnancy leaves no doubt that, for Sartre, the viscous signifies the feminine as the medium and mediation of being through the production and nurturing of a child.

> That [*ça*] didn't disgust her at all. It was a bit of life, like the sticky hatchings [*éclosions gluantes*] of springtime. It wasn't any more repulsive than that bit of reddish, odoriferous glue with which flower buds are imbibed. (1981, 464)

In addition to the in-itself, the viscous is what Sartre's being doesn't possess: "the viscous allows itself to be apprehended as what I lack" (1943, 668). Marcelle told Mathieu essentially the same thing: "[your life] lacks dark spots. There's nothing superfluous, nothing fuzzy or fishy left in it" (1981, 402). Sartre even writes of slime in 1943 with the very vocabulary employed to disparage Marcelle: "the viscous reveals itself as essentially fishy [*louche*]" (1943, 669). Although the existence of slime is somewhat autonomous from the existence of Jean-Paul (or of Pierre), it is intimately linked to him, in an inferior ("soft" and "base") position reinforced semantically by the use of passive constructions built on *se laisser* ("to let oneself"). The author attempts to impose himself as the ontological founder of the viscous. This, in turn, becomes the possibility of creating Sartre's own ideal self, giving him a feeling of fatherly bond with the viscous. He describes his relationship to the miraculous substance as one might imagine him speaking as a father of his child. "The originary bond between the viscous and me is that I project to be the foundation of its being, inasmuch as it is myself ideally" (667). Remember, when he says *I*, he means it. The viscous is not just *an* other (a new *other* being), it is *another Sartre:* "it appears as a possible myself to be founded" (667).[33] Who says Sartre never became a true father—the viscous is his offspring. Contrary to what he infers in *The Words*, Sartre *was* nothingness in the beginning, or rather, there was *no thingness* to Sartre.[34] He only began to make out the contours of his own being through his bond with the viscous (*le lien originel de moi au visqueux*), which brings us full circle (with a twist) back to the "bond of paternity" condemned in *The Words*. This "thing" that Sartre claims he can render "human" is the outline, or the beginning of *his own being:* "the viscous is the draft [*ébauche*] of myself" (668).

"Each human reality . . . is a direct project to transform its own for-itself into an in-itself-for-itself" (677)—a synthetic or hybrid being trained and ready for totality. As for the success of this all-too-human endeavor, Sartre is ultimately pessimistic—"man is a useless passion" (678) is the famous phrase. Yet his zealous apology of the viscous in "On Quality" constitutes an unequivocal statement that, for him individually, the ontological synthesis of the human and the nonhuman *can* take place. It does so through the mediation of the viscous: "the viscous appears already as the draft of a fusion of the world with me" (668). *Ebauche* ("draft," "sketch," "outline") is indeed a critical term, for, in describing the substructure that disappears, it leads us to another fundamental ambiguity in Sartre's ethical thought. Eluding closure on the key notion of his philosophy, he declared that the "*nothing* [that] founds freedom . . . cannot be described." This is consistent with Mathieu, who, like Roquentin, Hugo, and the others, is baffled by "being free for no reason" (*être libre pour rien*) and cannot understand how to transform phony freedom into the real stuff. On the other hand, it seems to me that, in "On Quality," there is something like the "fluid-speak" embedded in Mathieu's subconscious. By revealing to us his own intimate bond with the viscous, Sartre has done nothing less than draft the outline of the "indescribable" nothing. It is as if the child were the "nothing" that completes ethical being.

Far from simply dismissing paternity, as he does in *The Words*, Sartre divulges, through *The Age of Reason*, a deep-seated conviction that paternity is paramount to the human's project of seeking plenitude of being. Taking this position involves, for the quintessential writer for his time, exploring not social relationships in the broad sense, but the "current model" of father-son relationships so that it may be improved to the point where paternity may be endorsed. Sartre balks, in this text, at engaging in overt advocacy of paternity. Through Mathieu, Sartre's overt message is still a rejection of paternity. Sketches of acceptable reproduction of humanity are nevertheless discernible, intertwined with his ambiguous politics toward women. In *Being and Nothingness* he put forward, in a sense, his endorsement of paternity by two indirect agencies: that of the allegorical ethical Atlas responsible for the whole world, and that of androgynous being that results from the bizarrely privileged example of "the viscous." In *The Roads to Freedom,* "the viscous" takes over the subconscious of the text. Yet Sartre's inability to complete the saga novel at a period of his career dominated by extreme uncertainty about the possibility of ethics would seem to confirm that the author himself was blind to how close his own protagonist was to the total being and "real" freedom he sought.

Sartre's endorsement of paternity can be found at fleetingly more self-conscious levels of discourse in *Bariona* (1940) and, incongruously, in his political writings of 1952–54.

Notes

A version of this chapter appeared as "The Sartrean Viscous: Swamp and Source," in *SubStance* 64 (Spring 1991).

1. "You discover that it's there, in her, that the sickness of death gets fomented. You discover that it's that form laid open before you that decrees the sickness of death." Marguerite Duras, *La Maladie de la mort* (Paris: Minuit, 1982), 38 (my translation).

2. Serge Doubrovsky, "Sartre: retouches à un autoportrait," in *Autobiographiques, de Corneille à Sartre* (Paris: Presses Universitaires de France, 1988), 123–67.

3. Alphonso Lingus, *Libido: The French Existentialist Theories* (Bloomington: Indiana University Press, 1985), 13.

4. Gaston Bachelard, *L'Eau et les rêves* (Paris: Corti, 1942).

5. "Wasn't that rib instead a *side* of Adam?" Emmanuel Levinas, *Difficile liberté* (Paris: Albin Michel, 1963), 56 (my translation). The entire sentence reads: "Cette côte n'était-elle pas plutôt un *côté* d'Adam, créé comme être unique à deux faces et que Dieu sépara pendant qu'Adam, encore androgyne, sommeillait?"

6. In this dialectic's first moment—that of a *prematurely* vigorous child—Mathieu conforms to Sartre's portrait of himself as a little boy ("Poulou" in

The Words) assigning the adult Jean-Paul Sartre, world reknowned writer, a mandate to conquer the world with his pen (1964a, 145ff.).

7. This strange expression, *hard eyes,* is *les yeux durs* in French and audibly close to the words for *hard-boiled eggs* (*les oeufs durs*). My point here is that Sartre's unconscious cannot dissociate conception (eggs) and vision (eyes). One page before Mathieu's phantasm about bursting the placenta (his eye—and having nothing to do with it), Mathieu is described as having "calm and soft eye sockets [*ses orbites, tranquilles et mous*]" (1981, 409).

8. It is through *the Other's* gaze that the subject first become aware of his existence according to *Being and Nothingness.* In *The Words,* Sartre first encounters his own physical ugliness when he notices his extreme case of strabismus (1964a, 90–95). See also Alain Buisine, *Laideurs de Sartre* (Lille: Presses Universitaires de Lille, 1986).

9. One cannot help but be reminded also of Sartre's affinity for the poetry of Francis Ponge. Sartre's 1944 article, "L'homme et les choses," made him one of the first well-known literary critics to deal with Ponge (1947c, 298–357). In one of Ponge's pieces, "Le Pain," the poet sees himself as nearly indistinguishable from the loaf of bread: he is a universal, total being—both crust and dough; Francis Ponge, *Le Parti pris des choses* (Paris: Gallimard, 1942), 46.

10. Many studies have been written on narrative forms in Sartre's novels; see, for example, the afterword in Fredric Jameson, *Sartre: The Origins of a Style* (New York: Columbia University Press, 1984). Sartre had an uncanny faculty for adopting devices from a number of modernist contemporaries more original than he. One of these devices, quite apparent in *The Age of Reason,* is Joycean stream of consciousness, the best example of which is found in *Ulysses.*

11. Sartre equates virility with being "pure and hard" [*pur et dur*]—buzzwords adopted by the French fascists. In the short story "The Wall," Pablo is obsessed with "dying cleanly" [*mourir proprement*] (1981, 228–29). Beauvoir writes that Sartre "did not give up the tension and neatness of his existence as a captive [in 1940] without regret" (Simone de Beauvoir, *La Force de l'âge* [Paris: Gallimard, 1960], 550). In *The Words,* wielding a pen is as phallic a gesture as are phallic objects such as the books that stand erect on Sartre's shelves (Sartre 1964a, 37, 39, 164ff.).

12. On this particular use and definition of the word *phallic,* see Jacques Lacan, "La signification du phallus" in *Ecrits II* (Paris: Seuil, 1966), 103–15.

13. Later, when she shows the same photograph to Daniel, the narrator relates that "she looked like a dyke with her ungracious [*veule*] mouth and her hard eyes [*yeux durs*]" (1981, 561). See n. 7.

14. Mathieu thinks of her "beautiful mouth" as "impartial and severe [*juste et sévère*]" (1981, 404), qualities conventionally attributed to law-giving fathers.

15. His "flower" (what object is more traditionally thought of as being

feminine?) bows its head in shame for what it is "guilty" of and lays "cosily between his thighs [*cuisses*]," another feminine noun. For "douillettement," *Le Petit Robert* gives: "D'une manière douillette = 1. Qui est doux, délicatement moelleux et chaud. *Ant.* dur, rude. 2. Exagérément sensible aux petites douleurs physiques. *Ant.* courageux, endurant, stoïque."

16. Jean Cau reports this outburst directed at Sartre from Roger Stéphane: "Ecoutez, vous trainez un regret terrible. Vous voudriez être à la fois noir, juif, femme, coco et pédé" (Jean Cau, *Croquis de mémoire* [Paris: Julliard, 1985], 256).

17. A gesture repeated more than once in Sartre's work. Roquentin cuts himself in the palm; Hugo would cut off his hand to be Hoerderer (Denis Hollier, "The Handbook of the Intellectual," *Raritan* 1, no.2 [1981]: 73–88).

18. Another passage provides a lurid description of Marcelle's lips and tongue (just in case her tongue intervened in *this* kiss): "il sentit sur ses lèvres le riche velours de cette bouche et puis cette nudité glabre, chaude et preste, sa langue. Il se dégagea doucement" (1981, 697).

19. Luce Irigaray, *Ce sexe qui n'en est pas un* (Paris: Minuit, 1977), 105–16. Although an English translation exists, the pages references here are from the French version and the translations are mine.

20. "In the same vein of questions, one could ask (oneself) [*on pourrait (se) demander*] why sperm is never placed in relation to 'a' " (Irigaray 1977, 111).

21. This "kid" (*gosse*) who is more like a prostatic old man should not be confused with the phallic one. With Mathieu supposing what words must be going through Marcelle's mind, the original French is: "Le salaud, il m'a fait ça, il s'est oublié en moi comme un gosse qui fait dans ses draps" (1981, 409).

22. Some of the words Mathieu uses to designate the pregnancy are: "ces trucs-là" (410), "saleté" (406), "connerie" (406), "le mal" (408), and, especially, the distancing demonstrative pronoun "ça" (406, 409, 410, 437, 439, 440, 464ff.).

23. "It's blooming in all that crap she has in her belly [*Ca s'épanouit au milieu des cochonneries qu'elle a dans le ventre*]" (410).

24. Cf. Jacques Lacan, "L'instance de la lettre dans l'inconscient," in *Ecrits, I* (Paris: Seuil, 1966), 249–89.

25. Irigaray writes: "Woman never speaks identity. What she emits is fluent, fluctuating. Fogging/flowing [*flouant*]" (1977, 110). The related lexical item that Sartre embellishes here is *mare* ("puddle"), which is another term he uses in the novel.

26. Sigmund Freud, *On the Sexual Theories of Children* (1908) in *The Standard Edition of the Complete Psychological Works of Sigmund Freud* (London: Hogarth Press, 1973–74), 9:208, 219–20.

27. "Marcelle gripped the porcelain edge of the sink and stared at the bubbly liquid: actually it pretty much looked like sperm" (1981, 464)

28. "Marcelle was a swamp" (1981, 530), where the word used, *marécage,*

has a striking resemblance to *marée*. For Daniel, going to Marcelle's place is like being swallowed up: "he would enter the pink room, and let himself be ingurgitated [*engloutir*]" (684). The mood of these passages gets recreated in an entirely different context when Garcin says to Estelle in *No Exit,* "I don't want to sink down [*m'enliser*] into your eyes. You're moist! You're soft [*molle*]! You're an octopus, you're a swamp" (1960c, 176).

29. This is like the atmosphere surrounding Marcelle (1981, 395, 397ff.). The word *touffu,* also meaning "stuffy," evokes the thickness, density, and bushiness of fur. Either consciously or unconsciously, the narrator is identifying the summer with the warm, furry pubes in the cavity behind which Mathieu's preoccupation gestates. This narrator uses nearly identical imagery when describing Marcelle looking down at her swelling abdomen, which she refers to as "ces grasses prairies nourricières" (465).

30. At the beginning of *The Family Idiot,* Sartre's more than 2,000-page study on Flaubert, he just as flippantly refers to the object of his biography as an "example" among many from which he could have chosen (1971–72, 1:7). In point of fact, Sartre had been vigorously, almost obsessively, researching Flaubert since the early 1950s. Similarly, the viscous is not just any quality: it is one of vital importance in the overall argument of *Being and Nothingness* and, as my thematic analysis of Sartre's writings reveals, one of vital importance in Sartre's psychic preoccupations.

31. The dilatory quality of Sartre's writing in this chapter is reminiscent of Freud's fanciful delays at getting started in *Civilization and Its Discontents,* which, while he muses about the "oceanic feeling," reveal the extent to which he himself, despite denials, is subject to it. See Leo Bersani, *The Freudian Body* (New York: Columbia University Press, 1986), 13–14.

32. "Kids . . . are little voracious things; [he's] a little ravenous spirit" (1981, 437); "that little soft and pale cupping-glass sucking up [*pomper*] the world" (438).

33. In his rhetorical fervor, Sartre, I think, sees the viscous as the paradigmatic androgynous being. In this sense, the viscous is the point of convergence of the maternal, paternal, and filial: the viscous is "l'être partout fuyant *et* partout semblable à lui-même[;] qui s'échappe de toute part [et] sur lequel on peut flotter[;] sur lequel on ne marque pas [et] qui ne saurait marquer sur nous[;] qui glisse[;] qui est éternité [et] temporalité infinie[;] changement perpétuel [et] sans rien qui change" (1943, 669).

34. "Thinghood" (*Dinglichkeit*) being the ontological quality of things, which, in Sartre's language ("plenitude of being"), takes on much more positive force than in Heidegger's. Cf. Martin Heidegger, *Being and Time,* trans. John Macquarrie and Edward Robinson (New York: Harper and Row, 1962), 79–83.

Part Four

Paternity Endorsed

CHAPTER 6

Bariona or the Conversion to Paternity

> Il y a, dans l'appréhension même du visqueux . . . comme la hantise d'une *métamorphose*.
>
> —*Being and Nothingness*[1]

> on n'a pas assez réfléchi aux relations *réelles* de l'homme vivant avec l'homme encore à naître: *elles sont juste l'inverse de celles qu'on croit.*
>
> —*Notebooks for an Ethics*[2]

Contrary to his own claim (*The Words*) that freedom has to be limitless for existence to be tolerable, Sartre's conviction turns out to be that freedom, as he first explained it in the ethical language of *Being and Nothingness,* must be and ultimately is always counterbalanced by responsibility. This conviction abides throughout the rest of his literary and philosophical production. We have seen how Mathieu Delarue, like many other characters in Sartre's work, suffered from a prolonged limitlessness of freedom and endured it as an unbearable lightness of being. I have argued that Mathieu could have attained something like the plenitude of being he was searching for, which Sartre called "man's useless passion" in 1943, by endorsing paternity, that is by recognizing and taking responsibility for his child. Oddly, given the norm of Sartre's work, a woman elaborately prepared him for that weight-giving task. But the path to moral existence via paternity remains an unspoken solution, one that remains lodged in the recesses of the recalcitrant male character's mind, just as that solution must be wrested, through painstakingly close reading, from the deepest reaches of Sartre's text.

Nearly without exception, Sartre paints fathers in hideous colors. Here and there, however, even within the canon of his work, paternity appears in fleeting moments with unexpected favor. In three isolated episodes of *The Reprieve,* for example, paternity serves as pastoral counterpoint to the cruel atmosphere of the war novel.[3] It is 23 September 1938 as the story opens: Czechoslovakia is mobilizing against the Reich's agression and the Munich agreements are a week away. For Anna and Milan, two Czech resistance fighters, the concept of a future has no meaning.[4] Yet Anna is pregnant. In these desperate hours before the cession of Bohemia and Moravia, Milan, who has fathered the child, experiences moments of solace as Anna reminds him about their future baby: "she drew him up between her knees. The enormous tummy was touching his stomach" (1981, 738). This epiphany of joined maternal and paternal bellies would seem to deflect the narrator's warning that their total annihilation is at hand. For another character, Birnenschatz, a Jew from Krakow who has taken refuge in France, having had a child is the event of greatest import in life: "Good Lord, if my only accomplishment in life is to have made that little kid, I should think I haven't wasted my time" (814–15).[5] Finally, in a most touching scene stripped of any narrative irony, Georges, a French reservist who has been called up for active duty, is moved to reflect on the senseless repetition of human existence as he lovingly contemplates his sleeping daughter (840–41).[6] These consummate fathers are, in a way, the masculine correlates of Sarah, Pablo's mother, for whom "human life was sacred" (433).[7]

In *No Exit* (1944), we learn that an exemplary father was the victim of the crime for which Estelle has been sent to the hell that is the play's setting. By confronting us with a seemingly gentle but murderous mother, Sartre performs a reversal uncharacteristic of his overt treatments of parenthood: if one parent can be counted on to care lovingly for a child (even if that nurturing is sometimes subject to Sartre's ridicule), it is very nearly always the mother. Estelle's lover (she explains after being pressed by Garcin) took his own life after she drowned their infant daughter in a lake. In her rationalization of what happened, Estelle claims that having a child was Roger's idea, not hers.[8] Water, suicide, and birth intermingle once again, but in a movement opposite to this recollection of crisis in parenthood in the opening scene of *Nekrassov* (1955), where a couple of hobos, Irma and Robert, fish Georges out of the Seine after his attempted suicide.[9] Saving Georges's life fills the hobo couple with unmistakably parental emotions. Robert declares that he has been moved to save Georges by thoughts of what he himself might have been able to make of himself had someone given him a hand in life—even figuratively. Irma meanwhile exclaims that "it's as if [Robert] had given me a child" when she sees Georges beginning to help save himself instead of going limp in his first impulse to end it all (1955, 21).[10]

But although tableaux such as these may be part of what is considered the Sartrean canon and do present paternity as a fundamental human relationship, they are isolated and unsustained. It would be difficult to maintain that, by these vignettes, Sartre is trying to illustrate some major point in his thought. No theory can really take shape around them, and we would be putting words into Sartre's mouth by extrapolating a consistent set of remarks confirming paternity as a category in his ethics based merely on these scenes. However charming and intriguing they might be, these are minor episodes involving secondary characters.

The crisis of whether or not to endorse paternity (which in Sartre's thought is the deepest moral question) and the consequences of the eventual decision are also themes of major importance in several works *outside* the Sartrean canon. It has been confirmed by those close to Sartre that, although he was wildly careless about many of his writings, some of which were saved from oblivion only due to the care of dedicated followers, he actively promoted certain of his works and took pains to make sure they got published.[11] This politics of publishing and self-promotion was, in spite of the often cavalier attitude Sartre took with the sheaves of manuscripts he produced, instrumental in establishing his canon. He himself was an active participant in orienting not so much *how* we read his works (something arguably impossible to control) but *what* of his works would be read. To claim that Sartre strived to screen or censor any sustained positive view of paternity in the process that led to the establishment of a canon would be pure speculation. However, a correspondence clearly exists between the works that lie outside that canon and that elusive favorable position with respect to paternity. *Bariona, or the Son of Thunder*, Sartre's 1940 Christmas play, is the earliest work to exemplify this correspondence.[12]

Another means by which the Sartrean canon got established was through what we could call a more natural selection process valorizing commercial successes and stylistically polished products over writings where literary quality was of small import to the author (political diatribes and occasional pieces) and that, at their publication, only touched limited or specialized audiences. Within this second group we again observe a thematization of ethics through paternity. Some of the texts in this category hold a close thematic affiliation with that obscure play, *Bariona*. The period of "The Communists and Peace" (1952–54)[13] will therefore be the object of a discussion beginning here and culminating in the next chapter. In order to set the tone for examining such political texts, I would like to first discuss *Bariona* in anticipation of the following question: How did Sartre make the leap from something already as uncharacteristic for him as a Christmas play to written defenses of the Communist Party via ethical questions thematized by paternity?

Subhumans Dissected

The subjects Sartre treats in *Bariona* and in the 1952–54 period transcend what he calls their *subhumanity*. They learn how to coexist with others in an ethical manner and thus attain a higher level of being that is, if not mediated by an endorsement of paternity, at least a consequence of such a metamorphosis. Although in no other respect are these texts particularly close to Sartre's ambitious literary biographies, they all have in common their phenomenological—one might say surgical—approach to the deep-seated workings of their subjects. The ground rules for performing a "phenomenological ontology" of the human subject are spelled out in the chapter on existential psychoanalysis in *Being and Nothingness* (1943, 616–35). In a simple (if tautological) formula, this epistemological exploratory surgery to be performed on the human guinea pig consists of studying the observable factors that contribute to the subject's sense of possessing a being; existential psychoanalysis studies what constitutes being in its being. This is an enterprise from which Sartre never deviated. Whether falling within or outside the canon, virtually all of the works he wrote after *Being and Nothingness* may be viewed as phenomenological ontologies to the extent that, as fictional rehearsals, they prepare the way for Sartre's studies of historical subjects in the form of literary biographies. The subjects of those ontologies, whether fictional or historically attestable, are variations on a specific category of being that, with unflagging consistency, Sartre calls the *subhuman.*[14] Sartre's inquiries into the partial being of subhumans are not, it should be noted, limited to the rather obscure texts that will come under scrutiny here. In *Anti-semite and Jew* (1946), for example, he promoted a theory of interdependence, based on their antipodal subhumanities, between the two groups named in the translated title. *Saint Genet* (1952) discusses, ad nauseam, the ontogenesis of Jean Genet as a subhuman in the successive guises of bastard, thief, homosexual, saint, actor, and writer.

According to its dictionary definition, a subhuman resembles a human but is situated slightly below Homo sapiens in the evolutionary hierarchy. Sartre's understanding of the category of subhuman broadens this definition to include the *subject* of philosophy who constantly yearns for total being, with Sartre stressing the etymological roots of the word: that which has been "thrown down" or "put under." Sartre's subhuman is humanlike, but has been *sociologically* deprived of full humanity. Being unavoidably situated in the society of which he is the victim saps the subhuman of his potential for ontological fulfillment. The rationale for an evolutionary definition of subhuman is reversed: it is the subhuman's oppressed socioeconomic condition that reduces his mental and physical capacities, ultimately (over a series of generations of oppression) making him biologically deficient. It must not be ignored that (for Sartre) it is precisely because he is *not* in full possession of being that the subhuman is ontologically like *any* human subject. Indeed, because he is essentially dispossessed, he becomes the model for the subject of philosophy: if there is any chance that some given subject can attain full being, as indeed the Atlas allegory of *Being and Nothingness* implies any for-itself can, then Sartre's belief is that an embryonic potential (like that displayed in Mathieu's "age-being") is uniquely possessed by the subhuman because he is the only "human" who *knows* his subhumanity. It is the subhuman who, paradoxically, will show all humanity how it is done.

Bariona and Sartre's political texts of the 1950s are exemplary in evincing Sartre's preoccupation with the subhuman. In their uniquely un-Sartrean solution to the problem of universal subhumanity, which every subject struggles to overcome, they expose the unwritten Sartrean ethics in novel terms. In *Bariona,* Sartre puts into play the vicissitudes in the existence of a villager in Judea under the Roman occupation while in the political articles Sartre strives to provide an ontological answer to the question "What is a proletarian?" In searching for his answer, Sartre proposes a concrete solution for the subhuman's subhumanity. The list of subhumans that Sartre probed in his career ranges from bastards, actors, bourgeois militants, and fellow travelers of the Communist Party, to the Vietnamese and the Algerians in their struggles for national independence and, in general, all oppressed peoples fighting for identities divergent from those imposed by their European oppressors. Even the "family idiot," Gustave Flaubert, participates in this collection of Sartrean subhumans.

The X-mas Play

Bariona is set in Judea at the time of the birth of Christ. The play's main characters, however, are not the traditional actors of the Nativity whose events constitute the background and, very briefly, a catalyst for Sartre's tale. Bariona is the young and temperamental chieftain of a mountain village, and he has reached the limits of despair over the oppressive policies of the Roman governor. On the day the alien rulers impose yet another tax on his people, Bariona decides to defy the government with a drastic form of passive resistance: he orders his villagers to stop procreation. A poignant test case of Bariona's new law arises at once as Sarah, his own wife, comes to him announcing that she is pregnant.[15] Despite her pleas to let their child be born, he orders her to abort the pregnancy. Secretly, she will defy those orders.

In the meantime, news of Christ's birth has spread to Béthaur. The village inhabitants, still reeling from their chieftain's radical decree, prepare to depart for Bethlehem not only to venerate the putative Messiah but to experience vicariously the joy of putting a child into the world that has just been denied them. At this point Bariona hears final arguments for retaining hope for the future from two sources: Balthazar, an old sage who extolls religious faith,[16] and Sarah, who expresses her faith in the possibility of an improved world by banking on the offspring to come, thus countering Bariona's warning that the next generation will, in all likelihood, be condemned to the same subhumanity.

Impervious to these admonitions, Bariona heads for Bethlehem too—intent on murdering the holy neonate. At the play's climax, Bariona suddenly loses his will to carry out the infanticide because, in his own words, "in order to find the courage to extinguish this young life between my hands, I should have avoided catching a glimpse of him deep in his father's eyes" (Contat and Rybalka 1970, 620). This apparition, not of the child himself but of the *way* the father "cradles" the child in his own field of vision, is the beginning of a radical change for Bariona, the beginning of a true conversion. Step by step, he begins to advocate everything he had previously resisted. He acknowledges Christ as the Messiah, as one would expect from any Christmas play, but he also welcomes the imminent birth of his child.

There is something disquieting, however, in the play's ending. For, as Denis Hollier remarks, it is as if "the best of fathers are always the ones who die so their sons can survive."[17] The final scenes depict Bariona mobilizing his compatriots for war. In face of the massacre of the innocents instigated by Herod, Bariona claims as his fatherly and Christian duty the sacrifice of his own life in order to defend that of the infant Messiah. But agreeing to produce offspring does not entail, in Bariona's case, a father's continued relationship with the child. Just because his wife is having a child and comes to rejoice in that prospect does not ratify the requirement that he cohabit with the scion once it's been born. On the contrary, it seems that the faster Bariona vanishes from the primal family scene, the better off everyone will be. One might say, staying consistent with our metaphor, that Bariona takes paternity lightly: he endorses the biological aspect of paternity—the activity engaged in before the child's birth—

only to disappear before the postpartum parental responsibilities are in place for him to shoulder. Bariona's death will coincide with or *hinge upon* his own child's birth. Like the death of Sartre's father (as described in *The Words*), the birth of Bariona's child is as precisely coordinated as possible with Bariona's death. Bariona may have achieved the critical conversion to an acceptance of paternity, but he still does his son the fundamental favor (according to *The Words*) of discretely moving aside, passing to him the legacy of unlimited freedom.

Conversion to Conversion

The crucial significance of *Bariona* in Sartre's career can be gauged by its historical situation (in both individual and collective history) and Sartre's subsequent and curiously touchy attitude toward the play. These factors are submitted to detailed examination in Hollier's essay, "A Winter's Tale."[18] Among other allusions, the French subtitle of this collection of essays (*Sartre et l'an quarante*) implies that 1940 was quite simply of *pivotal* importance in Sartre's career.[19] In 1975, Sartre described his life as having been divided into two epochs—a "before" and an "after"—that hinged on his experience at war, with Sartre once again insisting that he created himself. The before and the after are like two articulated flaps radically different from each other but connected within the same person.

> The war truly divided my life in two. It started when I was thirty-four and ended when I was forty: it was my *crossover* from youth to maturity [*l'âge mûr*]. That's when I moved on from individualism and the notion of the *pure* individual . . . to the social and socialism. This was the true turning point of my life: *before/after*. (1976, 180; italics added)

According to Simone de Beauvoir, Sartre's brief imprisonment in Stalag XIID was, of all his war experience, the episode that marked him most.

> His experience as POW deeply affected him. It taught him solidarity: instead of feeling put down [*brimé*], he joyously

> participated in communal life. The rigors and the warmth of comradeship cleared up [*dénouèrent*] the contradictions of his antihumanism. (Beauvoir 1963, 16–17)

In analyzing some of the many statements made by both Sartre and Beauvoir concerning this period in Sartre's life, Hollier figures that what transpired in 1940, in that critical moment which Sartre stresses *between* the "before" and the "after," was not only a shift from his previous individualism to the later universalism, but also a shift of emphasis in writing and in life "from the unreal to reality" (Hollier 1986, 171). And, as *Bariona* is the only work Sartre actually began *and* finished during that crucial year as a prisoner of war, we are compelled to search in that work for the contours of the remarkably *real* transformation, as Sartre put it, from "youth" to "maturity," from "before" to "after." We must look to *Bariona* for the bare articulation of Sartre's own avowed conversion.

Although Sartre wrote, produced, and even acted in *Bariona* at one of the most pregnant moments of his career—a play which proved tremendously popular among the new comrades he made in prison (those prototypes for working-class affiliations he would nurture from that moment onward in his life), he never bothered to publish this first work for the theater. Sartre did nothing to even preserve the play's manuscript after the war was over, let alone have it become part of his canon. When asked about *Bariona* in an interview, Sartre dismissed it for unconvincing reasons.[20] He claimed it was a poor play. But as Hollier points out, *Bariona* is dramaturgically no less brilliant than most of Sartre's theater and arguably better than some plays—all of which he showed no hesitation whatsoever in publishing (Hollier 1986, 155). In reading back over Sartre's explanations, it seems that he was worried that the conversion to Christianity of the play's main character might lead people to suspect that, in a moment of weakness, he had himself undergone a similar crisis of conscience.[21] He stated unequivocally that the war *did* cause irreversible changes in his way of thinking, but why would anyone necessarily infer that those changes were of a religious nature?

Were a continued dialogue with Sartre possible, one might challenge his denials and sidestepping maneuvers by observing that, given the historical circumstances in which the play evolved, a conversion to Christianity in *Bariona* is simply to be expected in a play written to entertain Christian soldiers at yuletide. However, under close scrutiny, we find that *Bariona* is less concerned with religious conversion than with events (from which divine grace may or not be excluded) that lead to a *conversion to paternity.* Bariona's Christian "second birth" is a mere thematic pretext for his decision to embrace fatherhood. Paternity and Christianity are copresent as principle themes in *Bariona,* and it is equally unusual in a play by Sartre to see one represented in a positive light as it is the other. Sartre may have denied, in the interview setting, that he was tempted by a spiritual conversion, but a question about the all-too-obvious theme of paternity was apparently never posed and thus he was able to remain silent about this key issue in his statements about *Bariona.* While it would be rather farfetched to suggest, as he no doubt feared it would be, that *either* transformation underlie the conversion "from the unreal to reality" Sartre describes himself as having undergone during the war, I contend that from 1940 until his death in 1980, the concept of radical conversion *in any form* became an integral part of Sartre's philosophy. The idea that being could be radically altered, like the molecular structure of metals or the genetic makeup of cells, began to seize Sartre as a way of thinking a future means by which to overcome the duality of being and to facilitate the supposedly impossible synthesis of the for-itself with the in-itself. In short, Sartre's war experience—the "trauma" of forced togetherness—converted him to the notion of conversion.

Politics and Populationism

Bariona stages a bizarrely anachronistic Malthusian demographic economy. An obsession with populationism seems to color Sartre's thought as it takes its place alongside his unflinching interest in developing an ethics. The doctrine of Malthusianism, popular in late nineteenth-century Europe, grew from Thomas Malthus's theory that population increased geometrically while food production only progressed arithmetically. Malthus's latter-day proponents, excellent examples of whom ran most of the governments in Third Republic France, blamed overpopulation for virtually all social problems and argued that demographic disproportion between "humans" and "subhumans" was principally a phenomenon of economically or racially outcast communities. These theses are still plainly visible in France today, for example, in the racist politics of the National Front and its boss, Jean-Marie Le Pen. Neo-Malthusians recommend an aggressive program of population control within the subhuman sectors of society.

The inhabitants of Bariona's village observe with alarm that a combination of endemic poverty and a sort of self-imposed Malthusianism gone out of control in the wake of their leader's dejected policy change are moving their community toward extinction. Young people are fleeing the village for the city, the birth rate is falling (Contat and Rybalka 1970, 571) and infant mortality is high (611). The Roman officials governing the territory even express alarm over the rapid drop in the Jewish population in a discourse that one might imagine late nineteenth-century capitalists using if a decrease in the available work force had occurred.[22]

> But, were we to live in peace for centuries, don't forget that industry would requisition your children. Salaries have increased greatly over the last fifty years. This proves that the labor force is insufficient. I would add that this necessity of keeping salaries so high is a heavy burden on Roman management. If Jews would produce more children, the supply of workers would finally surpass the demand. Salaries could come down considerably and we could free up some capital for better use elsewhere. (584)

Bariona is anachronistic in two ways: speeches such as this come as if from the mouth of a neo-Malthusian political economist of high capitalism—a discourse obviously inconsistent with first-century Judea but also one which (except among extreme right-wing groups) was already long since spent in Europe by the time Sartre conceived the play. In any event, by confirming populationism as the ideological nucleus in the play, such rhetoric constitutes one more factor focusing the attention of the audience on Bariona's conversion to paternity rather than on his being won over to the Christian faith.

Hollier wrote that "the [populationist] positions taken in the Stalag were to know no further development after *Bariona*. They did, however, have something of a brief afterlife in 1953" (1986, 193). In fact, that afterlife of Sartre's populationist positions extended beyond 1953, as I will show in chapter 10. But as Hollier implies by these dates, Sartre's perception of the demographic circumstances in which Bariona's conversion to paternity occurs links the 1940 Christmas play to his political writings of 1952–54 that consecrated, if not his membership, at least his staunch support of the French Communist Party (PCF). In the nineteenth century, Marxists happened to be among the loudest critics of what they perceived as neo-Malthusianism being put into practice. They considered that the dominant class was attempting to ideologically shift the blame for poverty from the problems inherent in class society as a structure of oppression to the victims themselves of that society: the poor. Thus, when Sartre brought himself to claim, in "The Communists and Peace," that the French proletariat was courting annihilation through its Malthusian practices, he was mouthing a traditionally leftist point of social critique that had essentially spent its empirical usefulness before World War I. A cursory examination of the actual birth statistics in the period when Sartre was writing shows how factually off-base and theoretically hysterical his vociferations really were.[23] Of course, as one of the great polemicists of his time, Sartre was not often particularly concerned about attuning his arguments to facts. However, in deforming *these* facts about population, he was repeating about the proletarians of 1952 what he had written in 1940 about first-century Jews. Populationist concerns could not have sprung from the influence of a Marxist position in 1940. Apparently, Sartre really thought that "subhumans" of all sorts were, by definition, under threat of extinction. His mission, then, was to prevent this from happening because, to his mind, subhumans, as trailblazers of full humanity, were the saving grace of ethics. By advocating paternity in the name of proletarians in his political texts of the early 1950s, Sartre systematized in the social sphere, his idea that subhumans must *reproduce* as part and parcel of their being.

Between *Bariona* and the 1952–54 political texts Sartre wrote and published thousands of pages. In examining the similarities between these texts, separated by twelve years and by World War II, we must ask ourselves whether the later writings are merely a coincidental public rendering of the populationist concerns of a prisoner of war writing a Christmas play or whether this theme is more consistent in Sartre's thought than it would first appear. In order to save itself from the obliteration that worries Sartre in "The Communists and Peace," does the working class require the conversion to paternity programmed for Bariona and his cohorts? If so, will the proletarian, like Bariona and like Jean-Baptiste Sartre before him, make a child only to elude responsibility as a father and march off to die before the child is born? Before studying just how Sartre conceived of a proletarian conversion, it is helpful to review the historical, political, and psychological conditions that engendered Sartre's articles from his period of fellow traveling.

Conversion after Conversion

Before World War II, that is, before the before/after hinge in Sartre's career, before his conversion "from the unreal to reality," virtually no connection (let alone any exchange) linked Sartre with the PCF. His close and most admired school friend, Paul Nizan, became a fervent Communist militant as a lycée student at a period of history when most intellectuals in France were extremely reticent to work within the ranks of the PCF.[24] While Sartre, as he was later to admit, idolized Nizan in many respects, this particular area of his friend's activities had little effect on Sartre's political consciousness at the time.[25] Until the mid-1940s when he had passed his fortieth birthday, Sartre maintained himself in an aloof position of cautiousness regarding Party politics and was, thus, sometimes harshly critical of his friend's energetic and earnest militancy for the PCF.[26] Not only was Sartre not particularly interested in organized politics, let alone communist militancy, but he was not even well enough versed in Marxist theory to have engaged in serious debate with Party members. By war's end, however, still impressed by his 1940 initiation to group dynamics in the social melting pot of the Stalag, Sartre decided it was high time to open a dialogue with Marxism.[27] In the late 1940s we find him intensifying his knowledge of Marxist theory with the intention of becoming a viable and sympathetic critic while still remaining outside the Party.[28]

Meanwhile, during the months following the Liberation, the PCF, enjoying its reputation of being the "party of the Resistance," basked in a brief period of unprecedented popularity. The French Communists felt powerful enough to open their ears to an increased volume of informed critique from intellectuals like Sartre (who had become the most prominent figure on the French scene). And Sartre, on his side, decided it was necessary to disseminate his views on Marxist theory in order to fine tune the apparatus of revolution. In a few short months, however, the situation of the PCF had suffered a series of drastic reversals, sending it into a dogmatic retrenchment similar to its prewar defensiveness. The cold war was gearing up and France's economic dependence on the United States looked like it was clinched when, in 1948, the Ramadier government decided to adopt the Marshall Plan. The French government's official policies vis-à-vis the Soviet Union were adjusted accordingly and, in 1949, France joined in signing the NATO treaty that would, six years later, be echoed by the Warsaw Pact.

Having thus become increasingly beholden to the United States and in spite of President Auriol's attempts to maintain a semblance of economic and ideological autonomy, France's internal politics increasingly mimicked, at least for the moment, U.S. anticommunism, of which the McCarthy era would become the caricature. When General Matthew Ridgway, the commander of the U.N. Armed Forces and SHAPE,[29] visited Paris in 1952, the PCF organized a demonstration that was brutally repressed by the Pinay government. The venerated Communist deputy to parliament, Jacques Duclos, was arrested under trumped-up charges in the ensuing witch-hunt. This crisis spurred Sartre to switch his energy to all-out support of the PCF and condemn, in writing, any and all critics of the Party, be they from the right or the left. In his 1961 article eulogizing Merleau-Ponty, Sartre explained that this period took on the characteristics and significance of yet another personal *conversion:*

> The last ties were cut loose. My world vision was transformed. An anticommunist is a cur. After ten years of ruminating, I had reached the breaking point and only needed that one little push. *In the language of the Church, it was a conversion.* (1964b, 248–49; italics added)[30]

Only a handful of Sartre scholars knew, when "Merleau-Ponty" was published, about his obscure play *Bariona*. Yet the *presence* of the personal events of 1940 and the conversions upon which the play of that year hinges are obvious in Sartre's manner of describing, in 1961, the strong emotion that inspired his near acceptance of PCF membership. The results of this shift—this conversion, as Sartre again calls it—are reflected in the exhaustive political articles he feverishly published between 1952 and 1954 in *Les Temps modernes*.[31] Within three months of each other, the first two parts of "The Communists and Peace" were in print. Between them appeared the famous "Response to Albert Camus," ratifying the often misunderstood break between the two most popular postwar writers.[32] Then in early 1953, Sartre published his vicious "Response to Claude Lefort."[33] With the third part of "The Communists and Peace," appearing in 1954, the text comprises over three hundred pages of densely argued, sweeping diatribe against right-wing reactionaries ("anticommunist dogs") and leftist opportunists (labeled "viscous rats"). The attack on Lefort goes on for some ninety pages. Yet despite this characteristic long-windedness, the two texts succinctly demonstrate what has had to metamorphose in order for him to embrace his new political position.[34]

Although still officially outside the PCF, Sartre shifted from sympathetic critic to uncritical proponent of the Party's official line, the foundation of which was Stalin's application of Lenin's theses on the role of the Party. In a very general way, we can say that Lenin took as his jumping-off point the abstract Marxist privilege of the whole over the parts by affirming the specific and concrete privilege of the *proletariat* over individual *proletarians*. Marx himself had written:

> it is not a question of what this or that proletarian . . . at the moment *regards* as [his] aim. It is a question of *what the proletariat is,* and what, in accordance with this *being,* it will historically be compelled to do.[35]

This definition unfortunately paved the way to the Leninist position of judging the proletarian incapable of self-knowledge—a position whose implied correlate is that the "scientists" of class ideology (Stalin and company) alone held the secret of the proletarian's being and his destiny. In "What is to be done?" Lenin prescribed that the

Communist Party alone can help the proletarian rise above "trade-unionist self-consciousness" and attain "revolutionary consciousness."[36] The Party alone can articulate what the masses, unaided or unmediated, cannot. In psychological terms, the Party becomes the voice of the proletarian's "unconscious strivings"—an expression that Sartre employs frequently to make the same point.

In defending a cause, Sartre always proved the perfect zealot. Not only is the Party regarded as the vanguard of the proletariat in "The Communists and Peace," not only does the proletarian class not exist outside the existence of the Party, but the individual worker is virtually powerless if he refuses to identify himself with that Party. The worker is invited to enter the fold and warned that he will perish if he does not conform. Party stalwarts and independent French leftists alike agreed that the future of democracy and world peace lay in the hands of the proletariat. Where hardliners and dissidents clashed, however, was over the two crucial points of: (1) the possibility that the proletariat might manifest a unified will independently of the Party, and (2) whether (if [1] were possible) class dictatorship would be desirable, since it risks recreating the dominance of ideology over humanity. The Party's position, of course, was that the proletariat needed the Party to "represent itself." On the question of the dictatorship of the proletariat, the Party was cagier: extolling it as long as it did not entail the dissolution of the Party apparatus, and passing it over in silence if it did. Lefort and his colleagues in the "Socialisme ou barbarie" group advocated, more strenuously than the Party and outside the confines of class,[37] the dissolution of all class differences rather than risk the recreation of a new power structure. In opposition to this, Sartre takes faith in the Party one step further, claiming that the proletariat is ontologically *indistinguishable from* the Party and that, for a free world to be achieved, it is necessary to defend the Party tooth and nail—a party to which the proletariat is not subsumed, but with which the proletariat is one in its very being. While the sterility of Sartre's new political position was clear to Merleau-Ponty, who dubbed it "ultra-bolshevism,"[38] Sartre proceeds with an ontological description of the proletarian that is as elusive as the alliance he was trying to forge between existentialism and Marxism. In endeavoring to collapse the division between mass and individual (which is actually an untenable position for a Sartrean ethics, with its privileging of the individual subject), Sartre's text deviates from his original intent in much the same way that Bariona's politics of sterility became sabotaged by Sarah's determination to have a child. As this subversion of discourse proceeds, it is paternity, once again, that emerges as the dominant theme.

Such were the historical conditions under which Sartre wrote "The Communists and Peace" and the "Response to Claude Lefort" and the ideological framework (one might say with retrospect "straight-jacket") that he imposed upon himself, given the choices of that historical situation and the precedent of *Bariona*. In attempting to insert existentialism as a subjectivist critique that would operate within the ideological framework of Marxism,[39] Sartre's theoretical proletarian becomes endlessly tossed between the two incommensurable doctrines. As Merleau-Ponty meticulously argued in the *Adventures of the Dialectic*, the 1952–54 texts fail to merge the sociohistorical theories of Marxism with Sartre's preeminent given of radical freedom. While Marxism-Leninism dictated to Sartre that the proletarian has no ontological status outside the Party (i.e., class) structure,[40] the seemingly incontrovertible political apathy of a majority of French workers in 1952 and the subjectivist philosophy from which Sartre never would deviate drew his attention back to proletarians as individual subhumans just as in 1940, when the war shifted him "from the unreal to reality" and he wrote *Bariona*. When all is said and done, the object of concern that emerges from these Marxist polemical texts is not an ideal proletarian class but, rather, the real and palpable mass of proletarians taken in their individuality and whose being has yet to emerge, let alone be defined.

If Sartre had remained faithful to orthodoxy, the Marxism-Leninism that subtends the 1952–54 texts should have resulted in a characterization of the proletarian's being as one and indivisible under the "being" of the Communist Party. Sartre discovered, however, that to uphold this subservience of for-itself to in-itself as the solution to the problem of proletarian being would be a blatant contradiction of his compassionate focus on the masses, the "lost sheep" of the working class. This unavoidable multiplicity of individual proletarians who, out of despair, resist "their" Party (just as the townspeople of

Béthaur resisted Bariona's politics of despair) underscores his fundamental moral belief in a plurality of beings. As much as Sartre would have liked to convince everyone (including himself) to the contrary, the individual proletarian or subhuman does not accede to full being through a subsumption of his individual partial being into the overarching total being of the Party. Full humanity—synonymous with ethical being—is attained, rather, by means of a *coupling* with a fellow subhuman. The kernel of ethical being is not in a "vertical" relationship with a higher being (neither God nor Party) but in the recognition of sameness in difference that a "horizontal" relationship with another subhuman nurtures and that mediates the becoming-human of both of them. Whether, as in Sartre's texts, the term refers metonymically to the entire class or to an individual, the *being of the proletarian* is plural. A proletarian must be more than one or he is not: this is the message with which "The Communists and Peace" leaves us. And this plurality of being is not that of a group sacrificing its plural partial beings to a whole. Rather, it is a dialectical relationship between equal ethical beings.

Notes

1. "In the very apprehension of the viscous . . . there is something like a terror of *metamorphosis*" (1943, 672).

2. "Not enough thought has been given to the *real* relations between living man and the man yet to be born" (1983a, 90).

3. Jean-Paul Sartre, *Le Sursis* (1945) in *Oeuvres romanesques* (Paris: Gallimard, 1981), 731–1133.

4. "Mathieu was still waiting at the edge of a horrible future. At the same instant . . . Milan no longer had a future" (1981, 734).

5. According to a note in the Pléiade edition (1985–1986), Birnenschatz "was to take on [greater] importance in the projected follow-up of *The Roads to Freedom*" (1981, 1985–86).

6. Contat and Rybalka speculate that "Georges undoubtedly owes his existence to Sartre's phantasms about his own father" (Sartre 1981, 1989n). This episode, in which Georges takes leave of his daughter as he goes off to war, is analogous to the final scene of *Bariona*. Bariona says to Sarah, "when [our child] feels its immense loneliness and abandonment [*délaissement*], tell him 'Your father suffered all that you suffer and he died happy [*dans la joie*]' " (Contat and Rybalka, *Les Ecrits de Sartre* [Paris: Gallimard, 1970], 632).

7. Her husband, Gomez, a typical Sartrean adventurer (as such, a de-

scendant of the object of Roquentin's biography, the Marquis de Rollebon, and a predecessor of Goetz), was, according to Sartre's own standards, the worst father imaginable: absent but not dead.

8. *Estelle:* He wanted to give me a child [*me faire un enfant*].
Garcin: And you didn't want one.
Estelle: Right. But the child came anyway. He liked having a daughter. Not me. (1960c, 159–60; see also 145)

When one thinks that Estelle could have simply relinquished the baby to her lover for him to raise on his own, the recounted infanticide seems an unjustifiably drastic and unimaginative solution to their problem.

9. Jean-Paul Sartre, *Nekrassov* (Paris: Gallimard, 1955).

10. Later, Georges, a "ham actor" [*cabotin*] like so many other principal roles in Sartre's theater (and like the personality of Pierre Brasseur, Sartre's preferred leading man in the 1950s), joins in what he considers a "game of family," pretending to recognize the bums as his parents in his "new" life (1955, 32ff.).

11. This I have gathered from conversations with Jean Pouillon, J.-B. Pontalis, and François George.

12. The play is in print today only in Contat and Rybalka 1970.

13. Jean-Paul Sartre, "Les Communistes et la paix," in *Situations, VI* (Paris: Gallimard, 1964), 80–384.

14. The definition of *sous-homme* is slightly more specific to sociological considerations than that of "subhuman" in English. For convenience, I will nevertheless use subhuman because of the etymological commonality. The *Grand Robert* defines *sous-homme* as "he who has neither the qualities nor the freedom required for human dignity"; the *American College Dictionary* gives: "below the human race or type; less than or not quite human."

15. Bariona's wife and Mathieu's friend are, to my knowledge, the only two characters named Sarah in Sartre's published work. Unlike most of his other female characters, both Sarahs are unyielding advocates of motherhood. In light of the late Sartre's reflections on Judaism (see the "L'espoir maintenant" interviews), it would be tempting to speculate on his motives for giving the name of Abraham's wife and Isaac's mother to these two exemplary mothers.

16. The role of Balthazar was played by Sartre during the only staging of the play just before Christmas in 1940.

17. Denis Hollier, "A Winter's Tale," in *Politics of Prose: Essay on Sartre*, trans. Jeffrey Mehlman (Minneapolis: University of Minnesota Press, 1986), 189.

18. Hollier 1986, 149–200.

19. To make his point only on the level of professional work, despite Sartre's mobilization in September 1939, the "phony war" allowed him to pursue his intellectual career with astounding intensity. He read texts by Kierkegaard, Heidegger, and Hegel that had profound influences on all his

later thought. During 1940, he published *L'Imaginaire*, compiled much of the material that would become *Being and Nothingness*, and wrote the greater portion of *The Age of Reason*.

20. "It was a lousy play, sacrificing too much to long demonstrative speeches." Paul-Louis Mignon, "Le Théâtre de A jusqu'à Z," *L'Avant-Scène Théâtre* 402–3 (1968): 33–34.

21. "Seeing that I'd written a mystery-play, some came to believe I'd gone through a spiritual crisis. No!" (Mignon 1968, 33).

22. It is just this type of late nineteenth-century populationist hysteria that grips Sartre. One might suppose that he inherited this stance on population from his bourgeois upbringing at the hands of his maternal grandfather, Karl Schweitzer.

23. Statistics show that lower-class resistance to population expansion diminished drastically in France over the period from 1949 to 1965 (Colin Dyer, *Population and Society in Twentieth-Century France* [New York: Holmes and Meier, 1978], 152–59).

24. Literature about Nizan is abundant; good examples are William Redfern, *Paul Nizan* (Princeton: Princeton University Press, 1972); Pascal Ory, *Nizan, destin d'un révolté* (Paris: Ramsay, 1980); Annie Cohen-Solal, *Paul Nizan, communiste impossible* (Paris: Grasset, 1980). Before the war, the PCF could boast very few members of the intelligentsia within its ranks. For further information about intellectuals' roles from within the PCF before World War II, see Robert Harvey, "Georges Politzer: une caution posthume," in *La Liberté de l'esprit* 16 (1987): 299–309. See also Louis Althusser, preface to *Pour Marx* (Paris: Maspéro, 1965), 11–32.

25. Sartre recounts his memories of Nizan in several places, including the 1960 foreword to Nizan's novel, *Aden Arabie*, reprinted under the title "Paul Nizan" in *Situations, IV* (Paris: Gallimard, 1964), 130–88. Patrick McCarthy has written a thoroughly fascinating article about Nizan's long-term influence on Sartre: "Sartre, Nizan and the Dilemmas of Political Commitment," *Yale French Studies* 68 (1985): 191–205.

26. Sartre, doubtlessly like Mathieu, saw either politics in general or Party membership as threats to his personal freedom. And yet he admired such radicalism of conviction in Nizan, as Mathieu admired Brunet and Schneider-Vicarios.

27. Simone de Beauvoir, again describing the changes Sartre underwent in the POW camp: "before the Germans, before the collaborators and the indifferent ones they encountered daily, the anti-fascists of the Stalag formed something of a fraternity . . ." (Simone de Beauvoir, *La Force de l'âge* [Paris: Gallimard, 1960], 550).

28. For accounts of Sartre's conversion to Marxism, see Mark Poster, *Existential Marxism in Postwar France* (Princeton, N.J.: Princeton University Press, 1975); Arthur Hirsh, *The French Left* (Montréal: Black Rose Books, 1982); Martin Jay, *Marxism and Totality* (Berkeley: University of California Press, 1984).

29. Supreme Headquarters Allied Powers in Europe.

30. In "The Communists and Peace," Sartre speaks of this very same conversion in terms of a realization that the working class is both *something* and *nothing* (1964b, 166–67).

31. The sequence of articles with the same political tenor is:

1. "Les Communistes et la paix" (first part), July 1952;
2. "Réponse à Albert Camus," August 1952;
3. "Les Communistes et la paix" (second part), October–November 1952;
4. "Réponse à Claude Lefort," April 1953;
5. "Opération Kanapa," March 1954;
6. "Les Communistes et la paix" (third part), April 1954. Articles 1, 2, 3, and 6 are reprinted in Sartre 1964b; articles 4 and 5 in Sartre 1965.

32. An objective account of the Sartre-Camus break is almost impossible to find: M.-A. Burnier's version (*Les Existentialistes et la politique* [Paris: Gallimard, 1966]) is as thorough as any. See also the chapter entitled "Sartre and Camus: The Anatomy of a Quarrel" added to the English translation by Bernard Murchland, *Choice of Action* (New York: Random House, 1968), 175–94.

33. Lefort was the most important member of the small but highly influential dissident Marxist group "Socialisme ou barbarie" to have contributed to *Les Temps modernes*. Jean-François Lyotard's article on Hollier's *Politics of Prose* ("Un succès de Sartre," *Critique* 430 [1983]), shows how bitter the memory of Sartre's attack on Lefort remained, even to a former colleague of Lefort's thirty years after the attack was leveled. Sartre refused to the end to admit that, as his later political positions sometimes attest, his Marxism, in fact, evolved toward that of the group led by Cornelius Castoriadis and Lefort, especially on the subject of the role of the Party. Cf. Sartre 1976, 181–84.

34. For a more extensive analysis of these texts in their sociopolitical context, see Burnier 1966, 87–103.

35. Karl Marx and Friedrich Engels, *The Holy Family* (Moscow: Progress Publications, 1975), 44.

36. According to Lenin, the Party is run by what he variously calls "professional revolutionists" or "revolutionary intellectuals." Such a concept reveals some of the ambiguities of Leninism: by promoting the idea of an intelligentsia (mixed, it is true, with some proletarians) setting policy for themselves and the proletariat at large, Leninism would recreate a hierarchy of the sort it had intended to destroy. See, inter alia, the debate with Martynov in "The Working Class as Vanguard Fighter for Democracy," in V. I. Lenin, *What Is To Be Done?* (1902) (Moscow: Foreign Languages Publishing House, 1961), 421–36.

37. "Socialisme ou barbarie," founded in 1949 and dissolved in 1965, counted some proletarian members, all of whom had as much voice as the intellectual members. See Hirsh's chapter on the group (1982, 108–31) and Gregory Renault, "Bureaucracy to *L'Imaginaire:* Cornelius Castoriadis' Immanent Critique," *Catalyst* 13 (1979): 72–90.

38. The longest chapter of Merleau-Ponty's 1955 testimonial to his break with Communism is entitled "Sartre and Ultra-Bolchevism" and deals pointedly with Sartre's 1952–54 texts: "The ruin of the dialectic is accomplished openly with Sartre and clandestinely with the communists, and the same decisions that the communists base on the historical process and the historical mission of the proletariat, Sartre bases on the non-being of the proletariat and on the decision which, out of nothing, creates the proletariat as subject of history" (Maurice Merleau-Ponty, *Adventures of the Dialectic,* trans. Joseph Bien [Evanston: Northwestern University Press, 1973], 98). See also Russell Jacoby, *Dialectic of Defeat* (New York: Cambridge University Press, 1981). Claude Lefort, incidentally, was Merleau-Ponty's student.

39. This hope is made explicit in the conclusion of *Questions de méthode* (1976, 231–51), but is already at work here. After 1956, Sartre would drop his Leninist conception of the Party while continuing to work within a Marxist framework. Ironically, Sartre's political stance after the Soviet invasion of Hungary was a turn toward the positions of Claude Lefort, whom he had so harshly criticized in the 1953 article. The most elaborate defense of the possibility of an "existential Marxism" was sustained in Poster 1975, where the discussion of Sartre's 1952–54 texts is at 161–79.

40. Witness this dialogue between Sartre and an imagined Left-dissident (*gauchiste*) critic: "[Gauchiste:] So who do you say refused to go on strike? [Sartre:] Individuals, lets say a great number of them, even the vast majority of workers. —Isn't that what's called the proletariat? —No, it isn't" (1964b, 180).

CHAPTER 7

The Proletarian as Utopian Father: Sartre's Politics of the 1950s

> Le prolétaire ne se caractérise pas par sa profession, comme on le croit habituellement, mais par sa sexualité. Le prolétaire, c'est le prolifique, attelé au lourd chariot de la perpétuation de l'espèce.
> —Michel Tournier[1]

As the cold war reached its first peak in the early 1950s and after long hesitation and an abortive attempt to organize a political grouping called the Rassemblement démocratique révolutionnaire (RDR), Sartre decided it was time to work in direct support for "the vanguard of the proletariat."[2] The product of the ensuing furious activity is a series of four sweeping, sometimes vicious, polemical articles born out of what one writer has called "instinctual reaction [*réaction pulsionnelle*]" (Cohen-Solal 1980, 430). Sartre's epic political writings appeared between 1952 and 1954 in his mediatic organ and intellectual tribunal, *Les Temps modernes*. In this chapter, I will locate and elucidate the theme of paternity as it constructs itself in these writings and as it functions within the larger context of Sartre's ethical positions.

Activism versus Solitude

The avowed intent of the 1952–54 writings was to rally sympathizers among the French intelligentsia to the PCF at a moment when it was coming under fierce and unprecedented attacks from the government. Furthermore, Sartre idealistically hoped that his writings could find an audience within the working class: in addition to swaying Leftist intellectuals, he thought that these diatribes might rekindle the dwindling support of proletarians for the party that purported to be theirs. To achieve this goal (although he never seems to be addressing workers), Sartre embarks on a historical analysis of the proletarian as *activist*. This project of glorification, however, is quickly brushed aside to make way for a less heroic, at times rather dismal, yet much more compelling study of the proletarian as *defeatist*.

Under normal circumstances, in circumstances under which the proletariat displays the demeanor of solidarity witnessed at the great revolutionary moments of history, oppression falls upon the worker as a force imposed from outside his world by the dominant class. By 1952, however, this being-as-group called party activism, the principal feature of "normal circumstances," had been severely curtailed not only by government repression, it is true, but principally by worker apathy. Sartre describes oppression, in the case of the apathetic worker, as a corrosive agent eating away at his being from within. As the empathetic language of Sartre's Leninistic diatribes clearly reveals, the author is actually more fascinated with those pariahs of the working class who refuse party activism than he is with the party militants with whom he had virtually joined forces through his wholehearted support of the PCF.

In their own autonomous way, however, these apolitical workers are activists: they carry out their activism in the very private realm of paternity. And paternity proves, rather astoundingly in the context of this reputedly most political of periods in Sartre's career, to be a much more profound preoccupation than politics. In his attempts to explain worker apathy and lack of allegiance to the PCF in 1952, Sartre portrays these mavericks as family men caught up in their responsibilities as fathers and husbands.

> I can't go on strike because I have three kids and my wife just had an accident. (1964b, 182)
>
> . . . do people think that the strikers of 1920, 1936, 1947 were all unmarried and childless? (183)
>
> If he still happens to say to himself as he looks at his kids, "They'll see the revolution—not me," it's mainly a way of thinking about his own death. (192)[3]
>
> From time to time a statement is pointed out that can be taken as a general assessment of the situation: the worker recognizes that he's had it up to here with politics. . . . Today workers are heard to say, "I'm fed up with politics," or else women say to their husbands, "You'd do well not to bother with politics: what use is it *since nothing will be changed*? Politics isn't for the meek." For now, you will only hear these thoughts from the mouths of women—and of some men. No matter, it's a sign. (194; italics in original)

Conditioned, as we are, to the nearly uniform male orientation of Sartre's writings, these vignettes should strike the reader as lending a voice, stripped of cynicism, to women's concerns and even depicting women with the uncharacteristic compassion we saw only fleetingly in *The Age of Reason*. The working man's consideration for his spouse's well-being and for her opinion is altogether atypical of men's attitudes toward women in Sartre's writings. But in the 1952–54 articles, the tone becomes sympathetic toward the *women of the proletariat* and understanding of a husband who would listen to those women's advice. Apolitical outspokenness coming from a feminine voice constitutes a major force luring the already apathetic worker even further away from the PCF, thus eroding the original political intent of Sartre's articles. Exaggerating Leninist doctrine, Sartre insists that a worker outside the Party is a worker totally isolated. Yet his own glimpses into the worker's private life belie this putative isolation by surrounding him with wife and children and allowing him a feeling of solidarity and security within the *oikos*. As with Bariona, who was "converted" to paternity by his wife, solitude—that greatest horror of modern life—cannot affect the nonaligned worker as long as he aligns himself with the private sphere of the family group.

Multiply and Survive

By etymological definition, the proletarian is quintessentially a producer of offspring. The *proletarius* was a Roman citizen of the lowest class who served the state not by lineage, political skill, or the amount of property owned, but with the sheer quantity of his offspring (*proles*). The more children he and his wife produced, the more relative prosperity the *proletarius* acquired and the more he lived up to his social label. What obsesses Sartre as he writes in the early 1950s of proletarian destiny in crisis is the thought that this traditional proletarian fecundity might soon end. Against the logic of consumerism, which had modified Marxist economic analysis long before Sartre knew anything about it, he claims (in the 1952–54 texts) that the capitalist need for more human resources began to be satiated by the mid-1800s and that, from then on, instead of constituting a renewable resource for capitalist expansion, the increasing number of proletarians posed a demographic threat to the continued existence of the bourgeoisie.

> The trouble with capitalism is that it engenders its own grave-diggers and in the 1800s those grave-diggers had begun to swarm [*pulluler*]. Not only was the working class expanding due to the rural influx, on top of that it was making the most children. (1964b, 286)

Sartre asserts that wholesale massacres of teeming hordes of subhumans (such as the repression of the Paris Commune in 1871) were the first desperately primitive attempts to stave off a menace of proletarian proliferation.

> [But the] Versaillais had only assassinated a handful of people; their children suddenly discovered that those dead

> had a countless posterity. "This has got to be stopped" [the bourgeois say to themselves]. (288)

When capitalism discovered that exterminating workers was less like killing roaches than like cutting worms into segments and watching them grow back in even greater numbers, more subtle methods for depopulation, contends Sartre, had to be employed.

Sartre's obsession with neo-Malthusianism derives from this line of reasoning. In 1952, he feared, contraceptive practices were so widespread among workers that the demographic threat of the nineteenth century was reversed: population control was decimating the working class.[4] Seventy years before "The Communists and Peace," "countless" proletarians threatened the existence of the bourgeoisie. In 1952, the size of the bourgeoisie threatened to make the proletariat extinct. The rapid disappearance of the proletariat was taking place on two fronts: quantity and quality. By practicing contraception and even abortion, proletarian women and men had taken it upon themselves to shrink their own numbers.[5] Thus the ultimate goal of Malthusian policy—procreational "self-discipline"—had been attained and, worse yet, the very act of adopting family planning methods was a sure sign (to Sartre) that workers had mutated into bourgeois (the verb *s'embourgeoiser* is used frequently and ominously). "The Communists and Peace" was, to a large extent, a plea for the proletarian's conversion back to paternity—the proletarian activity par excellence.

To save the proletarian from extinction, Sartre calls for a return to the subhuman's former fecundity.[6] A lexical study of the descriptive, even lyrical, passages in "The Communists and Peace" reveals Sartre imagining himself as a nostalgic stroller through the teeming working-class districts of nineteenth-century Paris. In pushing for a normative proletariat, in telling his readers (as if they were workers) how the proletariat *should* live, Sartre deploys a liberal use of the verbs *pulluler, grouiller (de vie), regorger* ("to teem," "to swarm," "to crawl with," "to be alive, to brim over with" are some equivalents), and of the adjective *innombrable*.[7] Gradually attuning ourselves to the mood Sartre creates, we realize that he is persuading us semantically to take a favorable look at a quality of being that, in *The Roads to Freedom* for example, was absolutely revolting not only to Mathieu, but to virtually all the saga novel's male characters. The vocabulary of the (re)productivity that Sartre says would revive the proletarian and restore him to his true being contains the same terminology that epitomized Daniel and Mathieu's repulsion at Marcelle's pregnancy, fecundity, and the feminine in general. Mathieu was repelled by anything sticky or humid, just as the "viscous" was the repulsive "quality of being" that Sartre associated with the feminine.[8] Contact with that "viscous" was said to be a necessary step in the attainment of total being. Thus, paternity, undissociable from the viscous, became Mathieu's eternally missed opportunity both to attain a freedom ballasted by responsibility and, thus, to rise above his subhumanity.

In 1952, on the other hand, the proletarian's very survival depended on *this* subhuman's being able to restore the viscous to its proper function, as it were, as medium and emblem of reproduction. The primordial impotence of the apathetic worker is not merely political, as Sartre's overt message would have us believe: the proletarian weakness Sartre combats is primarily sexual. But the question remaining, as Sartre's occasional vignettes of private life suggest, is whether the proletarian can still produce children or whether he is condemned to childlessness. In either case, either through his association with fecundity and the viscous or through his inactivity, today's nonaligned proletarian is, within Sartre's value system, a "feminized" subhuman. Is Sartre now valorizing that "feminization"?

Scenes from a Proletarian Desert

The subhuman Sartre decided to rescue in 1952 had lost his virility. By practicing abortion and birth control, the proletarian was not only knocking at the door of extinction: worse yet, he was mutating into a bourgeois (*s'embourgeoiser*). And as Sartre's literary characterizations of the bourgeois demonstrate, there was nothing softer than their being. By adopting bourgeois-developed population controls, everything about the proletarian had begun to lack consistency. The adverb *mollement*,[9] used so frequently in *The Age of Reason* to describe Marcelle and then gradually in describing Mathieu, was now applied to the proletarian.[10] After attacking Claude Lefort, in the infamous

"Response" (1953), for having purportedly promoted the image of a "gelatinous" proletarian, Sartre *himself* turned around, through labyrinthine rhetoric to be sure, and acknowledged that, in the present state of affairs, the proletariat indeed had the consistency of jelly.

> The jellylike proletariat [*prolétariat-tremblotin*] is indeed out there, but this variable mixture of viscosity and pulverulence may just as easily produce separation, impotence, and solitude. All the mystical words that the eclectic sociologist employs to express his presentiment of the ineffable will not erase the fact that men can be reunited through solitude, through shared impotence, through resignation and that their manner of being-one-for-all can in fact be a mutual distancing, antagonism, or repulsion. (1965, 54)

Proletarian softness is not just a metaphor for the worker's unwillingness or inability to reproduce and, hence, a cause of solitude. This viscousness is not just a medium in which the proletarian risks drifting away from his fellow proletarians through antagonism and even repulsion, these "feminine" qualities are also those within which and through which he can discover solace in apposition with his peers. This is the sense of that most incongruous situation that Sartre describes by the oxymoronic expression "reunited through solitude." Even in the worst of circumstances, with impotence having become generalized, proletarians stick together in their "shared impotence" (*commune impuissance*). By acknowledging a soft quality in the proletarian and, in a wider sense, recognizing a feminine or feminized aspect of the masculine subject, Sartre discovers (against the wishes expressed in *The Words*) a way to advocate the restoration of proletarian viscosity to its *literal* function as reproductivity and thereby mediate total being.

Because these texts do not overtly convey Sartre's determination to revive proletarian fecundity, it is not readily apparent that remarks made about problems in the capitalist production of goods are subject to an inexorable slippage into observations about difficulties in the reproduction of proletarian offspring. However, among the several types of reproduction inherent to capitalist production, Marx did discuss biological reproduction or "perpetuation of the labourer."[11] But to Jean-Paul Sartre, Marxist apologist, this perpetuation becomes exclusively a product of biological functions. "We live poorly because we produce too little and at prices that are too high" (1964b, 260), Sartre rhetorically concedes to critics of the PCF. But instead of indicting proletarians for low productivity at the assembly line, Sartre shifts registers, invoking their unwillingness to produce *offspring*, calling them "derelict procreators" or "natality quitters" (*démissionnaires de la natalité*) in several instances.

Were the proletarian simply unwilling to reproduce himself, Sartre might see his self-appointed mission of converting him to paternity as merely a matter of reeducation. But the predicament is more serious: "softness" is a symptom of the proletarian's ingrained sexual, as well as spiritual, impotence. Impotence affects not only the lower but also the upper regions of the body. When Sartre repeats the Marxist thesis that the capitalist mode of production "empties the producer of his *substance*" (1965, 65), he stresses both the abstract essence of his being as commodity and, literally, a measurable quantity of matter. The same sterility afflicts, for example, the office worker whose fatigue "makes him a diminished man *in the literal sense of the term* [*au sens propre*]" (1964b, 332; italics added). Restoring such commonplaces to their literal (one might say organic) status is an integral process in Sartre's own investigation of the subhuman's being, and it amounts to an invitation for us to do so also. When he writes that the civil servant is a "diminished man," he means that he is both impotent and, quite literally (*au sens propre*), reduced in size. Sartre endows, as we shall now see, the very being of the subhuman with the properties of erectile tissue, that is, tissue that either increases or decreases in size and turgidity depending on whether fluid is accumulating in it or draining from it. As bizarre as the suggestion appears that, beyond mere comparison or metaphor, the being of Sartre's proletarian functions like a penis, this is nonetheless the most apt description of the subhuman's being as Sartre asks us to understand it in these articles from the early 1950s. A dysfunction in this being-for-reproduction causes the problem Sartre grapples with in these texts. His substance sapped, the being of the proletarian has been "reduced" to softness instead of rising to the role of incarnating the dialectic of both softness and hardness that was the hallmark of his original procreativeness.

Impotence to Fruitfulness: Mind over Matter

"Every evening in Levallois-Perret and in Charenton, the working multitude explodes and scatters. Another multitude, returning from all directions, replaces it" (1964b, 288). Reminiscing about the late nineteenth-century heroic period of proletarian history during which the first truly revolutionary stirrings were felt and when proletarian offspring subsisted in abundance, Sartre unabashedly invokes male ejaculation to stand for the explosion of the European worker population that first struck terror in the bourgeoisie concerning its own demographic status. Individual proletarians, like so many spermatozoa, were scattered (*s'éparpiller*) far and wide where they, in their turn, reinitiated spontaneous proletarian regermination. This fruitfulness that so fascinated Zola[12] is, by Sartre's reckoning, all but ended by 1952: "crushed by bourgeois forces, overburdened by the feeling of his impotence, . . . dead-tired, where might he find the seed of this spontaneity?" (246).[13] The sole answer to this rhetorical question lies in Sartre's belief that such a "seed" (*germe*) for renewing the proletarian's paternal instinct has ironically survived and is still potent enough to overcome the bourgeois infection of neo-Malthusianism. Sartre compels us to take his use of the word *seed* at face value because, in expressing his belief in some sort of proletarian eternal spirit, he once again invokes the images of erectile tissue and applies them to the source of sexual excitement in the upper body. The proletarian's somatic erectile forces have perhaps waned, but his brain is still rough and ready. His potential for hardness dwells—and as we shall now read, swells—in the deepest reaches of his psyche.

> There is a stiffening [*raidissement*], a hardening [*durcissement*] of the worker's mind [*conscience*]. Where does this erectile spirit [*conscience*] reside? In the unconscious . . . that's where it rises up, turgid [*s'érige turgide*]. (1964b, 213)[14]

We already have seen how literally Sartre takes the letter of Marx: when capitalism empties the worker of his substance, that substance is sperm. The proletarian thus loses his procreative forces under prolonged exposure to capitalism. Drained of his vitality, the quantifiable substance of virility diminishes: unable to produce his viscous quality of being, the worker falls below even his own subhumanity. But a proletarian is still a proletarian and the potential for an erectile force that can once again make him a procreator—*what he is*—inhabits his unconscious.

But if we assume for the moment (with Sartre) that something deeply embedded in the proletarian "unconscious" (strange terminology for someone so opposed to the concept) can still marshal such vital forces, then what exactly impedes the subject in bringing these forces to the fore and resuming the production of offspring? Let us read the continuation of the preceding quotation in seeking some clues: "[the erectile spirit] rises up, turgid and at first invisible, then scatters into thousands of refusals" (1964b, 213). The evocation of legions of negations emitted in what is meant to evoke some sort of ejaculation produced in the proletarian mind returns us to the theme of "derelict procreators" who have succumbed to bourgeois population control. In the late nineteenth century, when the proletariat was in its glory, during "the terrifying rise of the proletariat" (289), the working class disseminated *real,* fertile spermatozoa. Today, says Sartre, the class ejaculates seeds that say "no"—metaphorically referring to worker apathy in the form of abstentions at the ballot boxes of 1952. This proliferation of refusals underscores the inherent lack of uniformity of opinion among workers outside their families, a lack of unity that Sartre, despite his overt support for a Stalinist Party, already admires at this early date.[15] As for the image's metonymic value in designating the proletarian class, the "thousands of refusals" produced when the individual worker's unconscious detonates signifies the practice of contraception and abortion. As in *Bariona,* Sartre's 1940 Christmas play about paternity among the oppressed, today's worker refuses to let children be born.

The great danger Sartre warns about in these articles is in the proletarian procreational dialectic of hardness and softness only subsisting as an *imaginary* system faintly inscribed in the proletarian unconscious. When it was still a viable dialectic corresponding to organic reality, the worker, though oppressed, thrived in a mode proper for transforming his subhumanity into full being. The procreative forces of the 1952 proletarian go untapped: either they are repressed or, when they do resurface, they do so in a contraceptive or infertile mode.

Conversion Factors

Et la conception de cet être, de cet atome vivant lancé parmi les êtres, est auguste et sacrée, d'une incalculable importance, décisive peut-être.

—Emile Zola[16]

Throughout his career, Sartre believed that, in the subhuman, a particular aptitude for accession to full being could be gained through some radical conversion. At the 1952 flash point in Sartre's political involvement, his model in sustaining this thesis was the proletarian who, being the quintessential subhuman according to Marx, is historically ripe for ontological metamorphosis: " . . . he will not become *another man* except by a sort of conversion" (1964b, 247; italics in original). But, as with Bariona (the subhuman examined in 1940), the proletarian political conversion of 1952 must be founded on paternity, despite the professed politics of reconverting the worker to Party activism expressed in "The Communists and Peace" and "Response to Claude Lefort." The terms *conversion, metamorphosis,* and *transformation* that appear throughout the 1952–54 texts are elliptical designations for the very endorsement of paternity we saw taking place in *Bariona*—a homology of purpose we may hypothesize because of the two principles by which Sartre guides his argument: (1) a proletarian is, by definition, a producer of offspring, and (2) because paternity requires a constant readjustment with regard to the freedom of another being to whom one is unavoidably attached, it is the original process of perpetual conversion that serves as the model for the totalized individual within the social system.

Sartre argues that abortion, contraception, and sterility threatened the existence of the proletariat. But when he finally elucidates his position on what the being of the proletarian is, he does so by means of contrasting styles in procreation: "to be bourgeois isn't difficult: just aim well at the natal uterus. . . . Nothing harder, on the contrary, than to be proletarian" (1964b, 247). Unlike Bariona, who was an imperfect prototype for perpetual conversion through paternity because he sacrificed himself before his role as father had fully materialized as an interpersonal relationship, the proletarian has a collective historical past as procreator to live up to. He thus retains a class-generated "memory" of responsibility in the past and an idea of how universal responsibility could be instituted in the future. Once converted back to paternity, there will be no question of a return to the past and the wildly uncontrolled duplications of himself. The difficulty in this conversion to a new paternity is not in the act of procreation itself, but in the establishment of a new relationship between fathers and sons that would transcend the old norms of male struggles for dominance. The ideal proletarian father must not turn away in the last instance, as Bariona did, from his responsibility as father. The embodiment of procreation will once again procreate, but in doing so will concentrate on *who* it is he is creating in the process. The new paternity that Sartre envisions for the proletarian (and, through this model, for all humans) is a precarious but viable balance between hardness and softness, masculinity and femininity, lightness and weight, death and (re)birth, father and son, carrying and being carried.[17] This brings us to how Sartre articulates conversion in the 1952–54 texts.

The ontogenesis of the individual subhuman is homologous to what Sartre says concerning the history of the working class: he treats the individual proletarian as he does the collectivity known as the proletariat—an organic being that has not yet reached maturity. The proletarian's case is "a confused story, full of delays and *lost chances,* in which he seems to spend himself in making up for an *originary handicap*" (1965, 59; italics added). The resemblance between the proletarian's primordial backwardness that is caused by a series of "lost chances" and Mathieu's prolonged embryonic ontological state is no coincidence: Mathieu was simply another subhuman (a bourgeois leftist intellectual), albeit less successful at attaining total being, in Sartre's constellation of subhumans. Mathieu condemned himself to wait for his rise to full humanity to happen to him. But, whereas Mathieu spent himself aimlessly in trying to make up for his "originary handicap," the proletarian only appears to toil in vain. Due to the worker's privileged status among Sartrean subhumans, his backwardness is bound "to suddenly be metamorphosed" without anyone's noticing (60), as in that sudden burst of ejaculatory spirit discussed earlier. The 1952–54 texts then form a continuum with the unfinished *Roads to Freedom*, picking up where they left off, supplying answers to the enigmatic question of what Mathieu missed by not endorsing paternity.

There is agreement between an "early" and a "late" Sartre, that is, between the individualistic and the more social-minded Sartre—agreement in considering that the being of humans approaches completeness only when a practical basis for all future actions has been established autonomously and when the morality of these future actions is guaranteed by an equally "self-made" ethical system.[18] Sartre unconditionally maintains that proletarian conversion is the way to attaining total being: "the worker finds the source of his practical reality in his metamorphosis. Whatever he thinks or does, that source is his conversion" (1964b, 250). As for the ethical being that this metamorphosis might yield, the heroic worker movements of the last century prelude an answer, giving one the sense that conversion already inhabits the proletarian, again, as a potential force in his unconscious.

> Revolutionary syndicalism is the proletarian himself, exalted by his solitude and proud of his abandonment [*délaissement*] . . . he decides to pull all that is inside of him—even ethical values—from his own depths. . . . In 1871 . . . what is sometimes called syndicalist imperialism or worker totalitarianism is nothing less than the admirable turning inside out of a caste of pariahs. All they wished for was to be *something*. They were condemned to being *nothing*. Thus they demand to be *everything*. (282; italics added)

Retournement, which I have translated here as "turning inside out," also means reversal—that of the sociopolitical hierarchy. Had they not been exploited by the bourgeoisie, perhaps proletarians would have remained satisfied with their partial humanity. But the brokers of capital made life miserable for them, relegating them to a status outside "humanity," putting proletarians in such a dire situation that they now demand "to be everything"—to possess the full humanity that even their oppressors lack without knowing it. But, again, the universal reversal of the sociopolitical hierarchy can only take place if the individual proletarian commits himself to an internal reversal of old values—"one becomes revolutionary through an internal revolution" (246). Reversal, turning inside out, metamorphosis, transformation: all of these stand for the conversion to paternity and the exchangeability of the burden of responsibility between father and son that enables the subhuman to overcome his subhumanity and become fully human.

Woman as Vanguard of the Proletariat

"Between the class, as activity, . . . and the mass, as passive product . . . there must be a mediation. There must be *someone* . . ." (1965, 67; italics in original). How does the conversion take place? The proletarian cannot accomplish it alone. If he is not consistent anywhere else, Sartre is at least consistent here with the overt campaign he undertook in favor of Party mediation. Yet *someone* is an unexpected word in the context of a Leninist political stance in the early 1950s: *someone,* not *something* (e.g., the Party), serves as sponsor for the transformation that leads the proletarian out of his dilemma. Sartre adopted the Marxist dichotomy of class versus mass only to translate outward, from the private toward the social context, the two modes immanent to the subhuman's being: (1) when that subhuman procreates, he is active; (2) when he is sterile, he is passive. Activity entails evolution toward the goal of total being; passivity entails arrested development. By a similar translation, we may say that the internal conversion of the proletarian (cf. 1964b, 246) is not mediated by an outside other, but by another individual within the sphere of intimate empirical experience.

A woman, the mother of his child, is this intimate other who mediates the proletarian's conversion. The first of several indications that support this claim is that, in the 1952–54 texts themselves, Sartre makes a point of presenting the wives of workers as significant lobbyists in their husbands' decisions about politics. He sometimes even shows them as policymakers themselves, independent of their husbands' opinions. Second, because these texts follow thematically in the trace of *Bariona* and *The Roads to Freedom*, we can venture that, like the Sarah in each of those works, proletarian women will be influential in the key issue of conversion to paternity. Finally, and quite obviously, the female body is the biologically necessary medium for the "transformation" of individual (male *or* female) into parent.

This leads back, once again, to the chapter entitled "Of Quality as Revelation of Being" in *Being and Nothingness* and to the manner in which Sartre incorporated its imagery focused on "the viscous" into *The Age of Reason*. Recalling the detailed discussion in chapter 5, anything sticky and moist was a reminder of Mathieu's repulsion at women and, by association, his abhorrence of human reproductivity. In the 1943 text, after some rather lurid descriptions of "the viscous" in objects that supposedly show its inescapable importance in human reality and imagination and after putting forth the suggestion of a link between man and "the viscous" that strongly resembles the relationship between a father and a son, Sartre asserted that this "quality" is the means by which the for-itself gets a glimpse of the state of total being that he covets: "the viscous already appears as the sketching out of a fusion of the world with me" (1943, 668); "the viscous is myself in ideal form" (667).

Mathieu was comfortable in his sexual contact with women only as long as he avoided setting off conception. Practicing coitus interruptus with Marcelle allowed him to maintain an illusion of a sexual (and ontological) difference between man and woman based on entirely illusory hard/soft, solid/liquid, and active/passive dichotomies. This ideological comfort with phallic resistance, derived from a policy of nonreproductive sex, is directly translated from *Being and Nothingness*, where the for-itself (male) mistakes the *sticky* viscous for mere water: "if I thrust myself [*si j'enfonce*] into water, if I plunge into it, if I let myself flow, I feel no discomfort [or embarrassment: *gêne*] because I don't at all fear becoming diluted: *I remain solid within fluidity*" (1943, 672; italics added). In "The Communists and Peace," Sartre denounced just such facile but fertile intercourse, where the demarcations between masculine and feminine are as overdetermined as in the reproductive practices of the bourgeoisie: "to be bourgeois isn't difficult: just aim well at the natal uterus, then lay back and be carried" (1964b, 247).

As in so many other respects, *The Age of Reason* may be seen here too as a transitional text, for it lies at the turning point between the machismo displayed in *Being and Nothingness* and the more ambivalent writings of the early 1950s. Mathieu decided that he had become nothing better than the bourgeois genitors described so vividly when his accidental intrauterine ejaculation shattered his illusion of simplistic sexual dualisms: "Do those who have decided solemnly to be fathers, who feel like genitors, understand better than I do? They went at it blindly, with three prick thrusts [*en trois coups de queue*]" (1981, 411). Yet reproduction is not, according to *Being and Nothingness,* as comforting as all that (but then again, the for-itself knows he is a subhuman, while the bourgeois deludes himself into thinking he has it all). When the for-itself realizes that what he has sunk himself into is not water but "the viscous," he is overcome by the nauseating feeling that this contact has brought him face to face with death.

> If I sink into the viscous, I feel that I will lose myself in it, become diluted into a viscous substance myself, precisely because the viscous is solidification in process. (1943, 672)

In other terms, the loss of erection after ejaculation leads to man's sinking feeling that he has been absorbed or ingested by the feminine—that "fishy" (*louche*), ambivalent quality between the hard and the soft. Yet in the political texts of 1952–54, this contact and mingling with the viscous, because it constitutes a radical conversion of the *illusion* of sexual difference into the *truth* of ethical sameness becomes a requirement for total being. Sartre's paragraph on the necessary and terrifying "sinking into the viscous" ends with the statement that "the very apprehension of the viscous is like being haunted by a *metamorphosis*" (672; italics in original).

The progress that "The Communists and Peace" marks in Sartre's thought is one which dispels the *feared* metamorphosis founded on delusions about death, and it confirms the valued metamorphosis. After his derisive description of bourgeois-style reproduction, Sartre dramatically enunciates what the proletarian must overcome in order to procreate again: "nothing is more difficult than being a proletarian: he affirms himself only through thankless and onerous action, by overcoming fatigue and hunger, dying to be reborn" (1964b, 247). There are several interconnected meanings to this "dying to be reborn" reaffirming the key concept of metamorphosis while providing more details on what the change involves. By standing in parallel construction with the peremptory "aiming at the natal uterus" of the bourgeois paterfamilias, the idea of proletarian resurrection implicitly describes the renewed reproductive activities of subhumans. Not only does the proletarian risk his life, overcoming great hardships in order to reproduce himself, he does so in the act of procreation itself. Besides, the "little death" (*la petite mort*), the idea that orgasm is a scrape with Thanatos from which one narrowly escapes, is a fairly common expression in French. Although a hyperbolic commonplace for the popular notion that procreation perpetuates the species (as parents die off, their children replace them), we cannot fail to recognize in "dying to be reborn" the Biblical expression for resurrection, for the complete renewal of being mediated by radical conversion. In Sartre's ethical thought, there is undeniably a residual persistence of Christian ideology.

The phrases "to be proletarian" and "to affirm himself" indicate clearly enough that the proletarian father survives the "ordeal" after which he will engage in a relationship with his son. Proletarian paternity does not cause death, some form of which Mathieu undoubtedly feared: the experience, Sartre contends, confronts the subject only with a risk of death. This is extremely important because the endorsement of paternity meant certain death for the father almost everywhere else in Sartre's work. Bariona no sooner welcomed the birth of his child than he marched off to war. No sooner was Poulou born, according to Jean-Paul in *The Words,* than Jean-Baptiste died. As Hollier writes in *The Politics of Prose,* the reader of *Bariona* as well as *The Words* is led to conclude that "there is no father except a dead one" (1986, 89). However, the endorsement of paternity advocated in "The Communists and Peace" does not entail this quick exit by the father into death. Paternity, if it is to be a relationship at all, requires the father's survival. It is as if the *risk* of death, like the deferral of sexual pleasure, only increases the value of the father-son relationship. In his "Response to Claude Lefort," Sartre confirms that the risk of death is necessary for the proletarian to complete his transformation. Lending the proletarian a historical role in society, he says to his young opponent, is not enough unless he is allowed his "passion," which Sartre defines as "the possibility of suffering, of withering, of even dying" (1965, 57).[19] Conversion to full humanity, the metamorphosis into whole being, is not complete unless the subject is constantly reminded and even threatened by life's converse, death.

Notes

1. The proletarian is not characterized by his profession, as it is usually thought, but by his sexuality. The proletarian is the prolific: harnessed to the heavy chariot of the perpetuation of the species (Michel Tournier, *Les Météores* [Paris: Gallimard, 1975], 145; my translation).

2. For a recounting of Sartre's postwar debates with the PCF, eventually leading to his period of fellow traveling from 1952 to 1956, see Mark Poster, *Existential Marxism in Postwar France* (Princeton, N.J.: Princeton University Press, 1975), 125–44.

3. Even more enigmatic, and related to the first quote in this group (which also seems to refer to how baby workers are conceived) is the immediately preceding comment that "there are sometimes short-circuits in history . . . [the worker] must have been born during a black-out" (1964b, 192).

4. Another ratio that had become inverted, thus fueling Sartre's affinity for chiastic figures. The semantic organization of countless sentences in "The Communists and Peace" is that of the chiasmus.

5. Sartre writes as if abortion were a new procedure for the working class and in a tone indicating he thinks it the greatest offense to human dignity. Abortion was only made legal in France in 1974. Until then, only the wealthier strata of society could afford relatively safe abortions in clinics either in Nice (distant enough from Paris and where the practitioners could easily cross over into Italy to escape prosecution), Switzerland, or Britain where abortion had been legal since the mid-1960s. Illegal abortions were being carried out, often under deplorable health conditions, in great numbers among the working class until contraception and concomitant sex education were instituted in the late 1960s.

6. Even the Biblical themes of Bariona are not far off. God's admonition to man to "be fruitful, multiply, fill the earth and conquer it" (Gen. 1:28) is a strain heard throughout Sartre's studies of subhumans.

7. A typical example that incorporates these ideas is in a passage where Sartre compares the nonaligned workers to "molecular whirlpools, a multiplicity of infinitesimal reactions . . . a swarming of Lilliputian actions [*un pul-*

lulement de conduites lilliputiennes]" (1964b, 204). This atomization of the group is what Sartre actually fights *against*, as the *Critique of Dialectical Reason* will formally show, and yet it is to the prolific proletariat that he is calling upon workers to return.

8. Doubrovsky suggests that, in order to facilitate our reading of Sartre, we may quite simply and systematically replace the word *viscous* with *feminine*. See Serge Doubrovsky, "Phallotexte et gynotexte dans *La Nausée:* 'Feuillet sans date,'" in *Sartre et la mise en signe* (Paris: Klincksieck, 1982), 51 .

9. Roughly translatable as "feebly" or "indolently," but formed from the adjective *mou/molle* meaning "soft" or "flaccid." Related to it are the various ways in which Sartre describes the fatigue of the proletarian who is "reduced to his worn-out body" (1964b, 187). The word *épuisement* also underscores the draining of his "substance." The viscous, of course, is always near at hand: Sartre speaks of an "operation that the bourgeoisie pursues [to maintain] the working-class crowds in a fluid [thus helpless] state" (207).

10. "The worker still votes . . . but indolently [*mollement*]" (281). Related to the proletarian's indolence is his stagnation. "The country is mildewing from the bottom" (321). By metonymy, Sartre substituted the country for proletarian. This "mildewing" taking place "down below" (*par-dessous*) is an anatomical reference to the worker's sterility and also, in light of my reading of *The Age of Reason*, reveals his feminization. For Sartre, the female genitalia are a locus of rotting, a cloaca (see chap. 5).

11. Karl Marx, *Capital*, trans. Samuel Moore and Edward Aveling (New York: International Publishers, 1967), 1:571.

12. The fecundity of workers is the main reason Zola named his novel about miners in Northern France *Germinal*. One of his four secular Gospels was entitled *Fertility*.

13. It is remarkable that those who have analyzed these texts before, duplicating Sartre's suggestive vocabulary in doing so, do not go beyond his imagery to question its possible origins. As an example: "It was understandable to Sartre that the workers, weighed down, fatigued by the oppression of capitalism, would not rise to their historical task on every occasion" (Poster 1975, 171).

14. An analogous passage that anticipates some of my conclusions is found in *Notebooks for an Ethics:* " . . . proletarian minds are autonomous and unspoiled uprisings [*surgissements autonomes et frais*] not penetrated by bourgeois information. . . . Thus there is supercession that supercedes nothing and conservation that is not conservation" (1983a, 32).

15. Sartre's later support for autonomous leftist movements and for the proliferation of various (and not necessarily consistent) worker demands and programs would come only after his break with official PCF policy following Budapest. Such statements as "the masses demand nothing at all because they are nothing but dispersion" (1964b, 248) seem to run counter to the

belief in an *inherent* proletarian solidarity that is theoretically at the foundation of these writings.

16. "And the conception of this being, of this living atom thrown in among other beings, is august and sacred. It is of incalculable importance . . . decisive perhaps" (Emile Zola, *Fécondité* [Paris: François Bernouard, 1928], 1:102; my translation).

17. A footnote to the passage I have just examined reads: "the proletariat should be the carrier of human values" (1964b, 247).

18. Without being ordered to act by any other, man imposes upon himself a mandate by which he will perform acts gratuitously. Autonomous action or self-reliance is one of the most consistent principles of Sartre's thought.

19. Here again, as in so many other places, Sartre argues in complete contradiction with himself. A historical role for the proletarian is precisely what (as he argues throughout "The Communists and Peace") Party membership can furnish him (see 1964b, 153).

Part Five

Paternity Introjected

L'enfance comme création de
situations insolubles.
—*Cahiers pour une morale*

Je tourne encore mon esprit vers
mon enfant qui me lie à l'ordre
social, et dont l'existence aggrave
ma condition de serf. . . . Alors
ma respiration devient tout à fait
régulière car la tranquillité
m'apparaît comme le seul bien
souhaitable, dans un monde trop
méchant encore pour être capable de
se libérer, d'après les journaux.
—Francis Ponge[1]

Like Sartre's search in *Being and Nothingness* for a discrete, autonomous human subject who could embody the two aspects of being, his ethical search was for an interpersonal bond with as few of the drawbacks of alterity as possible: in an ideal world, total moral equality could exist between two beings. The full humanity into which the subhuman of the 1952–54 texts would be ushered by the maternal is a relationship of dependence on *another*. Sartre came to believe in a paternity (and thereby total being) that a father could endorse and endure, rather than having to escape through death. By surviving the conversion to this primordial intersubjective bond, the proletarian must not turn away from the bond with his son. From a gaze turned inward, a gaze with which he dwelled narcissistically on his own problems, the subhuman father would be compelled to look outward toward his offspring, who embodies the birth of the very same problems and passions in *an-other.* The aspect of conversion Sartre called *retournement* consists of the necessity for a father to "reverse," to "turn upside down" or "inside out" certain fundamentally held cultural principles for *reciprocity* to become possible.

To signify the acceptance of paternity, the word *endorsement* has been used throughout this study because the bond of paternity that Sartre foresees as leading to all ethical relationships is secured when two subjects mutually take responsibility for each other by taking an allegorical weight upon their backs. Fathers must regard their sons as beings who are both part of them and separate from them—both the same and different. An almost impossible balancing act of self-control, if it could succeed, Sartre assures us, this bond would form the basis for all other ethical relationships. The proletarian's utopian conversion would therefore transform his existence into unending compromise by permanently establishing a network of *differences* with which he would be compelled to reckon, differences caused by the fundamental *sameness* between himself and his son.[2]

The means by which Sartre sought this ideal bond involved rejecting the rotten duality handed down to us, searching for a new one, and embracing it as soon as it is found. His difficulties arose from the fact that the new bond had to be absolutely perfect or else Sartre would scrap it and begin anew. He expresses his vision of the new bond by variations on the reciprocal equation "toi c'est moi, moi c'est toi." Yet, just as the for-itself is separated from the in-itself by an incommensurable rift, Sartre's characters who strive for ideal intersubjectivity seem inevitably to fail in achieving that mutuality. The father-son relationship that the proletarian's conversion to paternity heralds is a tentative fulfillment of Sartre's requirement of identity and reciprocity. In order for that new being (which the subhuman creates for and of himself in creating a child) to be *total* being, the parent must dwell in interdependence with its child. This total being does not reside in the father nor in his son, but between the two generations. Total being is founded when reciprocity between *partial* beings is established in the milieu that surrounds them, defining their environment. Similar to Merleau-Ponty's concept of the "chiasmus of perception," or the way he conceived of the relationship between perceiver and perceived,[3] Sartre's total being is created from a doubling of the ethical relationship described in *Being and Nothingness,* then a turning of that doubled relationship on its head. The ethical subject (alluded to in 1943 with the now familiar allegory of Atlas carrying the weight of the world on his shoulders) lacked foundation or, rather, grounding in that this bearer of universal responsibility also needed himself to be supported by something or someone. Paradoxically, as in the legend of Saint Christopher, the ethical subject finds this support in Sartre's images of the child—the being who, as Lucien Fleurier, Werner von Gerlach, and other characters illustrate, is the *carried* being par excellence. Sartre's sketchy notebooks for an ethics corroborate this literary characterization of the child's being: "The child is first an object. We begin by being carried" (1983a, 22).

Jacques Derrida has also spoken of a reciprocal relationship that I find helpful in visualizing the Sartrean enigma of a new ethical bond. He compares two commentaries on Van Gogh's paintings of shoes.[4] An intricate controversy pitted Heidegger and Meyer Schapiro against each other over whether those shoes belonged to a city or country dweller, a man or a woman. Derrida calls this a controversy over the "restoration" (*restitution*) of the objects to their "wearer" (*porteur*). To the puns derived from the two meanings of *porter* ("to wear," "to carry," "to bear"), Derrida adds the ambiguity between that which *is carried* (or *worn—être porté*) and he who *carries* (*porteur*) and discovers that both the shoes, as object, and the indeterminate wearer, as subject, may be considered *porteurs portés* ("carried carriers").

> As soon as these abandoned shoes no longer have any strict relationship with a subject borne [*porteur*] or bearing/wearing [*porté*], they become the anonymous, lightened, voided support (but so much the heavier for being abandoned to its opaque inertia) of an absent subject whose name returns to haunt the open form. (265)[5]

> Let's be more precise: *subject*-shoes (*support* destined to bear their wearer on the ground . . .) (266)
>
> From then on, if these shoes are no longer useful, it is of course because they are detached from naked feet and from their subject of reattachment (their owner, usual holder, the one who wears them and whom they bear [*porteur porté*]). . . . (304)
>
> *To shoe* equals *to be.* (370)

This line of reflection progressively reveals a vital ethical inderdependence between object and subject that may be applied to the similar functioning of the ethical interdependence between for-itself and other in Sartre's ethical thought.

Derrida's observation that both objects and subjects are "carried carriers" (*porteurs portés*) may be depicted in the following manner: (1) a shoe supports and, in a sense, carries its wearer along the ground (it is a "carrier worn"); (2) a person who wears the shoe is carried by it (he is a "wearer carried"); and (3) since "the carrier is worn [*porteur est porté*] to the exact extent that the wearer is carried [*porteur est porté*]," the perfect reciprocity of Sartre's "toi c'est moi, moi c'est toi" has been achieved. The two partial beings would finally seem joined, yet not homogenized into an undifferentiated being. The infant human, who is by nature carried, provides the foundation for the adult human, yet avoids being crushed. This answers our query about who was meant by the "someone who must transform [the worker's] graveness weighting him down into an ascending force, [the someone] who must transform his suffering into demand" in Sartre's political writings of the early 1950s (1965, 67).

The infant would thus seem to have become the *carried carrier.* The socially conscious adult human, on the other hand, who is by nature a *bearer,* would seem to have acquired support from his offspring: the *bearer is borne.* Yet somehow, Sartre indicates, the son (i.e., the subject, the oppressed, the subhuman, etc.) is still disadvantaged in his new intersubjectivity with the other. A residue of "bad" alterity, a trace of paternal ascendancy survives every new interpersonal bond that Sartre can conceive. His earlier ideal of totality in solitude instead of reciprocity proves too compelling. Despite the evidence we have presented of an eventual endorsement of paternity as an ethical model, Sartre's visceral need to reject it appears overpowering.

Taken as a whole, Sartre's work resists refining the conditions under which paternity could become the accepted model for responsible existence. In his 1955 study of Sartre's theater, Francis Jeanson observed an inherent bastardy, in a provocatively broad sense of the term, in most of Sartre's characters.[6] This glorification of illegitimacy would appear to proceed from Sartre's well-known rejection of paternity, confirming isolation as the offspring's definitive position vis-à-vis the father. Yet Sartrean bastardy is a peculiar and complex state of being that strongly reaffirms a paternal agency, while it rejects outside authority from the conceptualization of a utopian ethical being. This uniquely Sartrean bastardy requires an introjected paternity, as the texts studied in the final three chapters show.

Notes

1. "I yet turn my mind toward my child who binds me to the social order and whose existence deepens my status as serf. . . . Then my breathing becomes altogether regular, for tranquility seems to me the only desirable good in a world still too mean to liberate itself, so the newspapers say" (Francis Ponge, "Le Monologue de l'employé," in *Douze petits écrits* [Paris: Gallimard, 1926]; my translation).

2. "To engender the proletariat . . . the worker has not only to deal with his own activity, but also with his inertia" (1965, 57).

3. These ideas are given their most compelling elaboration in the work left unfinished at Merleau-Ponty's untimely death. A passage in this project reads: "activity is no longer the *opposite* of passivity. From that, carnal relations from below no less than from above and the fine point. Intertwine" (Maurice Merleau-Ponty, *Le visible et l'invisible* [Paris: Gallimard, 1964], 323; my translation).

4. Jacques Derrida, "Restitutions de la vérité en pointure," in *La Vérité en peinture* (Paris: Flammarion, 1978), 291–436.

5. Jacques Derrida, *The Truth in Painting*, trans. Geoff Bennington and Ian McLeod (Chicago: University of Chicago Press, 1987). Page references in the French original are 302, 303, 347, and 423, respectively.

6. Francis Jeanson, "Un théâtre de la bâtardise," in *Sartre* (Paris: Seuil, 1955), 7–113.

CHAPTER **8**

Bastardy versus Family

We are all bastards,
And that most venerable man which I
Did call my father was I know not where
When I was stamped.
—William Shakespeare[1]

L'avenir appartient aux bâtards.
—André Gide[2]

Pronouncements of the death of God in the second half of the nineteenth century signaled a radical alteration in Western thought, precipitating aesthetic dislocations and disruptions that gave rise to modernity. Along with the vacuum of power created by the disappearance of the "father of all beings" came a questioning of the advantages and drawbacks of fatherlessness on the individual level. Much of the literature produced since the historical cleavage associated with God's death knell has strived, in one form or another, to provide a portrait of how someone fatherless—a bastard—fares in life. After the reign of paternal authority and filial legitimacy would come that of bastardy.

In France, André Gide was one of the first to seize upon this aspect of the modern condition. Throughout his fifty-five-year career as a novelist, Gide held that those best equipped for confronting existence were illegitimate children. As early as his *Nourritures terrestres* he argued, through the voice of Ménalque, that the morally spent institution of the family only served to impede one's freedom.[3] Nathanaël's guide toward authentic existence utters such invectives against the natal household as: "Nothing is more dangerous for you than your family" (Gide 1935, 44); "I hated homes and families" (67); and the famous "Families, I hate you!" (69). Gide's exaltation of fervor and his rejection of moral imperatives had tremendous influence on French youth a generation before Sartre. Lafcadio, the bastard in *Les Caves du Vatican* and champion of the "gratuitous act," was one of the most controversial figures in early twentieth-century French literature.[4] Right-thinkers of the period were outraged at this glorification of nihilism and declared Gide an obnoxious element in society. Gide later made a more ambiguous hero emblematic of modern man in *Les Faux-monnayeurs*. Already considering himself the "son of a nobody [*fils d'un croquant*]" (Gide 1925, 11), a sort of bastard by default, Bernard finds the following encouraging lines scribbled in the diary of his mentor, Edouard: "The future belongs to bastards. What meaning does the expression 'natural child' harbor if not that only the bastard has rights to what is natural" (113).

A bastard is not the genuine article. Before the institution of modern laws of legitimation, the bastard stood outside the law: he was, consequently, outside classification, like the insane in Michel Foucault's analysis.[5] Today, the term *bastard* is employed less systematically in reference to family legitimacy and connotes anything that is impurely conceived. Thus, *bastard* comes to designate the mongrel dog, and like this undocumented, impure element within a legitimate grouping, the *image* of the human bastard's deleterious effects on "normal" or "normative" society are all the more powerful for his being detached from any predetermined set of values—be they of class or race. His presence within the bourgeoisie is as insidious as that of a cur in a canine stud farm or of a parasite in a healthy body. Thus, Sartre's wish, expounded in the last chapter of *Saint Genet*, is that he would ultimately like to see the *born* subversive, Jean Genet, undermine the capitalist system and its rotten ethics by his mere presence within it.

Sartre adopted the Gidean preference for bastardy and widened its applications in his efforts to forge a paradigm for his utopian ethical subject. He universalized the designation *bastard* by opening it to the derivative connotations of betweenness, impurity, hybridity, and monstrosity. In its most extreme avatar, the Sartrean bastard becomes a bipartite monster composed of those conflicting forces that oppose fathers and sons in the bond of paternity, which they apparently elude. The Sartrean bastard's being will accommodate both the radically free fatherless child and the emburdened ethical subject. Sartre thus takes up philosophical applications of bastardy that Gide left in suspense.

In his difficulty envisioning a positive father-son relationship, Sartre turned his attention to the quintessential son without a father: the bastard. But paradoxically, *fathers* are not forgotten in the formulation of a peculiarly Sartrean bastard. Generational strife becomes an antinomian struggle *within* the bastard-subject. Anxious (following his personally momentous meeting with Jean Genet) to harness the ethical potential that ontological bastardy might generate, Sartre inaugurated a series of textual experiments with Genet more or less as his model. The conclusion of the *Saint Genet* period was that the self-generated ethical subject is unrealizable under present sociological, economic, and political conditions. Yet that ethical model is constantly imagined and revised in the protagonists of various plays and the subjects of literary biographies. When Francis Jeanson wrote of Sartre's "theater of bastardy" in 1955, he was referring to Sartre's drama and *The Words*. The term could, however, without exaggeration, be applied to his entire work from the time Sartre encountered Genet until his death in 1980.

In order to see how Sartre broadens the definition of bastardy through his theater and what this expanded concept offers him, we must briefly examine the evolution of Sartre's biographical studies as inflected by that key figure, Jean Genet. In this genre, the major works Sartre undertook and published are *Baudelaire,*[6] *Saint Genet, The Words,*[7] and *The Family Idiot*. Sometimes wildly speculative, these works go well beyond that search for truth in an individual's life which we normally call biography. Through these lives, Sartre attempts to elucidate one of the keystones of *Being and Nothingness,* "original choice of being," or choice as a property of being in the process of becoming. That choice is the domain of the child. In other terms, what one is given as a child and what one does with what one is given *marks* us. Each of Sartre's biographies (as well as his autobiography) focus principally on their subject's childhood. Of their four subjects, only Jean Genet was truly an illegitimate child. Through the lens of *Saint Genet,* however, Baudelaire, Poulou,[8] and Flaubert become bastards in the larger Sartrean sense: Sartre elucidates their choices of being as those that only a bastard makes.

When his essay on Baudelaire appeared, Sartre was accused of having completely misunderstood his subject, resulting in his heavy-handed dismissal of the poet.[9] But one needs only to reread the harsh criticism Sartre heaped onto virtually all late-nineteenth-century writers in *What Is Literature?*, taxing them for their "retreat from reality," to see that, in 1947, Sartre's critical stance with respect to Baudelaire was practically indistinguishable from his assessment, nearly a quarter of a century later, of Flaubert.[10] Sartre treats the author of *Madame Bovary* with a sensitivity that the reader of *Baudelaire* might not have thought him capable. The prosaic manicheism of Sartre's critical discourse in *What Is Literature?* is already counterbalanced by a more circumspect analysis of those same authors in *Search for a Method,* appearing ten years later.[11] Similarly, *The Family Idiot* reconsiders the original choice of Gustave Flaubert in conjunction with a sort of bastardy he acquired within a "normal" family. In this sense and by its moderation, *The Family Idiot* also retrospectively rectifies Sartre's rather peremptory and callous treatment of Baudelaire in 1947.

The crucial factor in precipitating this inflection between *Baudelaire* and *Flaubert,* as well as between the 1947 theoretical text and its 1957 counterpart, is, without doubt, Sartre's acquaintance with Jean Genet. One senses an irrepressible excitement in Sartre's voice throughout *Saint Genet,* bringing him to write of the author of *Miracle de la rose:*[12] "I am sure I know him better than he knows me for I have the passion of understanding men" (1952, 132). Six years later, he wrote almost the same thing concerning his relation to another "bastard," André Gorz: "I know him better than anyone else. I've always known him. I'm going to tell you what I know about him" (Gorz 1958, 36).

Saint Genet began as an introduction that Gallimard commissioned from Sartre in 1949 for a "Complete Works of Jean Genet."[13] By the time it was published in 1952, this introduction was so monumental that it swallowed up the entire first volume of Genet's *Oeuvres com-*

plètes.[14] Sartre had been acquainted with Genet ever since Genet accosted him in the company of Camus at the Café de Flore in 1944. Sartre had heard of him previously and was already in awe that an ex-con could write with such depth and in such elegant prose (Beauvoir 1960, 663ff.). When Sartre learned that Genet, an illegitimate child, had been raised by the state, this only redoubled a vicarious obsession whose amplitude is substantiated by the scope and sheer weight of *Saint Genet*.[15]

> Adieux beaux lys, tout en finesse dans vos petits sanctuaires peints, adieux beaux lys, notre orgueil et notre raison d'être, adieux, Salauds.
>
> —*La Nausée*[16]

In the novel that launched Sartre's career, he already was raising the *salaud* ("dirty bastard") to the status of philosophical category and it is one of the first terms one learns to recognize in studying Sartre's writings. With this single invective, Sartre designates the oppressors he will struggle against to the end. The unrepentant bourgeois is at the source of all the injustices perpetrated in the modern world.[17] The uncanny resemblance between different generations of *salauds* in Roquentin's famous visit to the Bouville Museum attests to Sartre's belief that this type of bastardy is rooted in family. As we saw with "Childhood of a Boss" in chapter 2, spoiled little bourgeois bastards, provided they follow the paterfamilias example, grow up to be bosses themselves: passive "flowerpots" become active exploiters. All bourgeois are born conformists and all conformists are *salauds*.

By coincidence, both *salaud* and *bâtard* are best translated by the American English noun *bastard*. In other words, *bâtard* and *bastard* share the same set of meanings with the one crucial difference that, in this country, the word also connotes the morally reprehensible individual designated by *salaud*.[18] If a *salaud* is, by definition, a bourgeois or, in general, any oppressor, the term also includes the notion of paternalism—a characteristic of patriarchal society. Since *salaud* evokes the father while *bâtard* supposes the father's absence, the two categories would appear to be mutually exclusive. However, the Sartrean *bâtard* introjects the fatherly instance (without there being a paterfamilias) and the two bastards intertwine to approach total being.

In positing the universal bastard as his model for the future ethical subject, Sartre brought himself face to face with the concrete problem of total responsibility that so many of his characters evaded. Free of the father, the bastard is freer than his legitimate counterparts. He may become a *salaud* by his own doing, but as Sartre's prototype for the ethical subject, he possesses a potential for becoming infinitely more emburdened morally than the legitimate son. The "immoral" Sartrean bastard, Kean, pleads, "I want to weigh with my own weight" (1954, 65). If the *bâtard* is free of the father, then the example of Orestes teaches us that we must ask where his burden of incalculable moral weight will come from. The predictable paths by which Sartre attempted to dispense with the *salaud* will aid in understanding the unpredictability of the *bâtard*.

Heidegger described our original ontological condition as one of "thrownness" (*Geworfenheit*), evoking the sensation of having been dumped into existence as into a medium that nevertheless supports us.[19] From our state of thrownness, Sartre would demand that we make an "original choice of being" that is as undisturbed by external forces as possible. However, most of us, being deprived of the "privilege" of being *bâtards*, are brought up under the aegis of a *salaud* and the first medium we encounter—the family—is consequently not neutral, but noxious. Therefore, the reprehensible behavior of our forebears is virtually unavoidable. And any form of filial piety leads to contemptible choices of being. As Lucien Fleurier illustrated, children who never question the path laid out for them before their birth eventually internalize the parental example. In the end, Sartre condemns those children along with the fathers who engendered them.

A reader familiar with *What Is Literature?*, where Sartre blamed modernist poets for retreating body and soul into unreality through art, picking up Sartre's *Baudelaire*, published in the same year, might justifiably wonder why one would write an entire book on a subject whose dismissal is already inscribed in the other work? As part of his struggle against the bourgeoisie, Sartre taxed the bourgeois subspecies of writers for not taking a more forceful stand against their own class. Sartre stops just short, however, of relegating them to the junkheap of *salauds* along with their fathers. Baudelaire's case posed problems for the system of thought Sartre espoused in *What Is Literature?*—problems that remain unresolved until *The Family Idiot*.

Like Poulou, Baudelaire lost his father at an early age. Like Poulou, he was raised by a surrogate father figure: General Aupick. According to the draconian logic of *The Words*, Baudelaire should, nonetheless, have been able to make a free man out of himself. Instead, even in the absence of the real father, he acts like any piously obedient son: "What is striking in Baudelaire is that, having received ethical notions from others, he never questioned them" (1947a, 53–54).

Could it be that Sartre now suddenly fears that *any* child, regardless of its relationship to the father, might succumb to this moral passivity? Is this the sentiment expressed in the following passage (taken from the *Notebooks for an Ethics*) being written contemporaneously with *Baudelaire*?

> The child is first an object. The phrase, "We start out by being children before being men" means that we start out by being *objects*. We start out being without our own possibilities. Taken up, carried [*portés*], we possess the future of others. We are *flowerpots* that are taken out and brought in. (1983a, 22)

It will be recalled that, in "Childhood of a Boss" and *The Condemned of Altona*, "flowerpot" alluded to the passive allegiance of bourgeois sons to the prescriptions of the paterfamilias. In the quoted fragment, it is no longer clear that Sartre is thinking exclusively of the legitimate, bourgeois child. The manipulator of the "flowerpots" is now an anonymous, plural other, not a singular father. If even a fatherless child (Baudelaire being an example) submits to passive conformity with a collective other, then something even more universally emancipatory than Poulou's "break of a lifetime" in losing his father must be at the foundation of the free-yet-responsible subject. These are the uncertainties that haunt Sartre's *Baudelaire*.

Sartre indicts the herald of modernism for making narcissism his "original choice." Yet a predisposition began to form the contours of a definitive being well before the young Baudelaire was entirely conscious or in control of what was happening.

> Baudelaire's original posture [*attitude*] is that of a man bent over—bent over like Narcissus. There is no immediate con-

> sciousness in him that is not shot through by a piercing glance [*un regard acéré*]. (1947a, 26)

Sartre maintains that as the subject evolves, he becomes increasingly conscious of his existence as a process leading to a choice of being. Baudelaire's definitive choice (which is not so different from that of Mathieu) is not as repellent to Sartre as the tenacious passivity with which the poet refused to deviate from his "posture": "through this tireless attention that he devotes to the very flow of his moods [*humeurs*], he starts to become the Charles Baudelaire we know" (26). He chose to exist as he perceived others perceiving him.

> He chose to *exist* for himself as he *was* for others. He wished for his freedom to appear to him as a "nature" and for that "nature" which others discovered in him to seem to them to be the very emanation of his freedom. (1947a, 243)

In reviewing the structures that fashion this choice, Sartre focuses on Baudelaire's flawed family configuration. "When his father died, Baudelaire was six years old and he was living in his mother's adoration" (18). At the death of his father, an oedipal idyll begins; eighteen months later, his mother remarries, ending Baudelaire's bliss. With some minor differences, this scenario duplicates Sartre's own childhood legend.[20] Sartre, however, would miraculously escape the inglorious *political* destiny of a Baudelaire. Sartre's condemnation of Baudelaire's choice differs little from his condemnation of any bourgeois son graced with both parents. His father's death and mother's subsequent second marriage sounds like the chance of a lifetime that delivered Poulou into unlimited freedom.[21]

> This sudden break [*rupture*] and the sorrow that resulted from it threw him without transition into personal existence. . . . This life [of bliss with his mother] retreated like an ebbtide, leaving him *alone and dry*, he lost his justifications, in shame he discovers that he is one, that his existence is given to him for nothing. (20; italics added)[22]

Sartre identifies and sympathizes with the heartbreak Baudelaire suffered. But, by Sartre's logic, no situation could have been more propitious for making an admirable choice of being than Baudelaire's sudden total contingency and the solitude brought on by the vanished father. Instead of seizing the opportunity, Baudelaire settled for less, "preferring the nervous excitation of desire to its fulfillment" (159). Baudelaire's narcissistic posturing eventually kills him. But cultivating petty and impossible desires is preferable to the terrifying satisfaction of desire through responsible action.

> Baudelaire, who had a feeling and a taste for *freedom*, took fright from it. . . . He understood that it led necessarily to *absolute solitude* and to *total responsibility*. He wants to flee from this anguish of the *solitary man* who knows himself *responsible without appeal for the world, for Good, and for Evil*. (84; italics added)

The feeling of loss before the absolute vastness of human responsibility and freedom deterred Baudelaire from a laudable choice of being.

The flawed family configuration in which Baudelaire was immured must have deeply disturbed Sartre because of its uncanny resemblance to his own "protohistory." Like Mathieu, Baudelaire both fascinates and disgusts Sartre. Baudelaire's irresolute manner of being puts him in the same problematic double bind where Mathieu found himself.

> He is full of himself. He overflows with himself. Yet *this "himself" is but an insipid and vitreous humor bereft of consistency and resistence*. It is a self without shadows or light that he can neither judge nor observe, a babbling consciousness which speaks itself in long whispering tones. (29)

Sartre has taken the commonplace about the mechanisms of narcissicm to its literal limits, portraying Baudelaire as an ontological monster, pregnant with his own being, yet incapable of delivering himself of it. Both womb and fetus, eternally undifferentiable from himself, Baudelaire is doubly repulsive to his biographer. Yet his ontological (and ethical) status is exactly that of the vapid Mathieu Delarue.

However disturbing it was to Sartre, what he called the "Baudelaire problem" inaugurated the space in which the ethical bastard would soon be developed. Willfully blurring any distinctions between fatherlessness and bastardy, Sartre reinforces the idea of bastardy in order to encompass a broader range of subhumans. Any child, even one in his own situation of being "orphaned of the father," will be considered as much a *bâtard* as the child that is born out of wedlock. Ultimately, bastardy may be a chosen or self-imposed state. Once elaborated, that peculiarly defined bastardy would be turned back to make sense out of the rather inexplicable harshness with which Sartre treated Baudelaire in 1947.

In the case of Baudelaire's loss of the father, this "bastardy" is exacerbated when he is subjected to the trauma resulting from his mother's remarriage. But Sartre does not choose to emphasize this trauma. The poet, left high and dry by this intolerable betrayal, became entrenched in his solitude. Suddenly confirmed in his belief that existence has no justification, that (like Mathieu and Sartre) existence "is given *for nothing*" (26), this poor bastard "bent over like Narcissus." Fifteen years or so later, describing the *same* lack of justification for his *own* existence in his autobiography, Sartre would be jubilant: "I never cease creating myself: I am the giver and the gift" (1964a, 30). Yet in spite of this exaltation, original choice can never spring from virgin soil. The milieu Sartre describes in *Baudelaire* is in place, ready to receive, to condition—one might even say *to adulterate*—young Charles as soon as he is born. Prior to interaction in the anonymous milieu of others, the subject is marked by his experience within the family. In this generational, thus hierarchical experience, the child is inevitably subordinated to the parents' will. All of the biographical investigations Sartre undertook subsequent to *Baudelaire* thus appear as attempts (made through imagining an emancipatory bastardy) to preserve intact his theory of original choice of being that was irrevocably disturbed by this, his inaugural biography.

Despite all of the fluctuations and contradictions in Sartre's political decisions, he proves consistent in the following line of thinking: (1) the relative morality or immorality of an action is immaterial to oppressors since they hold themselves accountable only to themselves; (2) these *salauds* justify their actions by circular logic and pragmatism; and (3) regardless of the consequences of his moves, the bourgeois considers any of the *means* he employs a birthright whose *end* is the reaffirmation of class legitimacy and sovereignty.

> Every member of the dominant class is a man by divine right. Born into the company of bosses, he is convinced, from a very early age, that he is born to give orders. A certain social function in whose mold he will flow as soon as he is of age. That function awaits him in the future and is the metaphysical reality of his person. (1949, 184)

But political action (including Sartre's) is demanded of him in the present and the *salaud,* a holdover of times past, represents a system waiting to be destroyed. The legitimacy of the *salaud*'s power can only be maintained in the present skewed world order.

When Sartre repeats Ponge's Marxist paradox that "man is the future of man," he envisions a utopian subject whose model both resembles and transcends the Gidean bastard.[23] The subject of the future will no longer be represented by an anachronistic son who invokes rights of legitimacy to justify exploitation. Just as the legal notion of illegitimacy is today nearly effaced as a social demarcation, bastardy has come to be a legitimate way of describing the modern condition. No preconceived paths hinder the bastard. There is no obligation to filial piety or to play the game of the *salaud*. Fatherless in the eyes of society, the bastard appears to be born without cause. Neither paternal nor filial guilt are his burden to bear. That he become a father and thereby reinstate the very cycle of emburdening that he has broken seems inconceivable. Nor is he a burden to a father: he is not a namesake.

Apparently burdenless, then, the bastard has no need to willfully disengage himself, as Mathieu did, in order to seek radical freedom. Yet Baudelaire's bastardly burdenlessness serves to demonstrate that fatherlessness is *not* tantamount to weightlessness. Baudelaire, as a narcissist (according to Sartre), was crushed by himself, by his own image, in the end. The goal for Sartre is to invent a bastard who avoids both being crushed and being weightless—a bastard who, as Kean demanded, carries his own weight. In the realm of legitimacy, namelessness is not anonymity: the extreme visibility of the *bâtard* causes him to incur the wrath of the ruling legitimate class.

Notes

1. This quotation from *Cymbeline* was used by Gide as the epigraph to one of the chapters of his *Faux-monnayeurs*.

2. André Gide, *Les Faux-monnayeurs* (Paris: Gallimard, 1925).

3. André Gide, *Les Nourritures terrestres* (Paris: Gallimard, 1935).

4. André Gide, *Les Caves du Vatican* (Paris: Gallimard, 1936).

5. Michel Foucault, *Histoire de la folie à l'âge classique* (Paris: Gallimard, 1972).

6. Jean-Paul Sartre, *Baudelaire* (Paris: Gallimard, 1947).

7. I include Sartre's autobiography in this group because autobiography often, and especially the way Sartre handles it, is a type of biography and because Sartre, by the time he wrote *The Words,* came to include himself among the bastards in the broadened sense of which I speak. See Philippe Lejeune, *Le Pacte autobiographique* (Paris: Seuil, 1975), 197–243.

8. See chap. 2 for a discussion of the differences between Sartre and Poulou (the nickname Sartre's mother always used to designate him).

9. These indignant protests missed the point. As Michel Leiris wrote in his foreword to *Baudelaire,* Sartre was attempting "to relive what Baudelaire's experience was from the inside instead of only considering the outside" (1947a, 9). Furthermore, as one critic points out, *Baudelaire* was originally written as a preface for the poet's *Ecrits intimes,* not for *Les Fleurs du mal* (Douglas Collins, *Sartre as Biographer* [Cambridge, Mass.: Harvard University Press, 1980], 74).

10. Jean-Paul Sartre, *Qu'est-ce que la littérature?* (Paris: Gallimard, 1947); see 154–62, for example.

11. See 1967, 82–85, 88–92, 194–208.

12. At the time of Sartre's study, Genet had not yet written for the theater and only his prose work is brought up in the body of *Saint Genet* (Sartre added an appendix in which he comments on *The Maids*). Also, the first text Sartre published on Genet was a 1946 advertising inset for an edition of *Miracle of the Rose* (Michel Contat and Michel Rybalka, *Les Ecrits de Sartre* [Paris: Gallimard, 1970], 146).

13. A very bizarre concept, on the part of the publisher, for a writer who was only thirty-eight at the time and not known to be suffering from any fatal illness.

14. For a useful discussion of this project and its consequences *on* Genet as well as *for* Sartre, see Jeffrey Mehlmann, "*Saint Genet:* I as Another," in *A Structural Study of Autobiography* (Ithaca: Cornell University Press, 1971), 167–86.

15. Goetz being Genet's fictional (and ethical) equivalent, Sartre's 1951 play, *Le Diable et le Bon Dieu,* is essentially an illustration for the stage of *Saint Genet*.

16. "Farewell, beautiful lilies, elegant in your painted sanctuaries, good-

bye, lovely lilies, our pride and reason for existing, good-bye you bastards" (*Nausea*, trans. Lloyd Alexander [London: New Directions, 1949], 129).

17. The *repentant* bourgeois exists, according to Sartre, and is a type of social bastard that will be examined in chap. 9.

18. A *bâtard* is also a type of bread, shorter and squatter than the *baguette*. Cf. my discussion of being and bakery imagery in chap. 5.

19. See Martin Heidegger, *Being and Time*, trans. John Macquarrie (New York: Harper and Row, 1962), 174. Sartre more or less adopted Heidegger's notion of *Geworfenheit* in *Being and Nothingness*. In Sartre's version of this primordial *engagement*, he has recourse (as we saw in chap. 5) to liquid imagery. "Je suis *délaissé* dans le monde, non au sens où je demeurerais abandonné et passif dans un univers hostile, comme la planche qui flotte sur l'eau, mais, au contraire, au sens où je me trouve soudain seul et sans aide, engagé dans un monde . . ." (1943, 614; italics in original). The relation of human being to a liquid medium of commitment is made more explicit by Beauvoir in "L'Existentialisme et la sagesse des nations," *Les Temps modernes* 3 (1945): "[l]a situation est à peu près à la liberté ce qu'est l'élément liquide au nageur: à la fois difficulté et point d'appui. L'eau résiste aux mouvements, mais sans eau il ne saurait être question de nager. Nous sommes donc jetés dans le monde et en situation dans le monde un peu comme Pascal disait: 'Nous sommes embarqués' " (398).

20. Baudelaire was at a more advanced age (postoedipal, one might say) when his father died. Sartre's mother eventually also remarried.

21. Sartre greatly minimizes the magnitude of moral burden General Aupick, Baudelaire's stepfather, exercised on his hypersensitive stepson.

22. These lines very nearly reproduce the words Sartre used in the autobiography to describe the troubled period of his own existence out of which sprang his *mandat impératif* (1963, 114, 145.). This is also like most of Sartre's other characters (see the discussion of Mathieu in chap. 5).

23. Sartre incessantly repeats the last lines of Ponge's "Notes premières de l'homme" as they appeared in the very first issue of *Les Temps modernes:* "L'homme est à venir. L'homme est l'avenir de l'homme" (75).

CHAPTER 9

Classy versus Classless Bastards

Sartre's momentous meeting with Jean Genet during World War II, leading to his mesmerized, highly imaginary study of the ex-con writer that appeared eight years later, advanced Sartre's search for a father-son model adapted to his conception of a utopian ethics in two important ways. *Saint Genet* first brought Sartre to the realization that, for more than a decade of writing fiction and theater, he had been creating beings whose character traits and decisions in life situations were fundamentally ambiguous and, as such, repellent to the characters keyed as "normal" who interacted with them. Through Genet, Sartre learned that the ideal moral characteristics he had been seeking rather gropingly through fiction were forms of illegitimacy and hybridity, of which bastardy is the most adequate and logical image. Once Sartre grasped the philosophical potential in his nascent conceptualization of bastardy, he initiated a process of refinement of differentiated manifestations of the illegitimate status as determined by class origins and affiliations.

Eventually, Sartre's distinction between a certain bastard with roots in the bourgeoisie and, on the other hand, unclassifiable bastards would enable him to reassess the rather peremptory judgment he had passed on Baudelaire for his "original choice of being." In a final reconciliation of these two types of illegitimate beings (the subject of the final chapter), Sartre attempted to envision them as a monstrous hybrid forming the coveted total being.

Bastards of Class

If we accept, with Sartre, that every individual born of the ruling class is a "dirty bastard" (*salaud*) and consider all the bourgeois who appear in his work as such, then his condemnation of the bourgeois *is not* without exception: not every *salaud* is beyond appeal. Despite their ineffectual efforts at commitment or at simply shaking the yoke of their family (or perhaps *because* of their impotence), Sartre's authorial sympathies are clearly on the side of such diverse bourgeois figures as Mathieu (*The Roads to Freedom*), Hugo (*Dirty Hands*), and Frantz (*The Condemned of Altona*). These characters rise to something of a hero status, at least in Sartre's sense of the term, because they gain a certain awareness of their infamous class identity whose guarantor (a visible or invisible father) has preened them for oppressing others. They manage, in spite of their vocation as *salauds*, to muster a degree of moral courage to fight their bourgeois destiny. They struggle to flee their own class by moving to embrace their otherwise "natural" victims in the class of the oppressed. This attempt, of course, does not warrant any undue optimism for better class relations on Sartre's part: Mathieu, Hugo, and Frantz's efforts to relinquish their credentials of legitimacy in order to undermine the system of oppression are all ultimately sterile. But it is that infinitesimally minute shred of ethical inspiration motivating these *voluntary* bastards that fascinates Sartre and makes them compelling to us as literary creations by eliciting our sympathy.

Francis Jeanson was the first to remark that, while not bastards in the strict sense, Mathieu and Hugo possess traits of illegitimacy on social and ethical levels that may transform these "enlightened" bourgeois into hybrid beings not wholly objectionable to Sartre.[1] We learn from the narrator of *The Age of Reason* that Mathieu is a lycée philosophy professor, yet never once do we see him at work. Instead, his private life is unremittingly served up for our scrutiny—a private life behind which we only reconstruct his social status as a legitimate son of the intellectual bourgeoisie. A large part of the ontological indeterminacy that Mathieu suffers derives from this very palpable class indeterminateness. Concerning this aspect of his "social bastardy," as Jeanson called it, Mathieu is lucid: "I write in Leftist journals in order to not be part of my class—to no avail: I'm still a bourgeois" (1981, 633). With Mathieu, the condition of social bastardy is one where the free time that the privileges of class status make available deteriorates into a frightening void of availability in which the subject develops an unrequited longing for commitment coupled with apathy in the face of necessity for action.[2]

Having committed crimes from whose punishment he would never escape, Frantz von Gerlach's sterile revolt against the prescriptions of his class was rendered definitive by a denial of freedom unequalled in any other Sartrean bourgeois. He became psychologically sequestered by the inescapable presence of an omnipotent father, from whom drug addiction was the only distraction. Hugo, whom we will have occasion to discuss further, incarnates Sartre's position (at least in the late 1940s) that for a bourgeois intellectual to engage in revolutionary activity is tantamount to an impossible breach in class-determined ontology. To varying degrees, each of these bourgeois characters "see the light" concerning their class destiny: they either go as far as carrying out what is considered evil behavior by their class or at least balk at stepping into the shoes of their forebears, betraying, in either case, the bourgeoisie. Yet they all fail to attain free, committed, and ethical existence. The sterile hybridity of a Mathieu and a Frantz, even that of Brunet or Schneider, is an existential state inseparable from a class origin with which Sartre sympathizes and identifies.[3]

Even revolutionaries like Brunet and Schneider-Vicarios (*Troubled Sleep*)—bourgeois protagonists who bring to tangible evidence the will to action that remains only latent in a Mathieu—succumb, nevertheless, to incontrovertible contradictions inherent in the bastardy of the Sartrean bourgeois intellectual. Particularly interesting in this respect is Schneider-Vicarios who, because he is so totally different from Mathieu, is quite possibly a personality that Sartre could imagine only after having reflected on the ethical significance of Jean

Genet. Schneider-Vicarios, whose very name and identity suggest hybridity,[4] is closely modeled after Paul Nizan, Sartre's admired friend who had quit the French Communist Party in extremis after twelve years of dedicated militancy.[5] After having been a Party stalwart (like Hoerderer in *Dirty Hands*), Schneider became disillusioned with the pretense of efficient planning at the expense of morality that was characteristic of vanguard Leninism and, by the time of his appearance in the novel, has adopted a cynically anarchistic position not unlike what Nizan's last troubled months must have been like. Far from a return to the politics of capitalism, Schneider's new stance constitutes both a deepened "illegitimacy" with regard to his class of origin and a reevaluation (for the better) of his pursuit of an ethical standpoint. Although no one character was adequate to any definitive model of Sartre's ethical subject, Mathieu, Schneider, and Hugo all embody a hybridity of being that places the subject (if he is bourgeois) in the nearly untenable dilemma, both ontological and ethical, that is described throughout *Being and Nothingness*. In the bourgeois bastard, this hybridity obviously attenuates the potential for concrete moral action. While a bourgeois *salaud* like Father von Gerlach perpetrates economic atrocities against the oppressed classes and lives his class position as a birthright, a Parisian intellectual bastard like Mathieu experiences his being, issued from the bourgeoisie, as one that carries the birthmark of the *salaud*. This blemish prevents him from acting on his being.

Bastardy as sociopolitical hybridity is most poignantly illustrated as the organizing force in Sartre's 1948 play, *Dirty Hands*. The work deals with a dilemma that had, at least since the Bolshevik Revolution, confronted many bourgeois intellectuals and that was becoming acute for Sartre during this period when the cold war was taking shape.[6] Hugo's is the dilemma of how to effectively and definitively repudiate the class of oppressors out of which he was born in order to embrace the party of the oppressed. There are obvious parallels between Hugo's desperate efforts to "dirty his hands"[7] and Orestes' quest for a weighty act of vengeance or Mathieu's half-baked plans for commitment. However, it is the intensity with which Hugo experiences the bastardy he chose for himself that distinguishes him from Mathieu and Orestes and sets the tone for seeing how differently Sartre's "classless bastards" confront the same problems.[8]

In shunning the class into which he was born by joining the Communist Party, Hugo creates in himself a four-way bastardy: (1) he symbolically repudiates the father (as synecdoche of the bourgeoisie) yet (2) bears his past as one would a scar: "I'm a rich kid, an intellectual, a guy who doesn't work with his hands" (1948, 94). From the proletarian side of the drama, (3) Hugo has indeed performed the ritual of joining the Party, the "corporation" of the class *other,* however, (4) because he is a turncoat of the class system, Hugo is prevented from achieving the crossover to a new identity by the very individuals he wishes to embrace as brothers. Thus, Hugo ultimately finds himself disenfranchized by both classes. Hoederer challenges the workers who ostracize Hugo, asking them what price he must pay for them to forgive him his origins. Georges, a proletarian party member responds that "there is a world between us. [Hugo] is an amateur: he entered the Party as a gesture or because he thought it was a good idea.[9] For us there was no other choice" (1948, 93). "We can't help it," another worker says to Hugo, "there's something that just doesn't click [*qui ne colle pas*] between us" (95). Hugo realizes that, at the root of his abortive class crossover, *voluntary* bastardy can never match the originary authenticity of the proletarian's innate social illegitimacy.[10] Yet what he has attempted is the very act necessary to satisfy Sartre's conditions for authentic existence, for *Being and Nothingness* tells us that we must choose what we are.

Hugo's dejection at finding himself an outcast of both classes takes on predictably Sartrean consequences as that frustration crystallizes in the more successful "bourgeois proletarian," Hoederer. Hugo's self-consciousness and anxiety give way to what Sartre, in his work on Flaubert, calls "self-derealization": everything, down to the simplest gesture, loses perspective and the only sensations Hugo experiences emanating from real objects are those he perceives vicariously through Hoerderer. Hugo admires his mentor's capacity for true action to such an extent that this Big Other[11] virtually becomes his nerve center: "Everything he touches seems real. He pours coffee into cups, I drink. I watch him drink and I feel that the true taste of coffee is in *his* mouth, not mine" (123). Hugo's awe-filled admiration for Hoederer, to which Hoederer responds in a paternalistic tone, suggest the latter's position as a surrogate father, transforming Hugo's murder of the Trotsky look-alike into a symbolic patricide.

The dynamics of psychological dependence that links Hugo and Hoederer foreshadows that between Frantz and his father. The only road to relief that either of these stifled sons can elect leads them to murder.

Hugo consciously fulfills the first requirement for ethical existence: incurring and bearing the costs of social illegitimacy if it is necessary to uphold moral decency. But Hugo's bastardy proves too wrenching to the man who is half outlaw-of-the-bourgeoisie, half pariah-of-the-working-class. He too easily falls prey to a new dependence upon the judgment of his would-be comrades and is diverted from the task of forging the principles of a new code of ethics. The fit of jealousy that prompts Hugo's assassination of Hoederer is an unfelicitous motive for two reasons: he has erred in thinking that Hoederer has seduced Jessica (1948, 224–25) and he disguises from himself the true motive of his action with its roots in father-son strife. Hugo thus regresses into bad faith. With regard to locating a new class- and self-identity by executing a Party-sanctioned action, Hugo is no more certain of who he is by the curtain's fall than he was at the beginning of the play. However, Sartre has succeeded in showing us, for the first time, an example of being that approaches something very close to the hybrid of *bâtard* and *salaud*. As a guiding force in Sartre's work, bastardy will henceforth designate a choice of being founded on moral ambiguity nurtured by our innate hybridity. Hoederer, commenting on Hugo's predicament, says: "I suppose you're half victim and half accomplice, like everybody else" (127). Hugo's elective bastardy, in other words, is not a mere aberration that results from a manichean world; it is a situation that universally conditions the modern subject's existence.

Classless Bastards

Mathieu, Hugo, and Frantz were born into the middle class and, despite their efforts at treason, retain the mark of the bourgeoisie. With Genet, Goetz, and Kean, however, Sartre achieves representations of total ontological indeterminacy that render class origins and allegiances irrelevant. Although the first trio may, in light of Jeanson's hypothesis of a Sartrean "theater of bastardy," be considered bastards in the figurative sense, it is the second trio's bastardy, in the *original* sense of a child who is refused legal recognition by a father, that inspired his analysis and enabled him to construct it in the first place. The differences in how the members of these two groups lived their bastardy are vital to understanding why Sartre utilizes the bastard as a philosophical model. And it is because of the preference that Sartre manifests for the second group that one must not dwell on the failures of the bastards of class, but rather turn to classless bastards in order to see where the search for Sartre's total ethical being will lead.

The Devil and the Good Lord, Saint Genet, and *Kean* were produced by Sartre as if from one continuous stroke of the pen, although the publication of each of these major texts is separated from the next by about a year and Sartre wrote several other articles between them.[12] Unable, as we know, to bring his "Ethics" to a conclusion, Sartre seemed to be offering the public these three literary works in rapid succession, as if to have them replace the intractable philosophical project.[13] In each of the texts, the same essential character appears with Sartre varying only the name and the literary vehicle employed to present him. Goetz and Kean are the only historical figures in Sartre's theater,[14] and a complex of factors makes Sartre's fictionalized biography of Jean Genet something of a work for the stage.[15] Both Kean and Goetz were originally played by Pierre Brasseur. In fact, *The Devil and the Good Lord* was composed by Sartre with this consummate ham actor in mind. The part-sincere, part-mocking versatility of the *cabotin* is one of the features Sartre tries to emphasize in Genet's personality, making it evident that he thought this to be one of the fundamental traits of the classless bastard. Each of these characters incarnates—with the apparent indifference of he who *plays* at existence—absolute evil and absolute virtue. Each of them, finally, is an illegitimate child and highly conscious of his bastardy.

As Sartre had already made clear in *Being and Nothingness,* all forms of prescriptive ethics were to be rejected. Throughout his career, he remained deeply disturbed by the stultifying incrustation of ethical norms upon society, and the posthumously published *Notebooks for an Ethics* only further corroborate this observation. But rather than create a new system that would hold bankrupt prescriptive rules of behavior in check, Sartre tries to imagine individual personalities capable of shattering the norms handed down by our forebears and submitting behavior to constant revision. With their seemingly untamed personalities, it is not surprising that Goetz and Kean—controversial figures modeled after Sartre's Genet—would be pivotal to his ongoing ethical considerations. As one philosopher has defined ethics as "a field outside all fields and presupposing them all,"[16] so Sartre locates Genet and his cohorts beyond the pale of bourgeois morality, making him paradoxically indispensable to the eccentric ethics pursued by their "creator."

For Sartre, the entirely unclassifiable bastard is Jean Genet. In *Saint Genet,* that "genesis of [a] monster who is perpetually other than himself,"[17] Sartre gave free reign to his "passion for understanding men" (1952, 158). As a living contemporary example of how original choices by real men should be selected and executed, the tangible object known as "Jean Genet" came as a revelation to Sartre. *Saint Genet* mobilizes bastardy both literally and allegorically as an explanatory grid for understanding Genet's entire existence, and shows Genet's literary enterprise to be the supreme manifestation of that existence in bastardy. Feeling free to treat Genet with the same offhandedness he employs with literary figures of the past, in meeting Genet, Sartre finally *lived* the experience of a bastard writer entering his field of personal acquaintances.[18] Genet eluded Mathieu's fundamental shortcoming: contrary to the hapless hero of *The Age of Reason,* "[Genet] is not an old child, but a man who expresses men's ideas in the language of childhood" (1952, 65).[19] Here we see clearly what Sartre was seeking to circumscribe in his earlier novel: an adult who avoids the pitfalls typical of adulthood by remaining childlike, a hybrid subject consisting of adult and child. And unlike Baudelaire, Genet manages to introject that artificially contrived paternity, taking the role of the mosaic father into his own hands and relying on this ethical prosthesis to create "new tables of the law" with the help of no one.[20] Genet's creation and internalization of the absent father lends another dimension to Sartrean bastardy. Bourgeois society is the collective father that Genet rejects. Yet, like the French population living under the German occupation, Genet, a victim unable to escape that society, has no alternative but to embrace this paternal victimization. By artificially transforming the imposed burden into one he can voluntarily endorse, by playing at loving what he hates, Genet subverts his oppressors and, thus, eludes the defeatist narcissism of Baudelaire. By approaching a creation of himself as a living hybrid of moral opposites, Genet approaches the total ethical being.

Ironically, it is not Genet's social status as everyone's pariah that intrigues and excites Sartre; after all, Hugo had already achieved that notoriety with no positive results. Genet's bastardy is one that Hugo lacked in several respects. As an illegitimate child he is exempt, in Sartre's view, from all problems deriving from the position of offspring in the paternity bond. As far as Sartre understands homosexuality, Genet will never have to deal with having a son, either.[21] Genet has committed petty crimes all his life, but as a traitor even to his fellow thieves, he incurs their censorship also. All of these particularities deriving from Genet's bastardy transcend Hugo's "betweenness." However, the most *awful* aspect of Genet's bastardy is that he achieves a perfect blend, in one person, of the *bâtard* and the *salaud*. Between Genet and the bourgeoisie there has developed a very unique economy of mutual parasitism.[22]

The Ambiguities of Awe

Sartre was awestruck at Genet. He and Jean Cocteau were instrumental in obtaining a presidential exoneration for Genet in 1948. When one reads the titillation in the voice that issues forth from *Saint Genet* and knowing Sartre's thesis concerning Genet's capacity for treason, one cannot help wondering whether Sartre thought with a certain pleasure that, in getting Genet's record cleared, the supremely evil saint might well repay him some day by a heinous act.

If I have selected and underscored the adjective *awful* to describe Genet's bastardy, it is because the word is one of those undecidable terms that enclose opposite notions. Both of the positions that Genet occupies in society with others, that is, in the realm where ethics is tested, are designated in *awful*. For well-thinkers, Genet both *inspires awe* and is *subject to awe*. As a scandalous homosexual ex-con producing literature that thrills the bourgoisie as they consume it, he instills awe in them. He even fills his fellow pariahs with awe by his treachery. However, trapped in this role, unable to escape the blame of anyone at all—both "actor and martyr" as Sartre's subtitle goes—he is victimized by everyone and, therefore, awestricken himself.

Genet is condemned to shuttle endlessly between inspiring awe and being awestricken, as he alternately embraces absolute evil and absolute virtue. This brutally shifting, indeterminate, and classless being is a dynamic type of bastardy created out of radical repudiations of former positions: Genet moves without transition from activity to passivity, from being subject to being object. One moment he is patiently constructing a religion of evil, the next he is demonstrating a curiously perverse potential for espousing virtue. Whereas Baudelaire eludes the sheer vastness of total responsibility "[wanting] to flee that anguish of the solitary man who knows himself to be responsible, without recourse, for the world, for Good and for Evil" (1947a, 84), Genet flies full force into the great moral dichotomy between whose two extremes the ethics of the future lies.

"Either ethics is bunk or it is a concrete totality realizing the synthesis of Good and Evil" (1952, 177). This totally open ethical system is a dynamic, exemplified in Genet, of virtue constantly challenging evil and of evil just as doggedly questioning good. This incessantly reversing system of valences, supposedly guaranteeing equality and reciprocity, mimics the mutuality of ideal paternity. Sartre would make the image he painted of Genet the precursor of his new fluid ethics, which uses Hegel's concept of supersession (*Aufhebung*) to convey the idea of perpetual moral revision.

> For Good without Evil is Parmenidean Being, that is, Death. Evil without Good is pure Non-Being. . . . I hope that the reader will have understood that what is involved here is not Nietzschean "beyond Good and Evil" at all but rather Hegelian *Aufhebung*. . . . It remains to be said that this synthesis, in the present historical situation, is not realizable. (177)

Obviously, what Beauvoir reported as his "discovery of the fertility of dialectics" in the 1950s aided in Sartre's progressive understanding of others: an implicit revision of his erstwhile condemnation of Baudelaire is already at work in *Saint Genet*. Although Sartre shelved his work in progress on the "Ethics" around the time he started writing on Genet, explaining that "the moral 'problem' comes from the fact that *for us* Ethics is simultaneously unavoidable and impossible" (177), that Ethics with a capital *E* is still high on Sartre's agenda when he writes of an even more acute form of ethical bastardy in *The Devil and the Good Lord*.

Goetz is an avatar of Genet, with Sartre perhaps even freer to invent because the model is not a living subject before him. Goetz is a "bastard of the worst type" (1951, 17), an adventurer with a keen sense of the polarity separating good and evil and whose brutality of character is brought to an actualization that remains mostly theoretical or potential in Genet. In the first half of the play, Goetz dedicates himself to evil for the sake of evil. Sartre appoints Goetz chief of propaganda for universal hybridity by having him systematically announce to everyone that they are no better than he because, like it or not, they are all bastards. The idealistic prelate, Heinrich, for example, tries to ignore his own dual existence that consists of conformity to Church dogma and loyal love for the peasantry. Brutally, Goetz unmasks the absurdity of such a denial by welcoming Heinrich into the fraternity of hybrids: "I salute you, little brother! I salute you in the name of bastardy! To engender you, the Clergy had to sleep with Poverty: what depressing intercourse!" (57). The shocked priest is initiated to the fundamental incompleteness of all being by coming to terms with his social bastardy: "a half-priest added to a half-poorman never made a whole man" (57). Far from denouncing the acceptance of such subhumanity, Sartre's very premiss is that no one can be ethical who does not first embrace incompatible opposites.

The vehicle of fiction allows Sartre to present, in Goetz, a bastard whose brutality of character transcends mere potential: a roll of dice suffices for him to switch from the practice of evil for evil's sake to that of radical goodness. Although he prefers playing out virtue rather than evil only when he is convinced of the Biblical theorem that virtue contains evil as a subset, it is because Goetz's very identity is composed of these opposites that he accomplishes such a quick conversion. Although his bastardy can appear as abject as that of Genet, who also embodied both meanings of *awful*, Goetz nevertheless escapes the martyrdom that characterizes his model's existence. This is because he attains absolute mastery over the polar opposites of which he is composed. On the one hand, he clearly perceives his own monstrousness: "I'm a double agent by birth . . . I am made up [like Hugo] of two halves that don't fit together [*qui ne collent pas ensemble*]: one horrifies the other" (1951, 57). Yet whichever extreme happens to be in dominance, he corresponds to and controls his identity ("I cannot be another than myself" [104]), thus Goetz becomes the first Sartrean character to achieve perfect self-sameness.

In remarking at the beginning of the play that Goetz is a "bastard of the worst sort," the Archbishop seems uncertain about what he himself means by that statement. At one point he explains that "[Goetz] is only happy doing evil" (17), but in another moment says that "the least one can say is that he's moody" (16). As if Goetz's move to absolute virtue were not brutal enough to convince us of the unpredictability of the bastard, he commits murder, even as a saint. This seemingly inevitable violence in the bastard reveals a fundamental flaw in either Sartre's model (the hybrid ethical being) or in the outrageous exaggeration to which Sartre seems bent on submitting the model's fictional prototypes. Sartre has indeed succeeded in showing us a being whose oscillations between good and evil are not whimsical, a being who embodies both his own incomplete self and that of other(s)—a total being who is the identity of the same and the other. However, in this total hybrid being, he has not succeeded in showing us that the temptation of destruction in order to prove one's totality is finally tempered. The compulsion to patricide, which infringes in the most definitive way both on freedom and upon ethics, is an inevitable feature of Sartre's fictional sons.

Notes

1. Francis Jeanson, "Un théâtre de la bâtardise," in *Sartre* (Paris: Seuil, 1955), 7–113.

2. Sartre will define this apathy as "stasis" in his *Critique of Dialectical Reason*.

3. Jeanson argued convincingly that the bastardy of Sartre's fictional bourgeois is fundamentally the same as the social illegitimacy that he characterized himself as having in *The Words*.

4. In *Drôle d'amitié* (untranslated), the unfinished fourth installment of *The Roads to Freedom*, Brunet discovers that Schneider's real name is Vicarios. The meanings of these two names create a complex constellation for interpretation. *Schneider*, meaning "tailor" in German (or "coward" or, by extension, "castrator"), is, in Latin, *sartor*, a vocable obviously close to *Sartre*. Contat and Rybalka note that, in one of Sartre's juvenile writings, "La Semence et

le Scaphandre" (The Sea and the Diving Suit), the author appears under the name *Tailleur* or "tailor" (Sartre 1981, 2089). Schneider's "true" name, Vicarios means "vicar" (Fr. *vicaire*, It. *vicario*, etc.), an ecclesiastic who acts in the place of another, thus corroborating the theory that this character is Sartre imagining himself as Nizan. It should also be evident from the relationship between Sartre and Genet how important *vicarious* experiences were for Sartre. For a further discussion on Schneider-Vicarios, see Hollier's discussion of "Le Castor," the nickname given Beauvoir by Sartre and his friends (Denis Hollier, *Politics of Prose*, trans. Jeffrey Mehlman [Minneapolis: University of Minnesota Press, 1986], 282).

5. For Nizan references, see chap. 6, n. 24.

6. See my discussion of Sartre's decision, in the early 1950s, to support the PCF and that decision's relation to the question of paternity (chaps. 6–7).

7. *Red Gloves* was a title Sartre had considered giving his 1948 play at one time. See Contat and Rybalka (*Les Ecrits de Sartre* [Paris: Gallimard, 1970], 180–81) for the amazing account of the illicit deformation of Sartre's play under the title *Red Gloves* in its New York showing.

8. Jeanson also considers Mathieu and Orestes to be social bastards.

9. Note the omnipresent theme of mere gestures, which are in contrast to actions. See Denis Hollier, "I've Done My Act: An Exercise in Gravity," *Representations* 4 (1983): 88–100.

10. Even Hoederer, whose origins are with the bourgeoisie, cannot always suppress a certain disdain for Hugo's putatively noble intentions: "[Hoederer] The central committee sent a message saying that you had never taken part in direct action. Is that true? [Hugo] Yes. [Hoederer] You must be champing at the bit: all intellectuals dream of action" (1948, 102).

11. A notion borrowed from Lacan that takes on these proportions in compelling ways in Slavoj Žižek, *The Sublime Object of Ideology* (London: Verso, 1989).

12. Notably, the publication of the first two parts of *The Communists and Peace* and the controversies and rifts involving Camus, Lefort, and Merleau-Ponty occurred between *Saint Genet* and *Kean*. For the order of events, see Contat and Rybalka 1970, 231–71; also see Michel-Antoine Burnier, *Les Existentialistes et la politique* (Paris: Gallimard, 1966).

13. On *The Devil and the Good Lord*, Contat and Rybalka write that "centered on ethical problems, [the play] is an illustration of the gradual awareness that Sartre acquired between 1945 and 1950 while he was writing his 'Ethics' and which he formulates . . . in the conclusion of *Saint Genet*" (Contat and Rybalka 1970, 235).

14. *The Devil and the Good Lord* was inspired by Goethe's 1773 play on the life of a sixteenth-century German condottiere, Götz von Berlichingen. Edmund Kean, of course, was one of the foremost tragedians of the early nineteenth-century British stage.

15. The work's subtitle is *Actor and Martyr*, referring to the career of the

patron saint of actors, Saint Genet. Jean Rotrou's 1646 tragedy, *Saint Genest* is also "embedded" in Sartre's title and is one of the first well-known examples of a play within a play in the French theater.

16. Angèle Kremer-Marietti, *La Morale,* (Paris: Presses Universitaires de France, 1982), 122.

17. Jeffrey Mehlman, *A Structural Study of Autobiography* (Ithaca, N.Y.: Cornell University Press, 1971), 171. Georges Bataille was one of the first to register the tombstone-like quality of this weighty study on Genet in "Genet et l'étude de Sartre sur lui," *Critique* 65–66 (1952): 819–32, 946–61; republished in *La Littérature et le mal,* (Paris: Gallimard, 1957). Mehlman, in his later study, renews this observation: "What are we to make of the fact that the initial and longest volume of the *Oeuvres complètes de Jean Genet* is written by Jean-Paul Sartre? Who then is Genet?" (Mehlman 1971, 167).

18. In his autobiography, Sartre proudly declares that he took the authors he read as his intimates, since he had spent his whole childhood only with them: "about Baudelaire or Flaubert, I express myself without mincing my words and when I'm blamed for it, I always feel like answering, 'Mind your own business: your geniuses belonged to me, I held them in my hands, loved them passionately and in total reverence' " (1964a, 60).

19. See the discussion of Mathieu's "age-being" in chap. 5.

20. The same expression is used in *Baudelaire* to describe a fundamental difference between his subject and André Gide: the later succeeded where Baudelaire failed because he "marched toward *his* ethics and did his best to invent a new table of law" (1947a, 60).

21. An interesting comparative study could be done by taking Daniel (*The Age of Reason*) and Genet as two examples and seeing what progress, if any, Sartre made in those five or six years in understanding male homosexuality.

22. On Genet's supposed final revenge through literature, see Sartre's brilliant chapter, "My Victory is Verbal and I Owe It to the Sumptuousness of the Terms" (1952, 602–44).

CHAPTER **10**

From Sacred Monsters to "Man as Son of Man"

> C'est vous qui avez pris un enfant
> pour en faire un monstre.
>
> —*Kean*

> je crois que tu nourris un monstre
> . . . un hybride de bacchante et de
> Saint-Esprit.
>
> —André Gide[1]

Monsters, whether possessing an attribute that the norm lacks or lacking what the norm possesses, are the embodiment of some unforeseen and, therefore, astonishing deviation from physical norms. In the efforts of the ancients to predict crises within the "normal" flow of historical events, their sages disemboweled sacrificed animals, revealing a *monstrum,* or omen that portended fortune or adversity. The same excitement mounting in the witnesses who waited suspensefully for the revelation and decipherment of the *monstrum* has also been exploited for monetary profit by the display of deformed humans and animals—biological "monsters"—in poverty-riddled boulevards and circuses. As with the pagan rituals of disembowelment, the nature of this monster's deviation from physical norms is hidden from the audience's view as long as possible in order to exacerbate the degree of surprise caused by the sudden view of an unpredictable mutation.

Monstrosity of character is a figurative derivation of this concept founded on vision. It is helpful to recall biological, physical monstrosity and audience reactions to it in order not to forget that moral deviations and acts that result from them are considered monstrous in the Western mind. Historical figures like Nero or Caligula, though not known to have suffered from any particular physical deformities, are considered monsters because their supposed crimes were as hideously unpredictable as the visible mutations of circus freaks. The Sartrean bastard's character resembles such deviant monstrosity.

The trope that Marx used to describe the operation he performed on the Hegelian dialectic illustrates the interrelation between the two halves of the moral bastard's hybrid character. Allegorizing his "philosophical father's" dialectic into a being with head (or Absolute Spirit) at the upper extreme and feet (labor, materialism) at the bottom, Marx demanded that, in order to move beyond idealism and capitalism, this hierarchy must be "turned on its head." Similarly, Sartre's admiration for Genet or for Goetz's capacity for evil within a morally bankrupt modern society is based largely on an elevation and glorification of the lower regions of civilization's body. However, like the dependence of the Marxian dialectic on the preestablished Hegelian dialectic, so the Sartrean monster's potential for evil must coexist harmoniously with an equally strong potential, in the same person, for virtue. The perpetual conversion of the Sartrean bastard is an internalized process whereby the instances of the "son" and the "father" alternate in the role of subjugating the other, keeping their respective forces in check.

This chiastically configured ethical being manifests itself, however imperfectly, in Goetz's conversion to virtue in *The Devil and the Good Lord*. During his period of absolute evil, Goetz dominated everyone in contact with him by subjugation. Yet however much the condottiere's oppression of subjects bears resemblance to the principle activity of the *salaud,* Sartre approves of his immorality because it occurs within a world where an individual's only choices are hypocrisy or a moral bastardy that includes evil. Like Genet's petty social-terrorism-turned-literary, Goetz's military despotism springs from a psyche where, in the apparent absence of any superego, the id is free to unleash what Freud called its "unknown and uncontrollable forces" (Freud 1973–74, 19:13). Even those characters legally and emotionally superior to Goetz are helpless before the power of his monstrous superiority: the First Officer, dissimulating his fear, declares that "[Goetz] disgusts me so much that I'd be horrified to harm him" (1951, 45); Goetz, thinking he recognizes loathing behind Catherine's façade, tells her "what I love about you is the horror I inspire in you" (47). So diabolical is Goetz's abjection that, as the play's title suggests, he is willing to measure it only in terms of the qualities of his "brother in universality"—God. To Heinrich, he shouts: "I don't give a damn about Satan! He receives souls, but he isn't the one who damns them. I will only deign to deal with God: monsters and saints are answerable only to him" (59). In this hubris, one can already discern the motives for his future conversion to saintly behavior. But for now he claims that, through an act of unspeakable violence, he will prove that no other agent can surpass him: (to Nasty) "This city is going to go up in flames. Then I'll ensure that I'm a pure monster through and through" (97).

Just as he is about to unleash total havoc, Goetz realizes that he has only familiarized himself with and controls part of his monstrous potential. The "pure" monster that he is striving to become must maintain his monstrousness even in a virtuous mode. Thus, the second half of *The Devil and the Good Lord,* where the moral dichotomy of civilization is inverted with respect to the first half, begins with Goetz deciding to transact a Christlike conversion by releasing the repressed powers of his dichotomous self. He learns that, to be monstrous as a doer of good deeds, one must become capable of wielding power from an inferior position—from the standpoint of the dregs of society. As in the conversion that Sartre prescribed for a dwindling proletariat, Goetz's mode of virtue is mobilized when an idealized superego (self-made, of course) takes control of a reckless id. In wishing to become a champion of charity, Goetz's new ethical configuration, where his capacity for virtue outstrips that of the timorous Christians who surround him, proves as awe-(fear and admiration)-inspiring as the evil one. Blind to the death and destruction that could indirectly result from virtuous acts, Goetz pursues his new politics to the hilt. The ultimate failure of his project (which is a steadfast feature of Sartre's works) derives from his incarnating virtue for purely narcissistic ends. We can see him wallowing in self-admiration in many exchanges.

> *Schulheim:* You're a murderer.
> *Goetz:* Yes, my brother, like everyone.
> *Schulheim:* A bastard [*bâtard*]!
> *Goetz:* Yes, like Jesus Christ.
> *Schulheim:* Scum bag! Excrement of the earth!
> *Goetz:* How God loves me! I accept everything. I'm a filthy bastard [*chien de bâtard*], a scum bag, a traitor, pray for me.
> (1951, 117–18)

A salutary mortification for the Christlike Goetz, the act of sustaining ruthless insults with supreme impassiveness serves as a mirror turning Schulheims's provocations against him and ultimately allowing Goetz to triumph over his frustrated "superior" from below. As humble saint, Goetz manages to debase others as effectively as he did earlier as a haughty sinner. Wielding power from the base as easily as from the top, Goetz commands the invertibility of his chiastic being.

Several characters attempt to assess the composition of Goetz's being. Among them, a puzzled Heinrich: "So there are two Goetz's, right?" to which Goetz responds cryptically, "Two, yes: one living one who does Good and one dead one who did Evil" (145). In spite of Sartre's monsters' uncanny power of control over their own being, Goetz, perhaps because he is an idealized object of Sartre's imagination rather than an example from reality that Sartre can examine, fails as a demonstration of ethical monstrosity, that is, of duality within unity. Of course, we know that there cannot be *two* Goetz's, but he deceives himself in believing, as he assures Heinrich, that a former evil Goetz is dead and buried. No, Goetz is a bastard, a hybrid, a monster capable of assuming two extreme ethical modes. Hilda seems to perceive this clearly and tries to set him straight.

> *Goetz:* What was [Catherine] saying?
> *Hilda:* That you were handsome, intelligent, courageous, that you were insolent and cruel, that at one glance a woman could not help but fall in love with you.

> *Goetz:* Was she telling you about another Goetz?
> *Hilda:* There is only one.
>
> (1951, 161–62)

Sartre's ideal ethical hybrid is but one being composed of two diametrically opposed configurations, each corresponding to subject and object: one in which the uncontrollable son (id) tends to dominate and silence the paternal law (superego), and the other in which the lawmaker brings moderation to the otherwise uncontrollable element. Together the two configurations form one chiastically shaped ethical being.

> Jeté je porte l'Autre, porté je m'élance. La figure du porteur porté pointe dans les descriptions de Sartre.
>
> —Benny Lévy[2]

In his study of Baudelaire, Sartre stumbled upon a bastardy with which he was unable to reckon. Monstrous bastardy was a concept that he was yet to elaborate and particularize, through his writings of the early 1950s, as a being that accomodates both paternal and filial instances. Baudelaire's original choice of being irritated Sartre to an extent that he felt compelled to publish an entire essay justifying his condemnation of that choice.

In Western societies, until this century, the illegitimate child was still denied all rights of inheritance. A legacy of sorts, however, was handed the Sartrean bastard, Baudelaire, in his critic's later biography of Gustave Flaubert. As the culminating work in Sartre's career, *The Family Idiot* functions as a gargantuan footnote to *Baudelaire,* significantly reconciling Sartre with the author of *Flowers of Evil* as he "sets the record straight" about Flaubert. *The Family Idiot* constitutes Sartre's final (but perhaps not definitive) reworking of the question of ethics and paternity.

In *The Imaginary,* one of Sartre's early essays on perception, he illustrates how his concept of the *analogon* works by recounting the story of a cabaret actress so accomplished as a mimic that she could actually *become* Maurice Chevalier.[3] A decade later, he chose the title *Saint Genet* for its resonance with Jean Rotrou's tragedy about the legendary Roman actor, Genesius, who, having relinquished his own *being* while incarnating the role of a Christian, was martyred by Diocletian. This thespian talent (or folly) gained for Genesius the distinction of patron saint of actors, the greatest of whom the French call *monstres sacrés,* or "sacred monsters." Each of the characters we have examined in part 5—Genet, Kean, Goetz—is a quintessential actor, and the image of sacred monster embraces all of the qualities that typify the Sartrean bastard: hybridity, ambiguity, saintliness, malevolence.

Combining his lifelong fascination with actors with the search for a model of total being, Sartre undertook, with *The Family Idiot,* to totalize the life of yet another "sacred monster," Gustave Flaubert. We know the weight Kean refers to in his appeal to "weigh his own weight" (1954, 65), to be the property of ethical being. According to Sartre's extensive exposition on the subject in *Flaubert,* the perfect actor learns, through the exercise of his craft and however ephemerally, to locate this proper ethical weight. If not the coveted total being that Sartre had always said was impossible, the sacred monster manages to attain "maximum being" (1971–72, 2:782). As for defining what constitutes this perfect actor, Sartre defers to Diderot (662) who, in *The Paradox of Acting,* asks rhetorically:

> The likeness of passion on the stage is not . . . its true likeness; it is but extravagant portraiture, caricature on a grand scale, subject to conventional rules. . . . What kind of actor will most successfully lay hold on this regulated bombast—the man dominated by his own character, or the man born without character, or *the man who sheds his own character to don another, greater, more noble, more fiery, more elevated*?[4]

Thus the "sacred monster," the perfect actor according to Diderot and Sartre, sheds or rejects his own character in order to don or endorse one of greater ethical import, one of greater weight. The role taken on by this incomparable master of being is tantamount to the introjection of the total other and, in a sense, the totality of others, as in the 1943 claim that the Atlas figure "carr[ies] the weight of the entire world" (1943, 612). Furthermore, because the "sacred monster" is a

Sartrean bastard, his role incarnated is that of the absent father: "An actor aims to manifest an absent or fictitious object through the totality of his person: he utilizes himself as the painter does his canvas and palette." (1971–72, 2:662). And, just as the "sacred monster" is at once painter, palette, and painting; author and work; father and son; he is also sculptor, stone, and statue. The quality of being that Sartre imputes to the Venus de Milo is, by analogy, that attained by the *monstre sacré.*

> . . . the woman of stone[5] . . . is the ideal of being: the figuration of a for-itself that would be like the dream of the in-itself. Thus sculpted stone, the indispensable mineral of a collective irrealization, no doubt possesses the maximum of being if we consider that, in social intersubjectivity, being is being-for-others when [the latter] is instituted. (786)

Is it thus, in this rather dismal image of the human as solitary (once again) and half-petrified, that Sartre brings to an end his search for total ontological and ethical being?

A Writer for His Time

The Family Idiot was not Sartre's final word on ethics, though the following rather unpleasant footnote on his ethical thought proves (Did we still need proof?) that stories do not necessarily all have happy endings. It is possible to discern a "last" Sartre (the Sartre who, in *Flaubert,* conceived of total being as our marriage with the world of object) who simultaneously holds to more *human* and *real* possibilities for thinking his "missing" Ethics. Having exhausted the paradigm of introjected paternity in the "sacred monsters" by turning them into statues of stone in their approach of total being, Sartre, who never left a stone unturned, became engrossed with an episode in his own recent history involving biological monstrosity.

Characterizing himself as a writer for his time, Sartre concerned himself with the historical moment of 1962 in an obscure, not quite posthumous piece of writing[6]—notes for a lecture given at the

Gramsci Institute in Rome in 1964. Of course, 1962 was the year of the Cuban missile crisis and Sartre, still more or less beholden to the Communist side of the cold war, followed that drama with intense interest. The Evian agreements, officially putting an end to the protracted Algerian Revolution, were signed in 1962 as well. But 1962 was also the year of what is arguably the greatest disaster of modern medicine. In that year, an epidemic revealed itself in ever so *visual* fashion under the now scorned name of *thalidomide.*

"A non-barbiturate hypnotic, [thalidomide] was generally withdrawn from the world market in the early 1960s after it was discovered that it produced teratogenic effects when administered to women in early pregnancy." Under "precautions," the pharmacist's handbook from which this description is excerpted warns that "thalidomide should not be used in women of childbearing potential."[7] Anyone even vaguely familiar with the thalidomide crisis should sense how understated that caution is. With the roots of the term *teratogenic* in mind, and, if we think back to the omen-seeking practices of the ancients, it is easy to see why I have stressed words like *discovered, obscure, reveal,* and *visual.* Formed of *genos* ("birth" or "origin") and *teratos,* meaning "monster," teratogenic designates substances that cause structural abnormalities (such as malformation or absence of certain body parts or organs) in living organisms. Sartre, speaking in 1964 about the untimely thalidomide,[8] describes it as "a medical product thought to be harmless [that] brings about embryonic modifications such that when the future mother uses it, she is certain to give birth to a *monster.*"[9]

Thalidomide was synthesized in West Germany in 1954 by Grünenthal laboratories. Preliminary testing had found it to be extremely effective as a sedative and as an antidote to nausea. Pharmaceutical companies, mostly in Europe, bought the so-called wonder drug, coining a predictable array of otherworldly brand names like Kevadon, Talimol, Contergan, and Softenon. Agitation and nausea being symptoms common to early pregnancy, doctors started freely prescribing thalidomide-based products to their pregnant female patients by 1958. The medical profession was so blindly zealous about the drug's versatility that it was even used in the treatment of such nonmedical disorders as "marital problems prior to and early in pregnancy."[10] Testing of this drug was tragically incomplete and the all-too-well-known "epidemic"[11] of "monster" babies was its devastating result. A limb reduction called *phocomelia,* so radical that what remains resembles the flipper of a seal,[12] was the teratological effect spectacularly present in over half the infants affected.

The health profession's inability, for nearly three years, to recognize the correlation between the spate of deformities and ingestion of thalidomide was one of three factors exacerbating the tragedy.[13] When doctors *were* finally tipped off to the probable connection, many were reluctant to prepare their patients for impending horrific events, preferring (in some cases) to drop them before the pregnancy reached its full term. The effects took place so early in pregnancy that damage often occurred before a woman even knew she was pregnant.[14] Thalidomide was finally removed from the market in Europe in November 1961, but not before precipitating upwards of 10,000 "monster" births.[15]

The thalidomide catastrophe was unprecedented in several respects. This was the first clear case of severe congenital deformities being caused not by biological or naturally occurring irregularites but by an artificial compound, synthesized by chemists, distributed by pharmacists, and administered by physicians. A drug thought to be a panacea was, in actuality, a poison,[16] the result of scientific "progress," not a cataclysm wrought on humanity by fate or divine providence, a "man-made epidemic" (Newman 1985, 143). This is the scenario of technological horror that captivated Sartre in 1962. The thalidomide events constitute just the type of limit-case he loved to tackle: fateful ignorance about the teratological effects of a product of man; quasi-inexistence of means to correct the malformations or even the social mechanisms (e.g., abortion) to avoid putting a severely deformed infant into the world. Yet it was not the issues of medical ethics raised by thalidomide that occupied Sartre's attention and imagination in 1964, but a sociological and legal debate triggered by the disaster.

Infanticide of a "Thalidomide Baby"

Sociologically, psychologically, and morally, "the mercy killing of a thalidomide child in Belgium" (Roskies 1972, 1) was by far the most wrenching public drama of the thalidomide period. The story of "the Liège infanticide," as Sartre calls it, began to unfold with the arrest, in August 1962, of a twenty-five-year-old woman accused of murdering her infant daughter born with acute phocomelia.[17] A few days after the traumatic birth, the desperate woman of low education and working-class origins, having decided that (in her words) "the child could not be happy as it was," mixed a formula of barbiturates, milk, and honey and fed it to the baby.[18]

Five people were indicted in November 1962 in this spectacular infanticide trial: the mother, her husband, her sister, her mother, and the family doctor who authorized the barbiturates for this purpose. The proceedings lasted six days during which the public repeatedly and vocally expressed its sympathy for the woman's action.[19] When the coroner stated that, if he had written the death certificate before the police intervened, he would have written "cause of death: natural" instead of "died a violent death," shouts of "How right you are!" and "There stands a man!" rose from the crowd. The virulence of the epidemic at the source of the alleged crime was poignantly underscored when the sister-in-law of the very doctor accused of accessory to murder gave birth to a thalidomide baby during the trial. Although the prosecutor argued that "except for her very grave malformations, [the accused woman's] baby was fit to live," two expert witnesses testified that the baby would not have survived longer than two years. Many mothers of thalidomide babies wrote "approvingly" or "understandingly" of the Liège woman's plight.

The all-male jury finally acquitted all five defendants to the approval of those who spoke out in Liège. If *Le Monde* can be taken as a standard of French left-of-center journalism at that time, Sartre is correct in observing that opinions were nevertheless mitigated: after urging for acquittal based on extenuating circumstances, an editorialist found "indecent the noisy demonstrations making a heroine out of a distraught mother."

The Vatican journal, *Osservatore Romano,* published an article during the week of the trial "against euthanasia." On the day of the acquittal, Vatican Radio sermonized that "eluding the moral law" can deceptively seem the humane solution, but that "it is the task of society and of the state, to facilitate observance of that law by all. It is the first guarantee of the common good."

Sartre's 1964 Lecture at the Gramsci Institute

Even more than the Algerian Revolution, for whose cause Sartre had risked his life, this infanticide trial governs the themes and tone of Sartre's second lecture at the Gramsci Institute.[20] The paper was written for a symposium on "Socialism and Ethics." Repeatedly, through the over 160 handwritten pages of lecture notes, Sartre insists on defining *ethical norms* on the basis of his own peculiar notion of history—not on the basis of systems held together by repetitive behavior.

Sartre has no quarrel with the traditional definition of ethics as one of the three normative sciences concerned with the determination of standards for good and proper conduct.[21] He adds to that definition, however, the condition that standards must in no way become rigid imperatives, but must change with the times. In doing so, he is in agreement with the social sciences, which, since their fairly recent inception, have shown how relative norms actually prove to be and point to the necessity for lending them dynamic definition. Psychoanalysis and, to an even greater extent, the antipsychiatric movements of the 1960s have given currency and legitimation to the idea (found in Nietzsche) that a *normal* individual is one who *contests* what society proposes as "normal" and who proposes new values that should be challenged and eventually overturned.

Sartre's vehement rejection, in the 1964 Gramsci lecture, of repetitive behaviors and their concomitant systems as legitimate foundations for ethics must be seen in the context of the ax he was grinding with structuralism. One might recall Sartre's jousting with Lévi-Strauss in the early 1960s over the latter's objections to the *Critique of Dialectical Reason*. Indeed, this lecture contains an all-but-overt allusion to Louis Althusser as the "Marxist who, tempted by structuralism, tries to kill [*mettre en sommeil*] the motor of history, that is, *class struggle*" (1964 ms, 36). Of course, structuralism is the first major shift away from the humanistic biases of existentialism in the history of ideas in France. In other terms, structuralism was the first system of thought to pose a serious threat to Sartre's jealously guarded position at the helm of France's intelligentsia. The early 1960s marked the time when Sartre's time was running out.

As a philosophy of history, Sartre says, structuralism (or "neopositivism," as he prefers to call it) not only shuns, but is incapable of, a totalizing moment. Totalization, as any reader of the *Critique* (or for that matter of *Flaubert*) knows, is absolutely crucial to Sartre's methodology. History, on the other hand, presupposes a subject capable of effective agency—a subject capable of innovating conditions for human existence no matter how daunting the structures or systems (i.e., the in-itself, the practico-inert) in place at the particular time. The peculiar difficulties in Sartre's notion of history spring from its idealistic projection into the future, and the subject's having to rely on an almost entirely nebulous notion of what he means by "fully human" or "unconditioned future" (1964 ms, 47, 54, 56ff.). In order to mark his distance from the project of structuralism, however, Sartre finds himself in a position of having to radicalize his already heavily teleological conception of history and, hence, of ethics.

Yet, to stave off the accusation that his challenge to emerging strains of antisubjective structural analysis is the rambling of a purely idealistic order, Sartre bolsters his claim that history, fueled by the will for an "unconditioned future," is the "true" foundation of ethics with several concrete examples. These real-life situations were either drawn from the events of 1962 or were events still considered by fellow travelers like Sartre to *make time,* that is, history, in that year. More than simple sequences of events interconnected within recognizable and namable historical conjunctures, Sartre's examples are "sets of behaviors" (24) that strain established norms, modifying established values, moving humanity toward that utopian ontological moment he calls "plenitude of being." The political and the social *feed into* the ethical. These "social objects" as he calls them (to remind structuralists that he is working their sandbox) are as diverse as *lycée* girls polled on the subject of lying, the torture of a prisoner of war, marriage among Aboriginals in Central Australia, the Canut revolt in Lyon, feudal lords preserving their honor, family strife in the Algerian War, and, most important, the thalidomide crisis.

Sartrean Analysis of the Liège Trial

The thalidomide-infanticide "social object"—the Liège trial—overshadows the other examples of norm bending that Sartre proposes.[22]

The victim of technological disaster, the "monster" baby fights against the same insuperable odds to attain "full humanity" as members of economically underprivileged classes—the Sartrean bastards. Even in his prognosis for the future of the Algerian Revolution, Sartre is thinking of the thalidomide babies, for it is the possibility of putting lots of viable new humans into the world that insures the victory of the oppressed over their oppressors. Sartre's populationist discourse in the 1952–54 political texts can be seen reemerging: he maintains that it was a "demographic surge" producing a "plethoric mass" of rebels that finally overwhelmed the outnumbered French in Algeria (1964 ms, 79–80). The time came for France's province-colony to liberate herself only when she took care to make kids.

Sartre's analysis of the Liège infanticide trial leads the eschatological foundation for his ethics into a crucial logical snare. Like the terror that revolutionaries unleash in the name of national liberation, the killing of hopelessly moribund monsters is denied status as repetitive behavior, but for entirely contradictory reasons. Hardly a case of humanist history and ethics, Sartre's argument runs amok in his irrepressible anti-Malthusianism. He tolerates the Liège infanticide only as an isolated and dated exception. To condone its ever being repeated would be tantamount to signing the suicide note for the proletariat and, concomitantly, to recognizing the triumph of the bourgeoisie. His fear of proletarian population decline is expressed in two arguments.

1. Any form of population control is bourgeois behavior: the proletarian who practices contraception or submits to abortion has succumbed to bourgeois customs and betrayed his class—for all intents and purposes he has become bourgeois.
2. To sanction the murder of thalidomide babies (before or after birth) is no better than killing *any* underprivileged child.

Proletarian population control implies that "every infant who is not bourgeois must be killed" (50). Infanticide is just "an extreme example of what have become routine contraceptive practices" (31). Hence the only difference between Sartre's position and that expressed by the Vatican following the Liège trial is that he has simply not bothered to invoke any preconceived "moral law" by name.

Sartre's Liège trial analysis undermines his figuring a basis for ethics. Departing from the ethical issues (especially medical ethics) raised by the case, he moralizes about the same implausible extinction of the proletariat through its adoption of bourgeois population control procedures: "Childhood diseases are on the wane and consequently contraceptive and abortive practices are on the rise" (30). He imagines a very specious class ambiguity within the infanticide mother in order to explain away this isolated case of murder that he is prepared to overlook: although the act was committed by a petty bourgeois woman, her motive had to be proletarian (58–59). In other words, if an act can be construed as proletarian in inspiration, it can be excused. Sartre is compelled to use these lines of argument because of the messianic image of the working class to which he clings: "When Marx writes that the proletariat carries in its bosom the death of the bourgeoisie he means that the proletariat is the pure future, beyond the system" (37). Whatever is proletarian about the Liège infanticide case is good because it is in direct opposition to bourgeois behavior. The proletarian in Suzanne Vandeput was prosecuting a noble revolt against an unacceptable state of medical technology. Only a bourgeois mother would treat a child like an object. Sartre's snag in logic consists, then, of his sense of history leading not to the long-promised ethics, but to his aberrant anti-Malthusian position in defense of the proletariat—a position entirely out of place with the demographic realities of his time.[23]

Sartre's anti-Malthusianism is mediated, as in the 1952–54 political texts, by the agency of women. While it is true that "the infanticide mothers [*sic*] of Liège lived out their attitude as a *real conflict of norms*" (32), their role in Sartre's ethical utopia would be, if we follow his argument, to bear lots of children. Flora Tristan wrote in the mid-1850s of these scions upon whom Sartre would like to see a future world built: "The most oppressed man can oppress someone else: his wife. She is the proletarian's proletarian."[24] Their labor is not to be expended on the assembly lines of the socialist state, but on the delivery table of a workers' paradise.

Sartre's Antipopulationism in Perspective

The little boy of *The Words* hardly knew his father, yet Sartre seems to have preserved an ideological and cultural legacy born of his father's generation. The fear of population decline is a fear peculiar in its intensity to early Third Republic France. In the aftermath of defeat by Prussia in 1870, the French bourgeoisie saw its only salvation against extinction in relentlessly striving for a higher fertility rate. Propaganda in favor of fertility and frantic populationist measures were advocated by political figures right, left, and center in the political spectrum.

Sartre's writings consistently show that he internalized this politics of fertility instituted by the French bourgeoisie of the late nineteenth century. But, of course, the aim of Sartre's politics of fertility was not to promote the bourgeoisie, for that would have been to promote the hated class of his father, which, because it is also *his* class, is a form of self-hatred. Sartre's anachronistic politics of fertility is intended to save the working class from purported extinction. This is the politics that was at the crux of the 1940 play, *Bariona*. If one substitutes first-century Jews slaving under the heel of the Romans for the proletariat laboring under capital, then Bariona's conversion to prolific paternity in order to conquer the enemy by sheer numbers becomes the ethical utopia (where working-class fertility flows unchecked) that Sartre painted in the 1964 Gramsci lecture. The same antipopulationism pervading *Bariona* and underlying the 1964 lecture infuses and commands *The Communists and Peace* where Sartre, between 1952 and 1954, anachronistically joined Marx against Malthus. Over those two, ten-year periods, Sartre's argument doesn't change one iota.

If we consider two canonical steps in Sartre's career in the perspective of the 1964 manuscript, we may conditionally state that ethics, by Sartre's definition, is utopian. I use the word *utopian* in the sense that there is no place for it in his time. In writing an ethics for "modern times"—Sartre's time—unavoidable prerequisites always seemed to hinder him. In 1943, immoral mechanisms seemed to pervade the for-itself's behavior. Yet, beyond its notorious pessimism, the implicit call in *Being and Nothingness* for an end to bad faith and the sadomasochistic foundations of love is in keeping with Sartre's nonessentialist human ontology and prefigures his later theories on praxis. In the 1960s, the implementation of the political, social, and economic equities stipulated in the *Critique of Dialectical Reason* would have allowed Sartre to finally write the ethics that his political philosophy frames. But the unpublished manuscript of his obscure speech in Rome demonstrates that Sartre, by this time, considered the ethics of the future to lie at the threshold of a sort of biological equality—an equality of human beings before nature, the absence of which human products like thalidomide sadly underscores.

Yet Sartre would also claim that, as an inexorable process of history in the making, as a product of the condition of the subhuman—the human bereft of ontological, political, economic, biological integrality, ethics, in the form of ever-changing norms, is paradoxically *present here and now.* In 1943, Sartre insisted in very Dostoyevskian terms that, no matter how hypocritical we might be, as soon as we act (which is to say as soon as we are *in the world*), we are responsible to all others because our every action reverberates throughout humanity. Similarly, ethical being is both foreshadowed and, in a way, already with us (according to the *Critique*) every time praxis rises up against the practico-inert in response to need. And here again, in this quirky body of lecture notes, in "man's animality" (73) in "the activity of the exploited classes" (62), the ethics that he could never quite bring himself to write—the *absent* ethics—is also, in a real way, *present.* With the thalidomide tragedy, never had it seemed so apparent to Sartre that man had become a product of a product of man instead of returning to the "natural" state of being, simply the product of man. Longing (alas, only nostalgically) for "a society where man is made for producing himself by reproducing his life" (141), glorifying a future state of humanity that resembles that of Rousseau's *bon sauvage* society, Sartre throws up his teleological ethics of history against the rising tide of what he saw as surrender to mindless repetition characteristic of the descendants of Nietzsche and Malthus combined. Sartre sensed that *les temps modernes*—modern times—were being superseded by postmodern times.

"Man as Son of Man"

If we set aside the desires for self-engenderment evident throughout Sartre's work, to what extent can one speak of a Sartrean desire to engender a son in order to create the human incarnation of a utopian ethical system? Peter Sloterdijk, writing on "moral illusion," refers to "the deep bond between Christianity and communism, of which the anarchists [like Sartre?] tried to remind us."[25] In order to resist bad faith and fight the practico-inert, Sartre essentially told his audience in Rome, man must elicit his primal energies. If the revolution cannot infiltrate and reenergize the biological, it is frivolous to talk about the political. "Man is made for producing himself by reproducing his life" (1964 ms, 141). What clearer expression could there be of a father's desire to be completed in the construction of his being than by his bringing a son into the world? In this sense, the Gramsci lecture is not only *posthumous* in that if and when it is ever published it will be after the death of its author. As yet another expression of the author's ethical thought, it offers a *posthumous method* of arriving at that utopian ethics. Corresponding to the admission that if true socialism is not possible today, perhaps it will be for the next generation, stands an implicit hope that if true ethics is not possible for me, perhaps it will be for my son.

"Son of man," an expression so frequently found in the Bible, comes from the Hebrew *ben-'adam* designating an individual, mankind in general, or an eschatological redeemer figure. Judging by the Synoptic Gospels, it was Christ's preferred self-designation.[26] Just as Christ used the expression *son of man* to refer to his activity and the exercise of his authority on earth as well as to an incarnation of himself after his crucifixion, Sartre, too, invokes it prominently in the Gramsci lecture (139), perhaps foreseeing his own eschatological return and rule in the form of *spiritual sons.* For to produce a perfect son—one who is filial and yet self-assertive, one who carries the paternal burden and yet *is* carried—would be tantamount to writing the ethics. If *I, Sartre,* cannot write the ethics of utopia, then perhaps Francis Jeanson, André Gorz, Benny Lévy, or some other son of Sartre can.

Notes

1. "I think you're nurturing a monster . . . a hybrid of bacchant and Holy Spirit" (André Gide, *Les Faux-monnayeurs* [Paris: Gallimard, 1925], 63; my translation).

2. "Thrown, I carry the Other: carried, I leap forward. The figure of the carried carrier rears up in Sartre's descriptions" (Benny Lévy, *Le nom de l'homme* [Paris: Verdier, 1984], 149; my translation).

3. Jean-Paul Sartre, *L'Imaginaire: psychologie phénoménologique de l'imagination* (Paris: Gallimard, 1940), 242.

4. Denis Diderot, *The Paradox of Acting*, trans. Walter H. Pollock (New York: Hill and Wang, 1957), 53. I have made minor adjustments to this translation.

5. "The woman of stone" (*la femme de pierre*), of course, designates the statue whose philosophical implications Sartre discusses in this passage: the Venus de Milo. However, would it not be fruitful to rethink this discussion in light of another translation for *la femme de pierre*, capitalizing *pierre*, rendering "Pierre's wife," and thus reinserting the ideas Sartre expounded in the last chapter of *Being and Nothingness* into this image of transformation?

6. The number of posthumously published texts by Sartre is rather astounding, especially for an author who published profusely in his lifetime: e.g., *Cahiers pour une morale* (1983), *Carnets de la drôle de guerre* (1983), *Le Scénario Freud* (1984), *Mallarmé* (1986), *Vérité et existence* (1989).

7. James E. F. Reynolds, ed., *Martindales's Extra Pharmacopoeia*, 29th ed. (London: Pharmaceutical Press, 1989), 1621–22.

8. Saying that thalidomide was untimely in the early 1960s implies that it had or has a place at some other time, which it does. It is now effectively and widely used in the treatment of certain forms of leprosy.

9. Jean-Paul Sartre, "Conférence à l'Institut Gramsci" (written on the first page of manuscript in a hand other than Sartre's). The lecture was given on 23 May 1964, according to Contat and Rybalka's chronology in (Sartre 1981). Page references are to the handwritten manuscript, hereafter referred to as "1964 ms."

10. Ethel Roskies, *Abnormality and Normality* (Ithaca: Cornell University Press, 1972), 46.

11. C. G. H. Newman, "Teratogen Update: Clinical Aspects of Thalidomide Embryopathy," *Teratology* 32 (1985): 133; Josef Warkany, "Trends in Teratologic Research," *Teratology* 3, no.1 (1970): 90.

12. "A flipperlike limb [that], with very great severity, result[s] eventually in only one or two fingers attached to a pendulous and very short limb" (Newman 1985, 136).

13. Having learned that 1961 was the year thalidomide products were removed from most world markets, I consulted the *Cumulated Index Medicus*

(an enormous bibliographic tool listing articles in all languages) working backward from 1963. In the edition for that year, I found references to more than 160 articles pertaining to thalidomide. However, the volume for 1962 does not even list a *thalidomide* rubric.

14. According to Newman, damage occurred thirty-five to fifty days after the first day of the last menstrual period (1985, 134). One mother who found out in the ninth month of pregnancy that she had taken thalidomide "wished vehemently for abortion, but she realized that it was too late" (Roskies 1972, 46).

15. In this country, the disaster was largely averted due to the repeated refusals to approve thalidomide for sale by Dr. Frances O. Kelsey, the first woman director of the U.S. Food and Drug Administration, who was commended in the press and eventually by President Kennedy for her vigilance. The story apparently broke in the United States in April 1962 with a news conference given in New York by a Professor Taussig. Although the United States was more or less spared, thalidomide-laden sedatives were distributed sporadically by the W. S. Merrell Co. and through doctors receiving it for testing. It was later found that many U.S. pharmacies had stocks of thalidomide. The drug took on cold war significance when the Soviet Union accused the Merrell Co. of selling it abroad for profit, even after the company suspected the teratogenic effects. By far the biggest scandal here involved an Arizona woman (Mrs. Finkbine) who was blocked from having a legal abortion and became a cause célèbre in 1962 by going to Sweden to carry out her wishes. The Vatican had its say, warning, on the day Finkbine aborted, that abortion was reprehensible no matter what the circumstances.

16. One cannot help but recall Derrida's discussion, in "La Pharmacie de Platon," of the paradoxical double meaning of *pharmakon;* see Jacques Derrida, *La Dissémination* (Paris: Seuil, 1972), 71–198.

17. *New York Times* reporters, for whatever reasons, display an odd indecision about the correct *name* to attribute to Suzanne Vandeput, the infanticide mother: Vandeputte, Vandeput-Coipel, Coipel-Vandeput, Vandeput, Coipel Van De Put.

18. The most detailed information I found concerning the Liège trial was in *Le Monde*, 5–13 November 1962.

19. It was the first time in Belgian history that television and movie cameras were allowed in court.

20. Sartre first spoke at the Gramsci Institute in December 1961 on "Subjectivity and Marxism."

21. The other two normative sciences are logic and aesthetics.

22. Thus, for example, the "risk of death" required for feudal lords, knights, or gentlemen to carry out acts of duty is compared to Sartre's image of the life of a thalidomide baby that would survive.

23. See Colin Dyer, *Population and Society in Twentieth-Century France* (New York: Holmes and Meier, 1978).

24. Cited in Claire Duchen, *Feminism in France* (London: Routledge and Kegan Paul, 1986), 2.

25. Peter Sloterdijk, *Critique of Cynical Reason* (Minneapolis: University of Minnesota Press, 1987), 41.

26. *The Eerdmans Bible Dictionary* (Grand Rapids, Mich.: William B. Eerdman Publishing, 1987), 962b.

Bibliography

Works by Jean-Paul Sartre Cited in the Text by Year of Publication

1940 *L'Imaginaire: Psychologie phénoménologique de l'imagination*. Paris: Gallimard, 1940.

1943 *L'Etre et le Néant: Essai d'ontologie phénoménologique*. Paris: Gallimard, 1943.

1947a *Baudelaire*. Paris: Gallimard, 1947.

1947b *Qu'est-ce que la littérature?* Paris: Gallimard, 1947.

1947c *Situations, I*. Paris: Gallimard, 1947.

1948 *Les Mains sales*. Paris: Gallimard, 1948.

1949 *Situations, III*. Paris: Gallimard, 1949.

1951 *Le Diable et le Bon Dieu*. Paris: Gallimard, 1951.

1952 *Saint Genet: Comédien et martyr*, Vol. 1 of *Oeuvres complètes de Jean Genet*. Paris: Gallimard, 1952.

1954 *Kean: Adaptation en cinq actes de Kean ou Désordre et génie, comédie d'Alexandre Dumas père*. Paris: Gallimard, 1954.

1955 *Nekrassov*. Paris: Gallimard, 1955.

1960a *Critique de la raison dialectique*, Vol. 1, *"Théorie des ensembles pratiques."* Paris: Gallimard, 1960.

1960b *Les Séquestrés d'Altona*. Paris: Gallimard, 1960.

1960c *Théâtre, I*. Paris: Gallimard, 1960. Includes: *Les Mouches* (1943) and *Huis clos* (1944)

1964a *Les Mots*. Paris: Gallimard, 1964.

1964b Situations, VI: Problèmes du marxisme, 1. Paris: Gallimard, 1964.
1964 ms "Conférence à l'Institut Gramsci." Unpublished manuscript, 1964.
1965 *Situations, VII: Problèmes du marxisme, 2*. Paris: Gallimard, 1965.
1967 *Questions de méthode*. Paris: Gallimard, 1967.
1970 *Bariona, ou le Fils du tonnerre*. In Michel Contat and Michel Rybalka, *Les Ecrits de Sartre*, 565–633. Paris: Gallimard, 1970.
1971–72 *L'Idiot de la famille*. Paris: Gallimard, 1971–72.
1976 *Situations, X*. Paris: Gallimard, 1976.
1981 *Oeuvres romanesques*. Paris: Gallimard, 1981. Includes: *La Nausée* (1938), *Le Mur* (1939), *Les Chemins de la liberté: L'âge de raison* (1945), *Le Sursis* (1945), *La Mort dans l'âme* (1949).
1983a *Cahiers pour une morale*. Paris: Gallimard, 1983.
1983b *Lettres au Castor et à quelques autres*. Paris: Gallimard, 1983.

Other Works Cited

Althusser, Louis. *Lire "Le Capital."* Paris: Maspéro, 1969.
Barnes, Hazel E. *Sartre and Flaubert*. Chicago: University of Chicago Press, 1981.
Bataille, Georges. *La Littérature et le mal*. Paris: Gallimard, 1957.
Beauvoir, Simone de. "L'existentialisme et la sagesse des nations." *Les Temps modernes* 3 (1945): 385–404.
———. *La Force de l'âge*. Paris: Gallimard, 1960.
———. *La Force des choses*. Paris: Gallimard, 1963.
Collins, Douglas. *Sartre as Biographer*. Cambridge, Mass.: Harvard University Press, 1980.
Contat, Michel, and Michel Rybalka. *Les Ecrits de Sartre*. Paris: Gallimard, 1970.
Derrida, Jacques. *La vérité en peinture*. Paris: Flammarion, 1978.
———. *The Truth in Painting*. Trans. Geoff Bennington and Ian McLeod. Chicago: University of Chicago Press, 1987.
Diderot, Denis. *Paradoxe sur le comédien* [1770], Paris: Flammarion, 1981.
———. *The Paradox of Acting*. Trans. Walter Herries Pollock. New York: Hill and Wang, 1957.
Dostoyevsky, Fyodor. *The Brothers Karamazov*. Trans. David Magarshack. Harmondsworth: Penguin, 1958.
Doubrovsky, Serge. *Autobiographiques, de Corneille à Sartre*. Paris: Presses Universitaires de France, 1988.
———. "Phallotexte et gynotexte dans *La Nausée:* 'Feuillet sans date.'" In *Sartre et la mise en signe*, ed. Michael Issachroff and Jean-Claude Vilquin, 31–55. Paris: Klincksieck, 1982.
Duchen, Claire. *Feminism in France: From May 68 to Mitterrand*. London: Routledge and Kegan Paul, 1986.
Duras, Marguerite. *La Maladie de la mort*. Paris: Minuit, 1982.

Freud, Sigmund. *The Standard Edition of the Complete Psychological Works of Sigmund Freud*, ed. James Strachey. London: Hogarth Press, 1973–74. Includes "Civilization and Its Discontents" (1930 [1929]), 21:57–146; "The Ego and the Id" (1923), 19:1–59; "On the Sexual Theories of Children" (1908), 9:205–26.

George, François. *Deux études sur Sartre*. Paris: Christian Bourgois, 1976.

Gide, André. *Les Caves du Vatican*. Paris: Gallimard, 1936.

———. *Les Faux-monnayeurs*. Paris: Gallimard, 1925.

———. *Les Nourritures terrestres*. Paris: Gallimard, 1935.

Gorz, André. *Fondements pour une morale*. Paris: Galilée, 1977.

Hollier, Denis. *Politique de la prose: Jean-Paul Sartre et l'an quarante*. Paris: Gallimard, 1982.

———. *Politics of Prose: Essay on Sartre*. Trans. Jeffrey Mehlman. Minneapolis: University of Minnesota Press, 1986.

Irigaray, Luce. *Ce sexe qui n'en est pas un*. Paris: Minuit, 1977.

Jeanson, Francis. *Sartre*. Paris: Seuil, 1955.

Kremer-Marietti, Angèle. *La Morale*. Paris: Presses Universitaires de France, 1982.

Kundera, Milan. *The Unbearable Lightness of Being*. Trans. Michael Henry Heim. New York: Harper and Row, 1984.

Lenin, V. I. "What Is To Be Done? Burning Questions of Our Movement." In *Collected Works* 5:347–516. Moscow: Foreign Languages Publishing House, 1961.

Levinas, Emmanuel. *Difficile liberté*. Paris: Albin Michel, 1963.

Lévy, Benny. *Le Nom de l'homme: Dialogue avec Sartre*. Paris: Verdier, 1984.

Lingus, Alphonso. *Libido: The French Existential Theories*. Bloomington: Indiana University Press, 1985.

Marx, Karl. *Capital: A Critique of Political Economy*. Trans. Samuel Moore and Edward Aveling. New York: International Publishers, 1967.

Mehlman, Jeffrey. *A Structural Study of Autobiography: Proust, Leiris, Sartre, Lévi-Strauss*. Ithaca, N.Y.: Cornell University Press, 1971.

Merleau-Ponty, Maurice. *Les Aventures de la dialectique*. Paris: Gallimard, 1955.

———. *Adventures of the Dialectic*. Trans. Joseph Bien. Evanston: Northwestern University Press, 1973.

———. *Le Visible et l'invisible*. Paris: Gallimard, 1964.

Ponge, Francis. "Le Monologue de l'employé." In *Douze petits écrits*. Paris: Gallimard, 1926.

Poster, Mark. *Existential Marxism in Postwar France: From Sartre to Althusser*. Princeton, N.J.: Princeton University Press, 1975.

Reynolds, James E. F., ed. *Martindale's Extra Pharmacopoeia*. 29th ed. London: Pharmaceutical Press, 1989.

Roskies, Ethel. *Abnormality and Normality: The Mothering of Thalidomide Children*. Ithaca, N.Y.: Cornell University Press, 1972.

Shelley, Pete. "Nostalgia." In *Love Bites*. London: IRS Records, 1978.

Sloterdijk, Peter. *Critique of Cynical Reason.* Trans. Michael Eldred. Minneapolis: University of Minnesota Press, 1987.

Tournier, Michel. *Les Météores.* Paris: Gallimard, 1975.

Virgil, *Vergil's Aeneid and Fourth ("Messianic") Eclogue in the Dryden Translation.* Ed. Howard Clark. University Park, Penn.: Pennsylvania State University Press, 1989.

Zola, Emile. *Fécondité.* Paris: François Bernouard, 1928.

Works Consulted

Aboulafia, Mitchell. *The Mediating Self: Mead, Sartre and Self-Determination.* New Haven: Yale University Press, 1986.

Althusser, Louis. *Pour Marx.* Paris: Maspéro, 1965.

Anderson, Thomas C. *The Foundation and Structure of Sartrean Ethics.* Lawrence, Kans.: Regents Press of Kansas, 1979.

Aronson, Ronald. "Sartre's Return to Ontology: Critique II Rethinks the Basis of *L'Etre et le Néant.*" *Journal of the History of Ideas* 48, no. 1 (1987): 99–116.

Bachelard, Gaston. *L'eau et les rêves: Essai sur l'imagination de la matière.* Paris: Corti, 1942.

Barnes, Hazel E. *An Existentialist Ethics.* New York: Knopf, 1967.

Barrow, Clyde W. "The Historical Problem of Political Organization in Sartre's Existential Marxism." *History of Political Thought* 7 (1986): 527–36.

Beaujour, Michel. "Sartre and Surrealism." *Yale French Studies* 30 (1964): 86–95.

Beauvoir, Simone de. *La Cérémonie des adieux.* Paris: Gallimard, 1981.

———. *Le Deuxième sexe.* Paris: Gallimard, 1949.

———. *Lettres à Sartre.* Paris: Gallimard, 1990.

Beigbeder, Marc. "Sartre: la chasse historique du salut." *Esprit* 110 (1986): 6–17.

Bersani, Leo. *The Freudian Body: Psychoanalysis and Art.* New York: Columbia University Press, 1986.

Blanchot, Maurice. *L'entretien infini.* Paris: Gallimard, 1969.

———. *La Part du feu.* Paris: Gallimard, 1949.

Boschetti, Anna. *The Intellectual Enterprise: Sartre and "Les Temps modernes."* Trans. Richard C. McCleary. Evanston, Ill.: Northwestern University Press, 1988.

Boudier, C. E. M. Struyker. "Sartre's Critique of Religion in His *Cahiers pour une morale.*" *International Philosophical Quarterly* 25 (1985): 419–24.

Bowman, Elizabeth Ann. "The Moral Impasse and the Possibility of the Human: A Study of Jean-Paul Sartre's Ethics and His Political Theater." *Dissertation Abstracts International* 48, no. 1 (1987) 136A–37A.

Buisine, Alain. *Laideurs de Sartre.* Lille: Presses Universitaires de Lille, 1986.

Bukula, C. R. "Sartrean Ethics: An Introduction." *The New Scholasticism* 41, no. 4 (1967): 450–64.
Burgelin, Claude, ed. *Lectures de Sartre.* Lyon: Presses Universitaires de Lyon, 1986.
Burger, Peter. "Passé simple: The Essay as Autobiographical Form in Jean-Paul Sartre." *Modern Language Notes* 102, no. 5 (1987): 1182–90.
Burnier, Michel-Antoine. *Les Existentialistes et la politique.* Paris: Gallimard, 1966.
———. *Choice of Action.* Trans. Bernard Murchland. New York: Random House, 1968.
Caleux, Anne-Marie. *Jean-Paul Sartre, Simone de Beauvoir: Une expérience commune, deux écritures.* Paris: Nizet, 1986.
Camus, Albert. *La Chute.* Paris: Gallimard, 1956.
Casey, Edward S., ed. *The Life of the Transcendental Ego: Essays in Honor of William Earle.* Albany, N.Y.: SUNY Press, 1986.
Cau, Jean. *Croquis de mémoire.* Paris: Julliard, 1985.
Caute, David. *Communism and the French Intellectuals, 1914–1960.* New York: Macmillan, 1964.
———. *The Fellow-Travellers.* New York: Macmillan, 1973.
Caws, Peter. "The Subject in Sartre and Elsewhere." In *Descriptions,* ed. Don Ihde and Hugh J. Silverman, 141–51. Albany, N.Y.: SUNY Press, 1985.
———. "Oracular Lives: Sartre and the Twentieth Century." *Revue Internationale de Philosophie* 39, nos. 1–2 (1985): 172–83.
Cohen-Solal, Annie. *Paul Nizan, communiste impossible.* Paris: Grasset, 1980.
———. *Sartre: 1905–1980.* Paris: Gallimard, 1985.
Colombel, Jeannette. *Sartre, I: Un homme en situation.* Paris: Le Livre de Poche, 1986.
Crittenden, P. J. "Sartrean Transcendence: Winning and Losing." *Australasian Journal of Philosophy* 63 (1985): 440–50.
Culler, Jonathan. *On Deconstruction: Theory and Criticism after Structuralism.* Ithaca, N.Y.: Cornell University Press, 1982.
de Man, Paul. *Blindness and Insight: Essays in the Rhetoric of Contemporary Criticism.* Minneapolis: Univeristy of Minnesota Press, 1971.
Derrida, Jacques. *La Dissémination.* Paris: Seuil, 1972.
Desan, Wilfred. *The Tragic Finale: An Essay on the Philosophy of Jean-Paul Sartre.* Oxford: Oxford University Press, 1954.
Descombes, Vincent. *Le même et l'autre: Quarante-cinq ans de philosophie française (1933–1978).* Paris: Minuit, 1979.
Detmer, David. *Freedom as a Value: A Critique of the Ethical Theory of Jean-Paul Sartre.* La Salle, Ill.: Open Court, 1988.
Diderot, Denis. *Est-il bon? Est-il méchant?* In *Oeuvres,* Paris: Gallimard, 1951.
Di Gona, Goriano. "Sartre, il moralista senza morale." *Humanitas* 5, no. 3 (1950): 244–46.
Dreyfus, Dina. "Sartre et le mal radical: De *L'Etre et le Néant* à la *Critique de la raison dialectique.*" *Mercure de France* 341 (1961): 154–67.

Drost, M. P. "Sartre's Concept of a Person as a Project." *Dialogos* 23 (1988): 97–108.

Dyer, Colin. *Population and Society in Twentieth-Century France.* New York: Holmes and Meier, 1978.

Ellis, Robert Richmond. *The Tragic Pursuit of Being: Unamuno and Sartre.* Tuscaloosa: University of Alabama Press, 1988.

Foucault, Michel. *Histoire de la folie à l'âge classique.* Paris: Gallimard, 1972.

Fourny, Jean-François. "La communication impossible: Georges Bataille et Jean-Paul Sartre." *Stanford French Review* 12, no. 1 (1988): 149–60.

———. "Sartre et le nom du fils." *La Liberté de l'Esprit* 4 (1983): 7–52.

Goldthorpe, Rhiannon. *Sartre: Theory and Literature.* New York: Cambridge University Press, 1984.

Gordon, Haim. "Sartre's Struggle against the Holy." *International Journal for Philosophy of Religion* 19 (1986): 95–103.

Gorz, André. *Le Traître.* Paris: Seuil, 1958.

Gosse, Edmund. *Father and Son: A Study of Two Temperaments.* Harmondsworth: Penguin, 1983.

Gourgaud, Nicole. "La dynamique du pouvoir dans *Bariona ou le fils du tonnerre* de Jean-Paul Sartre." *Kwartalnik Neofilologiczny* (Warsaw) 32, no. 2 (1985): 159–67.

Greene, Norman N. *Jean-Paul Sartre: The Existential Ethic.* Ann Arbor: University of Michigan Press, 1960.

Haarscher, Guy. "Autobiographie: Regard de l'autre et problème de la justification chez Sartre." *French Literature Series* 12 (1985): 145–53.

Harvey, Robert. "Sartre/Cinema: Spectator/Art Which Is Not One." *Cinema Journal* 30, no. 2 (1991): 43–59.

Hayman, Ronald. "Sartre and the Mice: A Reputation Reconsidered." *Encounter* 65, no. 5 (1985): 48–54.

Heidegger, Martin. *Being and Time.* Trans. John Macquarrie and Edward Robinson. New York: Harper and Row, 1962.

Helbo, André. *L'enjeu du discours: Lecture de Sartre.* Brussels: Editions Complexe, 1978.

Hendley, Steve. "Power, Knowledge, and Praxis: A Sartrean Approach to a Foucaultian Problem." *Man and World* 21 (1988): 171–89.

Hirsh, Arthur. *The French Left.* Montréal: Black Rose Books, 1982.

Hollier, Denis. "The Handbook of the Intellectual." *Raritan* (1981): 73–88.

Hornsby, Jennifer. "Sartre and Action Theory." *Philosophy and Phenomenological Research* 48 (1988): 745–51.

Houbert, Jacques. *Un père dénaturé: Essai critique sur la philosophie de Jean-Paul Sartre.* Paris: Julliard, 1964.

Howells, Christina. *Sartre: The Necessity of Freedom.* New York: Cambridge University Press, 1988.

Hunyadi, Mark. "Ma liberté, c'est le meurtre de l'autre: A propos des *Cahiers pour une morale* de Jean-Paul Sartre." *Revue de Théologie et de Philosophie* 117 (1985): 173–84.

Imboden, Roberta. *From the Cross to the Kingdom: Sartrean Dialectics and Liberation Theology.* San Francisco: Harper and Row, 1987.

Jacoby, Russell. *Dialectic of Defeat: Contours of Western Marxism.* New York: Cambridge University Press, 1981.

Jameson, Fredric. *Sartre: The Origins of a Style.* New York: Columbia University Press, 1984.

Jay, Martin. *Marxism and Totality: The Adventures of a Concept from Lukács to Habermas.* Berkeley: University of California Press, 1984.

Jeanson, Francis. *Le problème moral et la pensée de Sartre.* Paris: Seuil, 1965.

———. "Hell and Bastardy." *Yale French Studies* 30 (1963): 5–20.

Joubert, Ingrid. *Aliénation et liberté dans "Les Chemins de la Liberté" de Jean-Paul Sartre.* Paris: Didier, 1973.

Karst, Broniaslawa Irene. "The Problem of the Other and of Intersubjectivity in the Works of Jean-Paul Sartre and Witold Gombrowicz." *Dissertation Abstracts International* 46, no. 4 (1985): 972A.

Knee, Philip. "Solitude et sociabilité: Rousseau et Sartre." *Dialogue: Revue Canadienne de Philosophie* 26, no. 3 (1987): 419–35.

Lacan, Jacques. *Ecrits.* Paris: Seuil, 1966.

———. *Ecrits I–II.* Paris: Seuil, 1970–71.

LaCapra, Dominick. *A Preface to Sartre.* Ithaca, N.Y.: Cornell University Press, 1978.

Laplanche, Jean, and Jean-Baptiste Pontalis. *Vocabulaire de la psychanalyse.* Paris: Presses Universitaires de France, 1967.

Laurent, Jacques. *Les années 50.* Lyon: La Manufacture, 1989.

Lavers, Annette. "Sartre and Freud." *French Studies* 41, no. 3 (1987): 298–317.

Leclerc, Annie. "De Roquentin à Mathieu." *L'Arc* 30 (1966): 71–76.

Lee, Sander H. "The Central Role of Universalization in Sartrean Ethics." *Philosophy and Phenomenological Research* 46 (1985): 59–72.

Lejeune, Philippe. *Le Pacte autobiographique.* Paris: Seuil, 1975.

———. "L'atelier autobiographique de Sartre." *French Literature Series* 12 (1985): 129–44.

Levinas, Emmanuel. *Ethique et Infini.* Paris: Fayard, 1982.

———. *Le temps et l'autre.* Montpellier: Fata Morgana, 1979.

———. *La Théorie de l'intuition dans la phénoménologie de Husserl.* Paris: Alcan, 1930.

Lévy, Benny. "La cérémonie de la naissance." *French Review* 55, no. 7 (1982): 13–21.

Luce, Louise Fiber. "Alexandre Dumas's *Kean:* An Adaptation by Jean-Paul Sartre." *Modern Drama* 28, no. 3 (1985): 355–61.

Lukács, Georges. *Existentialisme ou marxisme?* Paris: Nagel, 1948.

Lyotard, Jean-François. "Un succès de Sartre." *Critique* 430 (1983): 177–89.

McCarthy, Patrick. "Sartre, Nizan, and the Dilemmas of Political Commitment." *Yale French Studies* 68 (1985): 191–205.

Marcuse, Herbert. "Existentialism: Remarks on J.-P. Sartre's *L'Etre et le Néant*." *Philosophy and Phenomenological Research* 8, no. 3 (1948): 309–36.

Marx, Karl, and Friedrich Engels. *The Holy Family, or The Critique of Critical Criticism.* Trans. R. Dixon. Moscow: Progress Publications, 1975.

McKinney, Ronald H. "Sartre and the Politics of Deconstruction." *Philosophy and Social Criticism* 13 (1987): 327–41.

Meszaros, István. *The Work of Sartre: Search for Freedom.* Brighton, England: Harvester Press, 1979.

Moi, Toril. "Existentialism and Feminism." *Oxford Literary Review* 8, nos. 1–2 (1986): 88–95.

Moreland, Richard. *Faulkner and Modernism: Rereading and Rewriting.* Madison: University of Wisconsin Press, 1990.

Morita, Shuji. "Sartre dans la salle obscure." *Etudes de langue et littérature françaises* (Tokyo) 48 (1986): 102–18.

Murat, Marie-Germaine. "Jean-Paul Sartre, un enfant séquestré: lire—ou l'enfance reconquise." *Les Temps modernes* 43, no. 498 (1988): 128–49.

Neu, Jerome. "Divided Minds: Sartre's 'Bad Faith' Critique of Freud." *Review of Metaphysics* 42 (1988): 79–101.

Ory, Pascal. *Nizan, destin d'un révolté.* Paris: Ramsay, 1980.

Pacaly, Josette. *Sartre au miroir.* Paris: Klincksieck, 1980.

Pilkington, A. E. "Sartre's Existentialist Ethic." *French Studies* 23, no. 1 (1969): 38–48.

Philonenko, Alexis. "Sartre et la logique transcendantale classique: Les essences et les normes." *Revue de Métaphysique et de Morale* 92 (1987): 503–25.

Plank, William. *Sartre and Surrealism.* Ann Arbor: UMI Research Press, 1981.

Ponge, Francis. *Le Parti pris des choses.* Paris: Gallimard, 1942.

Pucciani, Oreste. "Sartre et ses audiences américaines." *Les Temps modernes* 43, no. 503 (1988): 131–55.

———. "Sartre, Ontology, and the Other." In *Hypatia: Essays in Classics, Comparative Literature, and Philosophy Presented to Hazel E. Barnes on Her Seventieth Birthday*, ed. William M. Calder, Ulrich K. Goldsmith, and Phyllis B. Kenevan, 151–67. Boulder: Colorado Associated University Presses, 1985.

Quinn, Bernard. "The Politics of Despair versus the Politics of Hope: A Look at *Bariona*, Sartre's First *pièce engagée*." *French Review* 45, no. 4 (1972): 95–105.

Ramsey, Paul. *Nine Modern Moralists.* Englewood Cliffs, N.J.: Prentice-Hall, 1962.

Redfern, William. "Applying the Tourniquet: Sartre and Punning." *French Studies* 39, no. 3 (1985): 298–304.

———. *Paul Nizan: Committed Literature in a Conspiratorial World.* Princeton: Princeton University Press, 1972.

Renault, Gregory. "Bureaucracy to *L'Imaginaire:* Cornelius Castoriadis' Immanent Critique." *Catalyst* 13 (1979): 72–90.

Sartre, Jean-Paul. *Being and Nothingness.* Trans. Hazel E. Barnes. New York: Philosophical Library, 1956.

———. *Critique of Dialectical Reason: Theory of Practical Ensembles.* Trans. Alan Sheridan-Smith. London: New Left Books, 1976.

———. "L'Espoir, maintenant." *Le Nouvel Observateur* 800–802 (March 1980) 18, 56–60; 52–58; 55–66.

———. *Nausea.* Trans. Lloyd Alexander London: New Directions, 1949.

———. *Réflexions sur la question juive.* Paris: Paul Morihien, 1946.

———. *Situations, IV.* Paris: Gallimard, 1964.

Schrift, Alan D. "A Question of Method: Existential Psychoanalysis and Sartre's *Critique of Dialectical Reason." Man and World* 20 (1987): 399–418.

Sicard, Michel. *Essais sur Sartre.* Paris: Galilée, 1989.

Simons, Margaret A. "Beauvoir and Sartre: The Philosophical Relationship." *Yale French Studies* 72 (1986): 165–79.

Simont, Juliette. "Sur Jean-Paul Sartre: Raisons dialectiques américaines." *Les Temps modernes* 44, no. 507 (1988): 127–41.

Sprinker, Michael. "Politics and Theory: Althusser and Sartre." *Modern Language Notes* 100, no. 5 (1985): 989–1011.

Stone, Robert V. "Freedom as a Universal Notion in Sartre's Ethical Theory." *Revue Internationale de Philosophie* 39 (1985): 137–48.

Sweeney, Kevin W. "Lying to the Murderer: Sartre's Use of Kant in 'The Wall.'" *Mosaic: A Journal for the Interdisciplinary Study of Literature* (Winnepeg) 18, no. 2 (1985): 1–16.

Todd, Olivier. *Un fils rebelle.* Paris: Grasset, 1981.

Tournier, Michel. *Le roi des aulnes.* Paris: Gallimard, 1970.

Vedrine, Hélène. "Comment mettre Roquentin au travail . . . ou Bachelard et Sartre sur l'imaginaire." *Revue de l'Université d'Ottawa* 57, no. 1 (1987): 109–19.

Wahl, Jean. *A Short History of Existentialism.* New York: Philosophical Library, 1949.

Warnock, Mary. *Ethics since 1900.* London: Oxford University Press, 1960.

Wilcocks, Robert, ed. *Critical Essays on Jean-Paul Sartre.* Boston: Hall, 1988.

Wild, John. "Authentic Existence." *Ethics* 75, no. 4 (1965): 227–39.

Wilkinson, James D. "Jean-Paul Sartre and Raymond Aron." *Salmagundi* 70–71 (1986): 285–315.

Yaeger-Kaplan, Alice. *Reproductions of Banality: Fascism, Literature, and French Intellectual Life.* Minneapolis: University of Minnesota Press, 1986.

Žižek, Slavoj. *The Sublime Object of Ideology.* London: Verso, 1989.

Index